M000165821

# GHOST RIDERS OF BAGHDAD

# SOLDIERS, CIVILIANS, AND THE MYTH OF THE SURGE

## DANIEL A. SJURSEN

# GHOST RIDERS OF
# BAGHDAD

ForeEdge

ForeEdge

An imprint of University Press of New England

www.upne.com

© 2015 Daniel A. Sjursen

All rights reserved

Manufactured in the United States of America

Designed by Richard Hendel

Typeset in Utopia and Geogrotesque by Tseng Information Systems, Inc.

The views expressed are those of the author alone, and do not reflect
the official policy or position of the U.S. Army, Department of Defense,
or the U.S. Government.

For permission to reproduce any of the material in this book, contact
Permissions, University Press of New England, One Court Street, Suite 250,
Lebanon NH 03766; or visit www.upne.com

Library of Congress Cataloging-in-Publication Data

Sjursen, Daniel A.

Ghost riders of Baghdad : soldiers, civilians, and the myth of the surge /
Daniel A. Sjursen.

  pages cm

ISBN 978-1-61168-781-1 (cloth : alk. paper)—

ISBN 978-1-61168-827-6 (ebook)

1. Sjursen, Daniel A.  2. Iraq War, 2003–2011—Campaigns—Iraq—Baghdad.
3. United States. Army—Officers—Biography.  4. United States. Army.
Cavalry Regiment, 61st. Squadron, 3rd.  5. Iraq—Politics and government—
21st century.  6. Iraq War, 2003–2011—Personal narratives, American.  I. Title.
II. Title: Soldiers, civilians, and the myth of the surge.

DS79.764.B35S58 2015

956.7044'342—dc23    2015012184

5  4  3  2  1

*For my son,*

ALEXANDER JAMES MICHAEL SJURSEN (AJ)

*Life, to be sure,*
*Is nothing much to lose;*
*But young men think it is,*
*And we were young.*
— A. E. HOUSMAN

*I know we're not saints or virgins or lunatics; we know*
*all the lust and lavatory jokes, and most of the dirty people;*
*we can catch buses and count our change and cross the roads*
*and talk real sentences. But our innocence goes awfully deep,*
*and our discreditable secret is that we don't know anything*
*at all, and our horrid inner secret is that we don't care that*
*we don't.*
— DYLAN THOMAS

# Contents

# Acknowledgments

The very concept of an acknowledgments section makes me uncomfortable. It just seems an exercise in self-promotion and a recipe for trouble. Inevitably I will leave someone very important out, and for that I apologize up front. With that said, first off, I'd like to thank Marlboro brand cigarettes and Skoal Mint Dip, without which none of what follows would have been remotely tolerable. I'm skeptical of the idea that the important people in our lives "make us the men we are today," or whatever. Self-awareness of my own deep flaws and inconsistency—a trait I did not possess a decade ago—makes such rhetoric at best meaningless and at worst an insult to friends and family. Either way, this book and my life wouldn't have shaken out as it did without the following people:

I'll start with the pros. My literary agent (the possession of which is a ludicrous notion for a person with my utter lack of discernible talent) Gina Panettieri of Talcott Notch—for taking a chance on an amateur like me. Your sarcasm, wit, and straight shooting won me over from the start. Steve Hull, my editor at UPNE. Our shared vision and your patient advice made the decision to go with ForeEdge Books a no-brainer. And to my unofficial, but absolutely vital, editor—my wife, Kate. I'll thank her more later, but she belongs with the professionals. Kate read all my work before I'd dare show another human being, and gave me the time and space to lock myself away and write endlessly.

Then there's family. Thanks to my parents, Bob and Sue, who despite living separately made a pretty damn good team raising a pair of kids. To Amy—who is a far better sister and person than I deserve. To my uncles—Chris and Steve. I've spent the last thirty-one years trying to seem as tough as these New York firemen. My cousin and best friend—Kyle Killeen—AJ could have no better godfather. And dear cousin Krissy—the kindest, best listener in the world—an absolute joy to all who know her. I'd also like to extend special thanks to David and Susan Smith for trusting me enough to share their son's story with me. I can hardly imagine how difficult it must be to discuss such private matters, and your confidence meant the world to me.

To old friends. The fellas from Staten Island who shared neighborhoods and memories. Adam Pekor—to this day the smartest man I know and my longtime heterosexual life partner. Midland Beach boys: Peter Vadola, Anthony and Danny Rodriquez, Vinnie Whitaker, and company. The Port Richmond crew: Tom Loggins (RIP brother), Pete Salvione, and Rich Walsh—a bunch of guys who gave me enough stories to fill a lifetime. Assorted high school lunatics: John Palmer, Tony Holz, and Brad Resnikoff. My West Point brothers: great Americans who made the best of a shitty time—Danny Baringer, Al Trujillo, Logan Collins, Josh Banuelos, Josh Sik, Chris Kim, Marty Ellison, Gary Whidden, Ben Meyer, and Arg Nelson. Most of all to Ben Tolle—for the best of times shared over beers at NYC dive bars, stolen golf carts, rented Geo Metros, and discussions about the meaning of "Just to See You Smile."

To my brother lieutenants from Iraq—better men than me. Guys who'd likely tell a more effective story, but with the self-respect not to: Steve Migliore, Keith Marfione, Scott Maclaren, and BJ Laney. My platoon leaders and friends in Afghanistan. Blackhearts for Life—Alex Lamb, Jordan Rich, Pat Jones, and Scotty Boxler. Thanks for your sanity checks, courage, and for carrying an emotional wreck like me through a year in hell. Mostly, though, for your loyalty.

And for my—dare I say—mentors: first and foremost, to Colonel Matt Vanwagenen—by far the finest officer and man I've met in this crazy business. A guy who taught more by example, truth-telling, and friendship than all the rest combined. A constant reminder that when it comes down to a choice between being a good soldier and a good human being—to always choose the latter. Lieutenant Colonel Dave Defelice—a true cavalryman, brother, and friend. Colonel Greg Daddis—a true scholar in his own right, whose intelligence is sometimes intimidating, but always approachable. Thanks for running a great team, giving the instructors freedom to experiment and having the courage to be yourself in this crazy profession. Brigadier General (ret.) Bob Doughty—my entrance to the history profession and the first person (besides my wife) to read this work.

For my wife, Kate, and stepsons—Ryan and Brady. I often joke that

I'm a great guy to have a beer with, but an awful person to be married to. While all jokes have a kernel of truth, this one is realer than most. Thanks for your patience, love, and care. You are more than I deserve, and for that I'm eternally lucky. Mostly, though, for being a partner—still.

And finally, for my son, AJ—Alexander James Michael Sjursen. Though these stories will read like ancient history to you someday, it is my hope you'll always remember that you carry a proud name. Though you never knew Al, James, or Mike, and while my own example is far from perfect—I wish you to learn kindness and empathy from their lives and sacrifices. Be gentle, live freely, and know I love you always.

# Prologue

I started this book nine Decembers ago. It commenced on sleepless nights in Iraq during 2006 and resumed on long, lonely car rides moving from one army post to another. Swirling about in my head, the story hasn't—until now—translated into words on a page. One of the many reasons it took me seven years to begin in earnest is that I couldn't decide what I wanted it to *be*. Much to my chagrin, I've discovered I lack the literary skills to craft an effective novel. Nor do I possess the memory, documents, or will to write a comprehensive campaign history. Of course, I didn't want to do that anyway. I was certain what I didn't want this to be and what I most certainly hope it is not—that is, a self-referential memoir of challenges met, deeds done, and lessons learned. The bookshelves are full of those works, and I wish the authors well, professionally, and in life.

You've probably seen the books. If not, I'll summarize. The plot usually sticks to the following trajectory: boy receives classic Midwestern American upbringing. Boy attends West Point or some other military academy. Boy learns crucial lessons and becomes an *officer*. Officer applies these lessons to whip his new platoon into an elite fighting force. Officer takes platoon off to Iraq or Afghanistan, faces innumerable challenges, and stumbles. Eventually, of course, he applies his lessons, training, and gritty character to win in battle. In the process, the officer becomes a man.

This is not that book. I should hope this is a story altogether more human, more relatable. Full disclosure: with only minor detail changes, and though I often hate to admit it, the above officer could easily have been me. I come from New York City—well, Staten Island—so not exactly the Midwest. But I did go to West Point. I graduated and was commissioned as a second lieutenant in the army. I trained and took a scout platoon to Iraq at the height of the troop concentration known as the Surge. But as for the rest—becoming a man, learning many lessons, and applying them to win—I make no such claims. Yet I felt the need, you could even call it a pull, to write all this down. Why? I wish the motivations were either noble or easily articulated. The only truly honest reason I can muster is that I've never been able to forget Iraq—especially the first few months. Even after all these years, and a deployment to Afghanistan—which in many ways held more intense combat—and after two years at a civilian graduate school trying hard to forget the army, there it remains. Salman Pak, Iraq, just south of Baghdad, 2006–7. And my platoon, the "Ghost Riders"—2nd Platoon, Black Knight Troop, 3rd Squadron, 61st Cavalry Regiment, 2nd Infantry Division. Maybe I don't want to forget. Perhaps I'm holding on to something.

I propose to tell a brief story. It is about one platoon in Iraq. It focuses primarily on only half a dozen soldiers in that platoon. This tale spans just a few months in any real detail. I don't wish to be the main character. At least in my head, this is not a memoir (God forbid). That being said, I am the narrator. And truth be told, nearly all of this comes from memory, a few notes scribbled at the time, conversations with my soldiers and their families, plus a couple hundred photographs. Memory is a tricky thing. Were another soldier to write this, even someone within my own squadron, hell—my own *platoon*—it would be an entirely different story. Everything would change: the perspective, emphasis, recollection of sequences and events. So this is my version of the story—what has stayed with me.

I also aim to tell a wider story—grander, I suppose, than one platoon's trials and tribulations. The prevailing narrative about the Iraq War—when anyone bothers to think on it—seems to have developed along the following lines: the Surge worked, and we won. This might seem odd, given all the negative press during the campaign's first three years, and considering that our current president was elected on a veritably antiwar platform. Nevertheless, many intellectuals, senior military officers, conservative politicians, right-of-center media pundits, and common American citizens seem to believe it. The war was going badly, they've been told, but an enlightened general—David Petraeus—empowered by a sturdy commander in chief—George W. Bush—doubled down, stayed the course, and snatched victory from the jaws of defeat. In the process, everyone, it seems—except Nancy Pelosi and the fading congressional Democrats—triumphed. Army officers hate to lose, and avoided defeat while salvaging their reputations and—they hoped—their budgets. The political right, although they carefully distanced themselves from Bush-era personalities, still found vindication for a war they'd supported and regarding the use of force more generally. And the American people—well, they could go on acting like the Iraq War never happened, download a new iPhone app, and ignore the tragedies and sacrifices wrought by more than eight years of war.

The reality, examined in these pages, was far more thorny and complex. There were no simple resolutions or cookbook prescriptions for success.[1] Mostly, we muddled through, treaded water, and exploited any short-term opportunities available to protect and extricate ourselves from an altogether problematic war. *Ghost Riders of Baghdad* tells that story, one of scared, well-intentioned, and often confused soldiers grasping for solutions within the tangle of disarray that was Baghdad in 2006 and 2007. This book, in addition to honoring the men of Ghost Rider platoon, is really an attempt to answer three questions: First, who really serves in the all-volunteer military of an ostensible democracy, and what do those men look, feel, and sound like? Second, what did the business of counterinsurgency and refereeing a sectarian civil war actually consist of? And, finally, if most often forgotten, what exactly did all this mean for the Iraqi people? *Ghost Riders of Baghdad* describes what we saw, and what I believe the invasion wrought for Iraq and the region—unqualified catastrophe. That said, you won't find many unequivocal heroes or absolute villains in these pages. The war, I'm afraid, was never as clear as all that.

I began this book in the comfortable confines of my rented duplex during graduate school in the Midwest's liberal oasis of Lawrence, Kansas. Back then, ISIS was a new and seemingly unsubstantial threat. By spring 2014, however, the Islamic State of Iraq and Syria had burst across the west and north of Iraq, overrunning prominent cities such as Fallujah, Ramadi, and Mosul. Baghdad itself seemed threatened. Suddenly Iraq—until recently all but forgotten—was once again plastered on the screens of every twenty-four-hour news network. Politicians, pundits, and professors all weighed in with their analyses on the *meaning* of this new, brutal, and supposedly unprecedented movement. I was surprised by the rapidity of ISIS conquest, but not, truth be told, by its birth.

Should we be surprised that a generation of disaffected, nihilistic young men sprang from the chaos of America's decade-long occupation? *Fox News* and company would have you believe that ISIS is the direct result of President Obama's weakness and "retreat." Would that it were so simple. Such talk is more dangerous than the usual rancor of partisan politics. It indicates the inherently *American* flaw of overestimating our own role and placing ourselves at the heart of causality in international affairs. This, ISIS, is not just about *us*. The problem, and the tragedy, is bigger than Obama, the Surge, and our own political calculations. The narrative that follows is about obtuse misunderstanding, an ill-advised invasion, and the artificial structure of an entire region. The real issue was never Obama's decision to pull out U.S. troops in 2011, and the *genuine* tragedy belongs to the Iraqi people—the human beings living this horror, redux.

If at any point in the story I get to sounding self-righteous (perhaps the most common sin of the military professional, especially the volunteer)—stop reading. If you like me during every part, then I have probably failed. This book means to tell the truth, but I am aware that perception, bias, and incomplete memories are inevitable. So I may take some limited, mainly unconscious, poetic license. As I mentioned, I wish this could be a novel. But it is not. What follows is the truth, at least as I remember and perceive it. Maybe that is all the truth any of us ever get anyway. Enclosed are the memories of an adequate soldier and leader—one who as it turns out was probably never suited for this business in the first place—in one small portion, at one time, of one war. As many qualifiers as I've lumped into that—it remains the most important story of my life.

# GHOST RIDERS OF BAGHDAD

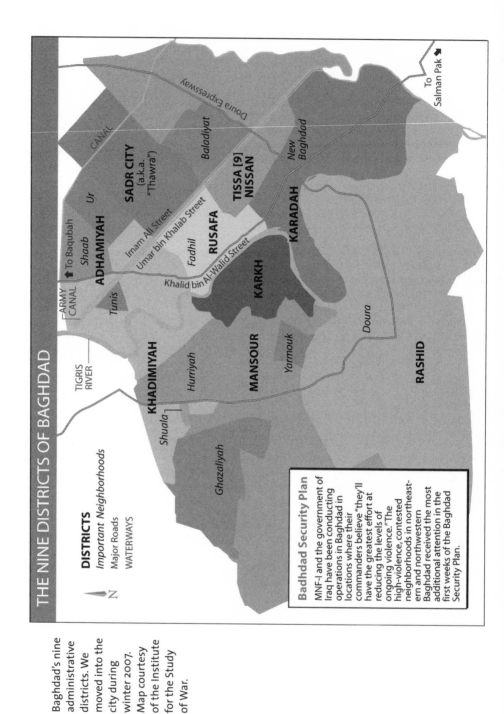

# THE NINE DISTRICTS OF BAGHDAD

Baghdad's nine administrative districts. We moved into the city during winter 2007. Map courtesy of the Institute for the Study of War.

**N**

**DISTRICTS**
*Important Neighborhoods*
Major Roads
WATERWAYS

TIGRIS RIVER

ARMY CANAL

Tunis

Shuala

Ghazaliyah

Hurriyah

**KHADIMIYAH**

Shaab ← To Baqubah

**ADHAMIYAH**

Ur

**SADR CITY**
(a.k.a. "Thawra")

Imam Ali Street

Umar bin Khalab Street

Fadhil

**RUSAFA**

**TISSA [9] NISSAN**

Baladiyat

Doura Expressway

CANAL

New Baghdad

**KARADAH**

Khalid bin Al-Walid Street

**KARKH**

**MANSOUR**

Yarmouk

Doura

**RASHID**

To Salman Pak ➤

**Badghdad Security Plan**

MNF-I and the government of Iraq have been conducting operations in Baghdad in locations where their commanders believe "they'll have the greatest effort at reducing the levels of ongoing violence." The high-violence, contested neighborhoods in northeastern and northwestern Baghdad received the most additional attention in the first weeks of the Baghdad Security Plan.

# PREFACE
## "No Shit, There We Were"
## Salman Pak Backstory

OCTOBER 2006

> Innocence is a kind of insanity.
> — GRAHAM GREENE, *The Quiet American*

I left Iraq with the nagging suspicion that we never understood the things unfolding around us. In fact, most nights at the FOB
(Forward Operating Base) when my head hit the pillow, I had the very
same intuition. Patrols, combat, and daily interactions with Iraqis left
me feeling empty. It was as though we operated in a constant haze.
A dense fog of ignorance surrounded us troops, our each action, our
every move. Sometimes I'd catch a smirk on a local's face or a com-
passionate but patronizing smile. These nonverbal cues seemed to
say, "Poor young American, you don't have the slightest idea what's
really happening here, do you?" And we didn't. I didn't. Try as I might.

Salman Pak was just one medium-size city. Prior to our arrival it
probably counted 150,000 residents—about the size of Paterson, New
Jersey. Estimates varied, but three years of war and the resultant refugee crisis likely halved that number. Fifteen miles southeast of Baghdad, "the Pak"—as the soldiers quickly christened it—was an urban/
suburban hybrid, the same way Paterson is simultaneously part of
and separate from the New York City metro area. It was only one
of several areas we patrolled during the fifteen months from October 2006 to December 2007. More than half the tour, in fact, was
spent within Baghdad's city limits. The "Surge" strategy, announced
in early 2007, led MND-B (Multi-National Division Baghdad—our
higher headquarters) to shift the squadron into the heart of the city.
Nonetheless, Salman Pak was our first sector, our first taste of com-

1

bat, and for me it will always represent Iraq. Like every square inch of the populated earth, especially the old ones—and it was certainly one of those—Salman Pak has history, a unique backstory. Few of my soldiers, or the senior officers, for that matter, knew much about the place. But the context mattered. We never seem to get that.

Our unit, 3rd Squadron, 61st Cavalry, took over the Mada'in Qada in November 2006. Baghdad proper is broken into a series of municipal districts, and the outskirts, sometimes referred to as suburbs (but don't picture Levittown, Long Island) were organized into *qadas*. (This is an Arabic term for a suburban administrative district outside the main city limits. Like the county versus city jurisdictions in the United States—that is, one who lives in Baltimore *County* rather than Baltimore *City*.) My troop inherited the southernmost portion of the Mada'in Qada, including the ancient city of Salman Pak, from the 1st Squadron, 61st Cavalry Regiment, of the storied 101st Airborne Division.[1] They'd arrived in 2005 and spent most of their tour targeting Shia militias, such as the Mahdi Army, and some of their elements maintained an unofficial truce with more dangerous Sunni insurgents.[2] 1-61 CAV took over from 3-7 CAV of the 3rd Infantry Division. The celebrated 7th CAV entered Salman Pak in 2004 and fought the Sunni insurgents while largely ignoring the less menacing Shia militias. Earlier, during the 2003 invasion, U.S. Marines fought through the city. A few died in Salman Pak, and a couple more perished fighting for a contested nearby bridge over the Tigris River. The marines faced a mix of regular Iraqi Army and Fedayeen guerrillas—an early indication, perhaps, of the burgeoning insurgency. Salman Pak was a problem from the outset, but the marines, like all who came after, were just passing through.

Each American unit did its best to quell the violence. Optimism was our charter. Every commander claimed success and advised his successor that one last push, some faith, and tactical continuity heralded victory. I'll give you an example. In April 2005, 3-7 CAV unearthed a huge cache of explosives in Salman Pak—a damn good find. The brigade operations officer[3] took the opportunity to declare: "The enemy appears to be on the run—we've neutralized anti-Iraqi forces' capabilities for using Salman Pak as a staging area."[4] More than a dozen Americans, killed around the Pak in subsequent years, might take extreme issue with this proclamation. In fact, Sunni insurgents infiltrated the area en masse after fleeing Fallujah in 2004.[5] By 2007, Salman Pak was considered a key Al Qaeda stronghold,[6] and it took a few thousand soldiers to regain some control in 2008. We were not that unit. Like those who came before us, chronically short of manpower, we did our best to hold ground and make small gains. We were treading water.

Salman Pak sits on the east side of the Tigris River at a dramatic bend, forming a huge phallus-like peninsula—dubbed the "penis"—and a second, less extreme, circular bend—known as the "ball sack." The outskirts of the city, especially down in the "ball sack," consisted of farmland, fishponds, and massive palm groves. The landscape was broken by hundreds of crisscrossed irrigation canals that severely hindered off-road vehicular movement.[7] Scattered outside the city were tiny villages with names like Ja'ara, Al Leg, Kanasa, and Duraya. The lush farmland contradicted most stereotypes of Iraq as a desert wasteland, but we shouldn't have been surprised. This was the heart of Mesopotamia—the "Land between Two Rivers"—from which the earliest civilizations sprang. People in Salman Pak clustered in advanced cities thousands of years before the Puritans built Boston. History matters.

Before the marines invaded, Salman Pak was a bastion of Saddam Hussein's Baath Party regime. The city held a headquarters building of Saddam's secret police, the notorious Mukhabarat. Tradition held that Salman Pak's Sunni and Shia communities lived in peace for centuries, but Saddam upset the balance in the 1980s. He rewarded his loyal Baath Party cronies—nearly all fellow Sunnis—with huge estates along the river.[8] Some were genuine mansions, though most were abandoned by 2006. Before Saddam, Iraq was a "republic"; before that there was a king. Earlier still, Iraq was a British "mandate"—a fun euphemism for colony. The British had followed Ottoman Turkish rule of the region. Anglo conquest, though, had snagged on Salman Pak. The city, it seems, has a history of troubling foreign occupiers. In November 1915, during World War I, a British army, fresh off a series of victories, broke itself on Salman Pak's forbidding defenses. Suffering a loss of forty-five hundred men, the Brits retreated.

Four hundred years of Turkish rule had preceded the battle. Some

750 years before that, the Arabs had burst from the Saudi Arabian desert, conquered the region, and gradually converted the people to Islam. Previously the city had been known as Ctesiphon, and it served as capital of the ancient Sassanid (Persian) Empire. In the sixth century AD, Ctesiphon was the largest city *in the world*. Salman Pak's defining structure—the Taq-i-Kasra arch—once formed a part of the massive royal throne room of Sassanid kings.[9] It remains the world's largest single-span, free-standing arch. In AD 363, the Roman emperor Julian invaded the region and laid siege to the city. Exhausted and struck with disease, the Roman army retreated in disorder, and the Sassanids pursued and killed Emperor Julian in battle. The Romans subsequently made peace and returned some Persian land. Before the Sassanid accession, Ctesiphon served as capital to another Persian dynasty—the Parthians. As the great Roman Empire spread east in the first century AD, its expansion was checked along the Tigris. Roman-Parthian wars raged on and off for centuries, and Ctesiphon changed hands several times; Rome, however, could never hold on to the city or defeat Parthia. Rome's legions had met their match outside Salman Pak.[10] Probably built in the second century BC, Ctesiphon possessed an epic history. Fast forward two thousand years, and most soldiers barely noticed. Iraq was Iraq—hot, dangerous, and shitty.

# 1

## Enter the "Ghost Riders"
## 2nd Platoon, B/3-61 CAV

FORT CARSON, COLORADO : MARCH 2006

> That though I loved them for their faults
> As much as for their good.
> — DYLAN THOMAS, "To others than you"

I was an accidental soldier. Admittedly, I played with GI Joes as a kid, read plenty of military history, and had considered enlisting since childhood. But as for a *career*, no thanks. Mostly, I think, I'd wanted to prove I was just as tough as my firefighter uncles and street-wise father. Exotic travel sounded pretty good, too. In hindsight it's easy to forget this, but back in early 2001, I assumed that a stint in the army would involve little more than tough training and an occasional trip to Bosnia or Kosovo. I counted on plenty of photo ops of cool Balkan landscapes and a few interesting stories along the way. Anything like 9/11 was beyond the scope of my imagination.

A soft kid, who liked hanging out with his mother more than most, I'd been posturing my whole life. Always scared around the rough boys in the neighborhood, I'd learned to act hard and fit in pretty early on. My dad—Bob "Butchie" Sjursen—grew up in Brooklyn's Sunset Park during the turbulent 1960s, when the Irish and Italian boys clashed with assorted Puerto Rican gangs for control of the streets. He taught me to stand firm, swing first, and hold my ground. I did my best. Raised in a house with no car or telephone, Dad was shot at and stabbed before his seventeenth birthday. With grit and natural intelligence, the guy managed to graduate from City College and worked two or three jobs at a time to wrench us into the lower middle class.

My parents divorced when I was seven, and unfortunately the split dropped us a few steps on the economic ladder. But my father dedicated himself—with every ounce of his soul—to being a full-time dad. My sister Amy and I bounced between my mom's small apartment, our grandparents' bungalow, and my father's condo. When I first started talking about enlisting in the army or marines, it was my dad who pushed me toward West Point. He'd done his research, too—in a pre-Google era, mind you—and explained how academy cadets were actually active-duty soldiers *and* college students. I promised to apply. Here's the thing: I thought you had to be either a blue-blood rich boy or some congressman's kid to get into the place. That might have been true fifty years earlier, but times had changed. The thick green packet, replete with a congratulatory letter from Congressman Vito Fossella and a keepsake plaque, arrived while I was at work in a local hardware store. That night, climbing the steep stairs to my mom's apartment, I heard her and some friends whispering over their wine and sensed something was up. They already knew—clapping broke out—and my mother cried. As close as we were, I don't think anyone was more proud than she was. You can't say no to that.

In May 2005 I graduated, took two months' leave, and attended the Officer Basic Course (OBC) at Fort Knox, Kentucky. After OBC I stayed on at Knox for a month-long Scout Leader's Course (SLC), preparatory training for platoon leaders in light reconnaissance units (Humvee rather than tank). I'd received orders to the 3rd Squadron, 61st Cavalry Regiment—"The Destroyers"—a recon unit in the 2nd Brigade of the 2nd Infantry Division. I showed up in March 2006 and on day one took command of a scout platoon. A lucky break—some guys waited months for an opening while toiling away in menial administrative staff jobs. The unit had only gotten back from their last tour in August 2005 but were already set to head back to Iraq in October. That's how it worked: the army ran on a conveyor belt. You were either at war, just getting home, or training to go back. Period. I was in for months of field training, punctuated by occasional booze-soaked holiday weekends, and plenty of stress. The countdown to Iraq began right then and there. It's how we lived. But first I had a platoon to meet.

On day one I had nineteen soldiers—eighteen Cav scouts and a medic. My second in command was a grizzled old (late thirties—ancient for the army) platoon sergeant—Malcolm Gass. Below that we organized into two sections of three trucks each. In addition to me and Sergeant Gass, we had four other truck commanders. The two most senior were the numbers three and four of the platoon—staff sergeants Damian South and Micah Rittel. Our junior sergeants were Ty Dejane and John Pushard. Then came the heart of the platoon: thirteen young troopers belonging to the undifferentiated yet proud mass we called "Joes."

▬▬▬ The first time I saw Specialist Alexander Fuller, simply "Fuller" within the platoon—first names are all but nonexistent among soldiers—he walked over, stood at stiff attention, and introduced himself. He was the only enlisted man to do so and was far more proper than any of the sergeants. My new platoon sergeant, essentially my second in command—and to most young soldiers the number *one* force in their lives—had given me a quick rundown of the guys in the platoon. He described Fuller with a few choice, military-speak adjectives: "high-speed," "squared-away," "motivated as hell," and "NCO-material." Fuller was young, just twenty then. He looked a bit older though. Medium height, medium build, dark hair cut close in an edged style. He had slightly olive toned skin that deviated just enough from his Anglo-sounding last name that some of the guys speculated he was part Puerto Rican, black, Asian, or *something*. He claimed not to know. Fuller would say he was *American* or "straight Boston, son." That settled it. There was something about his bearing, the mix of confidence and anxiety, something in that nervous smile. It was captivating. He stood stiff with his shoulders pulled back in perfect military posture and introduced himself. It was like something out of a movie and reminded me of a training vignette about "meeting your new platoon" I'd seen at West Point. This didn't happen in real life. In that moment I don't think I had an inkling that Fuller would be forever with me, but I guess you could say I liked him from the start.

▰▰▰▰ Private Edsel Ford was a pain in my ass from the day he showed up at the unit until the day we got to Iraq. His father had given him the strange first name as a tribute to the short-lived line of cars named for Henry Ford's only son. A significant commercial failure, the Edsel division lasted only from 1957 to 1960. Private Ford started slow; it took the war for him to flourish. A late arrival to the unit, he looked about fifteen, though actually he was in his early twenties. Of medium height and slight, he appeared almost frail as his oversized uniform draped awkwardly over his skinny torso. Everyone said he looked like Justin Timberlake—and he did! Fashion conscious when off duty, he frequented clubs and bars nearly every night of the week and twice on weekends. He was a legit dancer; come to think of it, Ford kind of thought he *was* JT. The kid was seemingly late to every single formation. He'd sleep in, miss PT, and spend the rest of the day getting "smoked"—forced to do physical exercises to exhaustion—by the platoon's sergeants. The thing is, he never seemed to sweat it. He'd stay quiet, take the punishment, smile at the end of the day and do it all over again. We thought he was hopeless. The one thing Ford *did* do well—besides break-dance—was medical training. It turned out he'd been a volunteer firefighter and a certified first responder back home. Looking at him, that was hard to believe, but years later one of the other soldiers told me that Ford had once said, "Hey, dude, if something bad ever happens when we get over there—I can no shit help you." He was right.

▰▰▰▰ Sergeant Ty Dejane was the junior NCO of the platoon, probably the least mature, but also the most popular with troops. DJ—as we called him—was from the town of Salem, Ohio, a hardscrabble district of abandoned factories and thwarted dreams. DJ was one of those young sergeants who could give two shits about getting some new lieutenant. He'd been to Iraq once before, was about my age, and exuded an air of "who gives a shit" when I first met him. DJ had had previous combat experience. He'd patrolled north of Baghdad in 2003 to 2004, assigned to the scout platoon of 1-12 Infantry in the 4th Infantry Division. That first tour started slow, but as the insurgency heated up in the late summer of '03, his platoon started to see contact with IEDs and some firefights.

███████ Sergeants, so goes the popular platitude, are the backbone of the army. And sure, that's true. But here's the thing: it's a lot more complex than that. Sergeants are essential. They stay in a unit longer than most officers and provide vital continuity. They've risen up from the ranks and know the soldier's life. Many are highly seasoned and their advice is invaluable. But some of them suck. They're not all created equal. NCO worship is no more rational than that of any other deified human group. Some are solid, others dreadful. A select few are exceptional. Staff Sergeant Damian South of Panama City, Florida, was my finest. Damian—we were quickly on a first-name basis—was twenty-six, just three years older than me, and close enough in age to feel like a peer.

Damian had lived with his father, a diesel mechanic, after his parents split up and had moved all over the Southeast before settling in Panama City, Florida. In high school he played football, joined the Air Force ROTC, and always planned to enlist in the military. That's just what the men in Damian's family did. His father was a former marine and a Vietnam vet, his uncle an army Special Forces Green Beret, and his grandfather a twenty-three-year veteran of the U.S. Navy—including service in World War II. Damian had originally signed a contract with the air force, but after he shattered his ankle wrestling with some friends the military was put on hold. He kept trying to join the army but each time was rejected on account of the old injury. In the meantime, he worked as a bouncer in a local club and spent some time studying criminal justice at Gulf Coast State College. Exceptionally bright but never a focused student, Damian quickly tired of school. It was 9/11 that changed everything. Suddenly the army starting accepting nearly *everyone*, and almost overnight he received an injury waiver. By January 2002, he was on his way to basic training.

Damian was young, energetic, physically fit, and wildly popular with the troops. He led by example in every way—technically skilled, tactically aware, fastest runner, best athlete, and the most charismatic. About six-foot-three, he had the outsized personality to match. Ironically, he'd been a Cav scout for only about a year.[1] He'd first enlisted as an Air Defense Artillery (ADA) specialist—not generally considered among the elite combat branches. Nonetheless, he *had* been to Iraq before, with the 4th Infantry Division in 2003 to 2004. With the Iraqi Air Force all but nonexistent, most ADA units converted to armored infantrymen, and Damian's platoon was no exception. He spent a year in the northern city of Tikrit, learned his trade, but saw little direct combat. Back in those early days large swaths of Iraq were relatively quiet, and it was fairly normal to serve a whole year without losing a man. Soon after, the army phased out Damian's particular ADA specialty, and he had to switch jobs. He chose 19D—cavalry scout.

There was just something about the guy—I guess you could say we got along from the start. Damian was smart and witty, by far the brightest guy in the platoon. He was young and relatable but simultaneously mature. Damian hung out with the soldiers but stayed a step above their nonsense. He treated officers with respect and never acted better than me, despite his greater experience. Turned out we shared an acquaintance, too. During his last tour Damian's platoon leader had been Lieutenant Ronald "Ronnie" Iammartino, a fellow West Pointer and Staten Island native. Ronnie was a senior during my freshman year, so our overlap was short. Nevertheless, he was good to me. Plebe year sucks, what with the hazing and lack of off-post privileges, and there weren't very many New Yorkers around. Ronnie would always say, "Hey," and talked to me like a normal person— something surprisingly refreshing back then. He'd once pulled me to the side and said that, when no one was around, I didn't need to call him "sir," because, "after all, I'm really just Ronnie from Rose Avenue, ya know?"[2] I did know. Damian's and my shared affection for Ronnie built some key early trust between us.

■■■■■ By design, the closest relationship in a platoon is supposed to be between the lieutenant and his platoon sergeant. Mine, eighteen-year veteran Sergeant First Class Malcolm Gass, was in his late thirties. He knew the job, could acquire anything the platoon needed—we called him the scrounger[3]—and had a shortcut for everything. Gass was just what we needed from a senior sergeant, but he could have been my dad. Technically. As a result, Damian quickly became the guy to whom I'd go with a question or concern. He was my rock. He talked about getting out of the army after this stint, and, given that I was a brand new lieutenant without a clue, I spent an inappropriate amount of time trying to convince him to stay in. He didn't. But that came later. Right then, we needed a "senior scout," and Damian was it. Senior scout is not an official military rank, and it exists only in the cavalry. In our world, it's the biggest honor and responsibility a sergeant can have. To simplify: the senior scout is the section sergeant in the lead vehicle on all patrols. He has immense influence on route selection and has the freedom to call an audible (make a last minute change) mid-mission. As the first set of eyes on everything the unit sees and eventually does, the senior scout is often the difference between success and failure, life or death. He's a guy you better trust. Choosing Damian was a no-brainer. We took to hanging out off-duty and drinking beers at a local dive—the Hatch Cover. Trust is built on booze and bullshitting as much as it is on rank or training. Don't let anyone tell you otherwise.

Richard "Ducks" Duzinskas put up with a lot of shit. Ducks was our most experienced young soldier. He'd been in the army for three years and had deployed to Iraq in 2004 to 2005. You'd think that'd earn him a ton of respect from the new guys. It didn't. He'd been with our brigade on the last deployment but hadn't seen much combat compared with some of the other scouts. During that tour, Ducks's personality conflicts with a couple of sergeants resulted in a reassignment to headquarters duty in the intelligence section. That was a blow to his confidence and standing among his peers. It would stick with him.

Ducks was a genuine guy, well spoken, kind, and friendly. He was the sort of soldier who *liked* sitting in the lieutenant's office talking about the job. I enjoyed our long discussions and immediately recognized his uncommon intelligence. Smarter than your average "Joe," Ducks—if he'd shaved a couple minutes off his 2-mile run time—would have fast tracked to sergeant. He felt that his physical fitness tests—limited by some lingering injuries—combined with the ire of a few sergeants were holding back his career. That may have been true, but Ducks would need to improve his scores before we could promote him. He had other strengths, though: he could shoot. Ducks was adept with weapons, studied the manuals, and knew his machine guns inside and out. Leadership was a different beast; he'd need to prove himself to the young troops and earn some respect.

██████ Private Edward Faulkner came from the small town of Elon, in the North Carolina Piedmont. He was a bit older than the other Joes, already twenty-two when he arrived in 2nd platoon. Quieter than most of the guys, he held a piercing dry wit in cautious reserve. I needed a driver for my HMMWV (High Mobility Multipurpose Wheeled Vehicle) and picked Faulkner. I don't know why exactly. He was new, inexperienced, and traditionally platoon leaders take a seasoned driver. I guess I liked his self-deprecating humor and humble mannerisms. At one of his first training events, I saw Ed—though I took to calling him Eddie after he told me he'd briefly worked as a plumber back in Carolina—sitting alone on the side of a huge dirt hill. He was smoking and looking rather serene. I climbed up to join him. We smoked a few cigs, shot the shit, and mostly just took in the view. Such a simple moment, but it stuck with me. The good ones do.

██████ Private First Class James David Smith was Texan to the core. It's not a surprise. When I started at West Point back in 2001, I swear it seemed like *half* the cadets were from Texas. That was impossible, of course, since the military academy accepts applicants based on congressional apportionment, but it seemed like Texans were everywhere—probably because they were so loud about it. The same held true in the regular army, and Smith could have been the state spokesman. Hailing from the Fort Worth suburb of Hurst, he was a high school wrestler who loved the rodeo and four-wheeling. Smith's arm sported a Lone Star flag tattoo, just above script of the name "Sadey." Smith ran hot, with all the typical impulsiveness of a single, nineteen-year-old dude. It was too easy to get under his skin. In a platoon full of ball breakers, it was inevitable that they'd start in on him.

"Yo Smith, like, who the fuck is Sadey—your cow or some shit?"

[This always ended the same way.]

[Smith, chest puffed out, nose to nose with said heckler, yells,] "That's my niece, asshole, now take that shit back or I'll beat your ass!"

[Random sergeant breaks it up before things come to blows.]

Same old. All of five-foot-ten and 170 pounds, Smith wasn't a huge guy, but he was well built, scrappy, and always prepared to fight. The guys didn't know why he cared so much about that tattoo. I did. I wrote letters to the parents of all my troopers just before our deployment. I wanted them to know what their sons actually *did* in the army, introduce myself, and tell them how proud I was of their kids. Kind of cheesy, I guess, but I was, and am, an eternal romantic—about everything. David and Susan Smith were among the few parents to write back. They thanked me and were glad to hear James was succeeding. They expressed some concern about his decision-making and impetuosity. Sadey, I learned, was James's niece—his only sister's daughter. She meant everything to him. The Smiths said they'd be out to Colorado to see him off in October and hoped we could meet. I read the letter twice and put it down, feeling a weight of crushing responsibility. This was their only boy, just a few years younger than me, and now, somehow in my charge. I was in over my head.

# Citizenship and Sacrifice
## Reflections on Military Service

I volunteered for the army on my birthday.

They draft the white trash first 'round here anyway.

— STEVE EARLE, "Copperhead Road"

THE OTHER 1 PERCENT: THE ORIGINS OF 2ND PLATOON

Soldiers come and go. They switch units, transfer posts, get promoted, and return to civilian life. That's just part of the game. About thirty-five guys served in the platoon during my time there. That said, about twenty core guys stayed together for the majority of our training and the Iraq deployment. Just how representative they are is, I suppose, debatable. But my experience in later units and another deployment makes me think the platoon was fairly standard.[1] So who were these guys? It's an important question, actually. These individuals did the country's dirty work. Two-time volunteers, they first picked the army, and then chose a direct combat job. They trained for war and went wherever the president—and, one assumes, by extension, the American people—told them to go. Let's start with origins—their hometowns.

Confession: I like to spend my down time in the trendy neighborhoods of bigger cities. You know, the artsy districts; places where they bring infants or golden retrievers into pubs, and play board games at the bar; where the guys have superfluous facial hair and girls rock gratuitous hats and glasses. Hipsterville, USA. These days every city has such a place—personally, I like Carroll Gardens, Brooklyn, and Westport in Kansas City—but they're everywhere. I like being away from the army when I can, and pretending to be a normal person. In truth, I don't love the hipster styles, and the trendiness can be a bit much. Nevertheless, the great thing about hipsters—unlike frat boys—is they don't fight in bars and can quote *The Princess Bride* (which is key). Anyway, I digress.

One thing I've noticed after thirteen years in the military world is that no one in the army seems to come from anywhere *near* these places. Almost none of my soldiers hailed from big cities. New York, Los Angeles, Philadelphia—you just never hear those answers in the ubiquitous "Where ya from?" conversations. Statistically, some soldiers are from those places, but not at all in the numbers you'd expect and not at a proportionate rate given huge populations. Besides me and Ducks, no one hailed from a city with more than 100,000 people. With one exception—Artis—2nd platoon comprised nineteen white boys, mostly from small-town USA. (This is not to imply that there are no, or few, minorities in the military. Actually, the army is broadly representative and progressive on racial matters—more on this later. But 2nd platoon, and a surprising number of other combat units, did adhere to my racial and demographic description.) So we didn't have any New Yorkers (besides me), San Franciscans, or Los Angelinos; instead, the platoon counted three Texans, three Kentuckians, and two guys from North Carolina. Plus lots of other southern(ish) locales: West Virginia, Florida, Arkansas, Georgia, and Virginia; a smattering of Midwestern places: Missouri, Ohio, Indiana, and Illinois. Our outliers were Arizona, Massachusetts, and Maine.

My guys came from places you've never heard of—towns and cities that don't get their own reality TV shows, areas without much opportunity. You haven't been there. Spots like Thomasville, Georgia (Pop. 18,143; 35.2 percent poverty rate), Stuarts Draft, Virginia—"Warehouse Capital of the USA"—(Pop. 9,125), Corbin, Kentucky (Pop. 7,304; 19.8 percent poverty rate), Radcliff, Kentucky (Pop. 21,688; 21.4 percent poverty rate), and Myerstown, Pennsylvania (Pop. 3,062).[2] Some soldiers came from solid families, many were very bright, but by and large they struggled. At least a bit. These weren't the sons of bankers, doctors, or hotshot lawyers. They all came to the army as a result of some combination of desire and necessity. Neither can be ruled out. The 2nd platoon counted one bachelor's and one associate's degree plus a smattering of community college credits. For some, the army was a means to an affordable education; for others, health care and a steady paycheck. But they were all volunteers, and the moment they stepped into the recruiting office, they were special. Whether motivated by cash, schooling, or patriotism, each of them made a conscious decision to take on the burden of service. Young enlisted soldiers fight, suffer, and risk death in far-off lands—for $18,000 a year.[3] We should at least know who they are.

DUTY, FREEDOM, FAIRNESS:
PATTERNS OF NATIONAL SERVICE 2007

The way a nation wages war—the role allotted to the people in defending the country and the purposes for which it fights—testifies to the actual character of its political system.
— ANDREW BACEVICH, *Breach of Trust:*
    *How Americans Failed Their Soldiers and Their Country*

The incidence of military service both reflects and affects social structure.
— JOHN SHY, historian

Once upon a time, the sons of senators, presidents, and newspaper magnates served in uniform. When duty called, elite families sent their young men off to war. Some 453 Harvard graduates died in World War II, just 35 fewer than the number of West Point dead.[4] As late as 1956—during peacetime—400 out of 750 Princeton graduates served in uniform. Contrast that with 2004, when nine Princeton grads joined the military, the *highest* number of any Ivy League school.[5] Until quite recently, Harvard, Yale, Brown, Stanford, and Columbia banned ROTC programs from campus, indirectly deterring many of the nation's elite students from even *considering* military service. After 1973, the geography of the ROTC program shifted south and west. So did the enlistment pool. The military today is out of balance—far more southern, western, and rural than the population at large. Military posts in the Northeast and on the California coast closed down and shifted personnel southward,[6] to bases named, ironically, for Confederate Civil War generals—Fort Hood (Texas); Bragg (North Carolina); Gordon and Benning (Georgia); Polk (Louisiana); Lee, A. P. Hill, and Pickett (Virginia); and Rucker (Alabama). Unless one is exposed, in some fashion, to the armed forces enlistment is highly unlikely. We do only what we know.[7] The sons of

16

Wall Street bankers, affluent professionals, acclaimed athletes and political elites failed to follow the military southward.

It was not always so. Once the Sulzbergers—scions of the *New York Times*—sent sons off to war. Movie stars left Hollywood and donned a uniform. Henry Fonda, Clarke Gable, Tyrone Power, and Jimmy Stewart served in World War II.[8] So did the athletes. Baseball legends Joe DiMaggio, Hank Greenberg, Bob Feller, pro boxers Joe Louis and Gene Tunney served, along with a few hundred more. Red Sox slugger Ted Williams flew combat missions for the Marine Corps in two wars—in the South Pacific in the 1940s, then Korea in the early '50s. In Korea, he flew wingman for future astronaut John Glenn.[9] Eight former MLB players died in World War I, two in World War II, and one in Korea.[10] Nineteen players from the NFL perished in World War II.[11] The draft ensured that the rich, famous, wealthy, and powerful would serve alongside the middle class and the poor. During World War II, most elites avoided the draft—they volunteered. It was the thing to do.

Celebrities in uniform are one thing, but the willingness of politicians to serve is far more significant. After all, presidents direct the troops and congressmen ultimately approve (in theory) and fund the wars. And not too long ago, most of the American political elite shared the burden of service. As recently as 1991, 70 percent of U.S. senators were military veterans.[12] Less than a quarter-century later, that number has more than halved with no sign of its changing course.[13] The trend is also reflected among the chief executives. Before President Clinton, nearly every modern president was a military veteran. George H. W. Bush was the lone survivor after his plane was shot down in the South Pacific.[14] Jimmy Carter was a Naval Academy graduate, John F. Kennedy a highly decorated navy officer, and, of course, Dwight Eisenhower gave the better part of his adult life to the army.

Moreover, U.S. presidents once sent their own sons off to the fight. Teddy Roosevelt offered up four sons to the army.[15] Teddy, Jr., the eldest boy, won the Distinguished Service Cross in France during World War I after being gassed at Soissons. In World War II, after fighting across North Africa, he was the only general to land at Normandy on D-Day. He died of a heart attack in his tent weeks later and received a posthumous Medal of Honor. Kermit, the second son, couldn't wait to serve. He volunteered for the British Army before the United States entered either war. In the first war he fought against the Ottomans in Iraq; in the second he distinguished himself in Norway and North Africa. Plagued with alcoholism and depression, he committed suicide later in the war. Archie Roosevelt was wounded in both world wars, once in France and later by a grenade in the Pacific. Teddy's youngest son, Quentin, had the unfortunate distinction to be the only presidential son to die in combat—shot down behind German lines in World War I. The boy's death crushed his father, who never fully recovered.[16]

During World War II, a serving president, Franklin Delano Roosevelt, had four sons in uniform. The eldest, James Roosevelt, had flat feet and a draft exemption but still volunteered for the Marine Corps. He worked intelligence for a Marine Raider unit and earned the Navy Cross and Silver Star. FDR, Jr., served as a naval officer in the European theater. He won the Silver Star during the invasion of Sicily and was also wounded in action.[17] John, the youngest son, served on the USS *Hornet* aircraft carrier and earned a Bronze Star. Elliot Roosevelt flew three hundred reconnaissance missions over Europe with the Army Air Corps. On one such flight, he actually witnessed fellow officer Joseph Kennedy, Jr.—older brother of JFK—die in an explosion.[18]

The Kennedy boys also served. In addition to John and Joe, young Bobby actually enlisted in the navy before his seventeenth birthday. He eventually served on a ship named in honor of his oldest brother. The list goes on. Dwight Eisenhower's son John graduated from West Point on D-Day and served in both World War II and Korea. Even LBJ had a son-in-law in Vietnam, future senator Chuck Robb. Robb served two tours, one as Rifle Company commander, and earned the Bronze Star.[19] Then the tradition stops. Not a single child of a serving president has worn the uniform since, and shockingly few congressmen's sons serve. Contrast the impressive war records amassed by FDR's sons with the unapologetic lack of service by the five Romney boys. Queried while on the 2008 campaign trail about his prowar stance and lack of personal or family military service, Republican hopeful Mitt Romney countered: "My sons are all adults and they've . . . chosen not to serve in the military . . . and I respect their decision in that regard." He then added: "One of the ways my sons are showing support for our nation is helping me get elected, because they think I'd be a great president."[20] How times change. And should my example sound partisan, I wouldn't count on Sasha, Malia, or any future Obama son-in-law serving in uniform, either. Just a hunch.

Looking back from 2014, the past generations' elite and celebrity service seems astonishing. The nation has been at war for thirteen years and just one professional athlete joined the army. Arizona Cardinals defender Pat Tillman's death might have highlighted the changing patterns of national service, sacrifice, and citizenship, but instead the controversy surrounding the military's cover-up of his friendly fire death dominated the media narrative. Today's soldiers are neither the most destitute nor the most well off. They don't reflect the stable upper middle class. The most affluent, influential, and famous citizens aren't represented at all. No, my soldiers came from small towns—primarily in the Deep South, mid- and far-West—and many had few other opportunities. The uncomfortable reality is that most Americans—especially on the coasts—don't come into contact with any of the kids who served in Iraq. And if they do meet a veteran, they probably don't even realize it. It's unlikely that most affluent Americans would give most vets a second thought, except to hire them to clean the family pool or hand some fast food out a drive-thru window. Deep down, I doubt that's the country most of us *want* to live in. Only it's the one most of us know—the new normal, at least since 1973.

The end of the draft was a direct result of the unpopular Vietnam War. Nevertheless, it's important to realize this represented a conscious decision by President Nixon to stifle a powerful protest movement and extend the war.[21] All Americans were complicit. The prowar hawks, led behind the scenes by Nixon, wanted more freedom to do what was necessary to salvage victory from the sinking fortunes in Vietnam. Antiwar "New Left" Democrats wished to unilaterally end both the war and the draft. Few young men were excited about mandatory military service, and conscription was wildly unpopular by the late 1960s. The army establishment, and even many young officers, also welcomed the end of conscription. A new professional force would jettison their responsibility to train, discipline, and motivate disruptive, reluctant soldiers. This was an army, after all, dealing with unprecedented racial, political, and class strife in the ranks. During the war, nearly one hundred officers were killed by their own men in the notorious "fragging" incidents. The new All-Volunteer Force (AVF) was thus a compromise that pleased nearly everyone. Vietnam dominated the debate. Besides, the rebirth of the professional army and its stellar performance in the 1991 Gulf War formed an undisputed—if misplaced—consensus around the decision's wisdom. Few considered the long-term consequences of ending the draft. We're living with them now.

In the midst of the nation's longest war, nothing is asked of the American people. Not military service, not taxes, not sacrifice. The *other 1 percent*—the fewer than one out of a hundred Americans on active duty—fight our current wars of choice. Presidents use this new professional force at will, without fear of a popular backlash, even when things go bad. The "liberals" in Congress, well, they're mostly too afraid to look soft on defense to do much of anything at all. Besides, as fewer and fewer (especially Democratic) congressmen have a military record, they face what you might call a credibility crisis. And the people? They're mostly consumed with minutiae and distraction. Some of it is normal—the economy is rough, real wages are stagnant, and life is hard. But the people are also cognizant of and reliant on their utter lack of obligations. The combination feeds widespread indifference.

War, as such, is an abstraction. The media doesn't report much on Iraq or Afghanistan because it doesn't sell anymore. War is now chronic, routine, and thus boring. Look at the nonstop, days-long coverage of (admittedly tragic) school shootings, or of the Governor Chris Christie (R-NJ) "Toll-gate" scandal. Turn on the television and you can't escape it. But what about the daily firefights, IEDs, and casualties in Iraq or Afghanistan? Or the countless number of humanitarian patrols and schools built? Or, for that matter, the numerous failures—strategic and tactical—of our officers and soldiers? Sure, there's an occasional story, but for daily coverage you might as well watch BBC *World News* or *Al-Jazeera*—because, in truth, the Brits and Arabs do a better job covering our wars than we do. Consider it another way: how many coworkers at the proverbial "water cooler" discussed Phillip Seymour Hoffman's death or speculated at length about the sex of the royal baby? Compare that with the number of meaningful discussions of the war, its merits, faults, and consequences. Distraction sells.

By the way, beyond just shock value and fascinating vignettes—this all matters. Charles Moskos, the preeminent military sociologist of the last forty years, wrote that "citizens accept hardship only when their elites are viewed as self-sacrificing."[22] Enlistment rates ebb and flow—mostly contingent on the economy—but even back in the booming 1990s, Moskos polled a group of army recruiters on whether they thought doubling their budget or having Chelsea Clinton enlist would better boost enrollments. The recruiters overwhelmingly picked the latter.[23] You see, it's about fairness. Human beings learn by example, sense hypocrisy and respond accordingly.

# 3

# Life as a Countdown
## Drinking, Training, and Otherwise Getting By

FORT CARSON, COLORADO : MARCH TO OCTOBER 2006

### THE GREATEST (TROOP) STORY EVER TOLD

My first weekend as platoon leader, I was fast asleep when the phone rang. I checked the clock—4:00 a.m.—didn't recognize the number, but picked up. You couldn't miss the voice, a mix of ghetto street slang and a New England accent—Fuller. It felt like home.[1]

"Hey, Sir . . ."

"Yes, Fuller?" [I mumbled.]

"Yo Sir, Artis in jail, cuz!"

He gave me a couple of scattered details, and then my platoon sergeant called in on the other line. I switched over to get the *official story*. It turned out that Private Artis, one of my other troopers, had in fact been arrested for an alleged breaking and entering. Nothing makes an officer's weekend like a good old B&E. My platoon sergeant was already on his way to pick him up, so I was off the hook until Monday. But it was my job to inform the captain—never a fun assignment. I tried to fall back to sleep and thought about how a *specialist*—Fuller—was the one to call me with the news. At the time it seemed strange.

Weeks later, Fuller gave one of his legendary performances recounting the full story of Artis's arrest. We were out conducting urban training in a mock city. Of course, this "city" consisted of about a dozen shipping containers with some Arabic signs hung around town. I never saw such a place in Iraq, but hey—budgets are budgets, and we got the idea. The platoon was done for the afternoon, and all the junior enlisted soldiers were hanging in one of the double-wide containers, smoking cigarettes and ducking the wind. The sergeants were in a nearby container, doing the same. Most of the officers shadowed the company commander in the headquarters area. That was the way of things. But not me, I was a *soldier's* officer, a man of the people. I came from the working class end of Staten Island—the type of place where half the streets are named for firemen killed on 9/11. I grew up with some rough kids, lived in small apartments, and struggled just enough. I was *one of them*. Or so I liked to believe. Truthfully, I still do. I walked into a circle of soldiers, sat down, and bummed a smoke. In the center, Fuller re-enacted the whole story:

"So yo, Artis got this girl he's fucking, right. Beat ass bitch, I mean BEAT."

[Artis interjected,] "C'mon, Fuller, c'mon, she ain't THAT bad, man."

[Fuller proceeded,] "What?!? Are you kidding? Son, this girl's got some nappy-ass short hair, dyed red and shit, with some serious bald spots, bro."

[Artis laughing, conceded,] "Arright, true, true, she ain't so great, I guess."

[Fuller continued,] "So Artis calls this girl for a hook-up and she like tells him to let himself into her place—like the door's unlocked and shit—so he's like, arright, cool, and so he does. He heads over there and she's kinda late and not pickin up her phone, so he's like fuck it, I'm *gonna* get comfy. So this dude takes off all his clothes, man—gets buck ass naked and shit."

[Laughs and hoots, Artis explained,] "So what man? I was tired bro—LT be runnin the shit out of us every DAY—besides I wanted to make it easier when she got home."

[Fuller laughed and went on,] "So this guy gets himself butt-naked and gets in her bed, under the sheets and everything. So she still ain't home and Artis heads to the fridge!"

[Artis interrupted,] "I was hungry, man. I got me some Go-Gurts!" [Hysterical laughter.]

[Fuller:] "Only thing is, this bitch has a man, and he lives there. She didn't expect to see the dude that night, but they're together now and she can't call to warn ol' Artis. So this girl and her man pull up to the house, and they come in, and here's Artis' big black ass—naked as all hell—in their fuckin' HOUSE."

[Shrieks of "Ohhh shit!" and "Fuck!" from the crowd.]

[Artis jumped in:] "And this bitch, she act like she don't even KNOW me—she's like screaming and playing like I'm an intruder. So they call the COPS. And they put me in the car and cuff me and everything. And I'm yelling out at her, like 'C'mon, girl, how you gonna DO me like that?!?'"

The mental image of naked, jolly old Artis munching on a Go-Gurt and led away by the cops was too much. The whole platoon burst into an uproar bordering on hysteria. In that moment I felt close to them, like I was sharing in privileged information. Of course, I already knew about the arrest. I'd been awakened to deal with it. And I knew the charges were eventually dropped. But this was the first time I'd heard the *whole* story, and no one could tell it like Fuller. He and Artis played off each other like a polished comedy act. They were perfect. I'd been platoon leader just short of a month. There was nowhere I'd rather be.

### GLORIFIED BABYSITTING: DOMESTIC VIOLENCE, COCAINE, AND OTHER EXTREME BEHAVIOR

A platoon leader's official job description reads as follows:

> Responsible for training the platoon to fight and win in the contemporary operating environment. Responsible for the training, mentoring, and tactical leadership of two scout sections to ensure they are prepared for all contingencies. Responsible for $2 million worth of MTOE equipment and property. Responsible for maintenance of assigned equipment and facilities.[2]

Sure, we do all of that. The duties *not* mentioned, however, and the ones that take up inordinate amounts of training time, are social work, criminal investigation, counseling, and babysitting. Consider one full work day, just a few months before our deployment to Iraq. A new soldier, who shall remain nameless, got into some trouble the preceding night. Hearing riotous commotion next door, neighbors called the police. When MPs arrived at my soldier's house, as per standard procedure in domestic disturbances, they forced him to leave and placed him under arrest. This was bad, not just for the soldier but for the unit. The incident hit the police blotter, read each morning by the battalion commander, and was inevitably seen as a black eye for my troop commander. This is typical army. Everyone is trying to have the best unit and constantly competing with their peers. In a world in which officers receive a report card every year, determining their prospects for promotion, *everything* becomes an evaluation. Even the off-duty habits of your soldiers. I suppose lieutenants and captains should get some rope, *physically tie* naughty soldiers to their hip, and take them home for the weekend; because in truth, that'd be the only way to keep dozens of men in their late teens and early twenties out of trouble. Oh, but we do love our quixotic battles with human nature.

The next morning, said soldier was out of jail and back at work. He was given a forty-eight-hour "no contact" order with his wife by the troop commander, and I was sent to escort him back to the house. My mission was twofold: (a) supervise while he grabbed some clothes and essentials, and (b) conduct a "health and wellness" inspection of the home. Basically, I was supposed to take some photos and write a report on the suitability and sanitation of the soldier's quarters. We got to the front door and couldn't miss the sight and smell of the overflowing trash bin outside. They'd missed a few weeks of trash pickup, I guess, because about a dozen garbage bags—some torn open by stray animals—were strewn across the front yard. He let himself in and the place was a wreck. Pizza boxes, trash, clothes, and beer cans were everywhere.

His wife, on the couch watching TV, calmly greeted us as though *nothing had happened.* She didn't even get up or introduce herself. I looked down at the carpet and noticed a dark red blood trail. Taking one more look at his wife, I realized that her hand was wrapped in a blood-soaked dish towel. I asked if she needed medical attention, and she waved me off. Super sleuth that I am, I followed the trail of blood upstairs. It led to the bathroom, then turned bigger and brighter. She'd punched the glass medicine cabinet and sent shards of shattered glass and blood across the room. I snapped a few shots. My soldier collected his stuff. I felt like a detective on CSI as I followed the trail to a bloody doorknob. Turned the handle, looked up, and—"Oh shit, I'm sorry ma'am"—slammed it shut. On the floor in the sparse room sat a single mattress. Two half-naked women—one passed out cold—lay on the unmade bed with a few liquor bottles littering the floor. I skipped the photography. My soldier and his wife were each about twenty-one and a hot mess. He was gone a few months later, chaptered out of the army after pissing hot for cocaine on a random drug test. It happened. Ask any young officer and they've got the same story, plus or minus a few details. All told, that was an ok day—I sort of dug the drama—and it beat working.

Some kids were straight crazy. I had another soldier—we'll call him "Jones"—who probably cost me and the sergeants a few hundred hours of our lives. Time you never get back. For brevity's sake, I'll review the charges. Jones forgot to shave, rarely bathed, slept through his alarm, refused to train, heard voices, talked to himself, and eventually climbed out a barracks window and threatened to jump. The last incident brought police, an ambulance, and a permanent trip to the psych ward. Just before that, Jones had pulled his greatest stunt. Out on field exercises at Fort Carson, the platoon was gearing up for the impending deployment. Jones was considered a flight risk of sorts by this point. He'd missed a few days of work and had been acting more bizarrely than usual. We had him under watch. The truth is, I didn't want to take him out to the field—the guy was a drain on our time and energy—but the commander didn't want to reward bad behavior. So there he was in the tent with the rest of the platoon, guarded in two-hour blocks by a sergeant. Late one afternoon, during Fuller's guard shift, Jones had to piss. Fuller walked out to the portable latrines and watched him head in. Less than a second later, Jones rushed out of the port-a-potty and took off for the woods line. Fuller yelled for help and gave chase. The manhunt culminated in a few dozen soldiers chasing one deranged kid across a vast expanse of Colorado wilderness. We never caught him.

Hours later, long after the sun went down, an exhausted Fuller stumbled back to base camp. Our grizzled platoon sergeant, Malcolm Gass, razzed Fuller about his failure.

"What the FUCK, Specialist Fuller, I thought you were a PT stud; you can't catch one measly private?"

[Fuller struggling to catch his breath:] "I, I, tried . . . Sergeant. You, you, can't outrun crazy, son!"

Indeed you can't. Jones—who couldn't keep up in a *single* training run—had bested our fastest sergeants and dozens of HMMWV mounted patrols. Turned out he'd beat feet several miles to the west and off the military reservation. Reaching a busy state highway, he'd hitchhiked a few days straight until he made it home to *Kentucky*—1,180 miles. You had to respect the commitment. In the process, Jones had stopped our squadron field exercise and subsequently frozen operations in the *entire* Fort Carson training area. All rifle and artillery ranges stopped for fear that Jones would stumble into the line of fire. The interruption lasted about twenty-four hours and came to the attention of the division's two-star general in charge. Needless to say, Ghost Rider platoon had finer days. Shuffling to the battalion commander's office to explain, I wished I'd used that damn rope.

### BULLIES, BLOODY NOSES, AND ASSORTED TEAM-BUILDING TECHNIQUES

One of the best training events I've been a part of was our squadron's "Destroyer First Responder" exercise. Over the course of a few days, each platoon received instruction on various medical procedures and buddy-aid techniques. We then applied this knowledge during simulated exercises. Everything was done under combat conditions. Case in point: we practiced administering IVs to one another at night while in the back of a moving HMMWV. My partner, Staff Sergeant Micah Rittel, of Myerstown, Pennsylvania, wasn't known for his steady hands. A dedicated NCO with the finest intentions, he also had a nervous streak. My forearm bore the brunt of it. Daylight revealed several bloody holes—about a baker's dozen—on my right arm. But the highlight of "Destroyer First Responder" was nasopharyngeal airway training.

Also known as the nasal trumpet, the "nasal," as we called it, was a surprisingly long rubber tube used to open an obstructed airway in unconscious patients. The nasal facilitates breathing and prevents a wounded soldier's tongue from inadvertently blocking the throat. A vital first aid technique, sure, but the insertion was *brutal*. Every one of us had to practice inserting and receiving this long-ass, thick tube up our noses and down our throats. Nobody wanted to be first. Then the chant began: "L-T, L-T, L-T!" I'd wished they were New York

Giants fans circa 1990 chanting for All-Pro linebacker Lawrence Taylor, but alas, the guys wanted *me* to be first. You've got to give the people what they want. I lay down and watched SSG Rittel douse one end of the nasal with Vaseline. This was going to suck. He shoved that bad-boy up my nose and I swear it entered my brain. My leg reflexively raised in the air and, ironically, I felt like I *couldn't* breathe. Within a second it was over. The cheers were deafening. The boys loved that shit.

Everyone took turns "taking the nasal," and the fellas screamed and cheered for every iteration. Two things: (1) today, only trained medics in the army practice the nasopharyngeal on *live* patients, and (2) only *my* platoon could—and did—turn this disgusting process into a rite of passage. In the peculiar world of soldiers, getting a tube stuck up your nose signified team building, a challenge met and shared by all. From that day forward, every new arrival had to face the nasal. At day's end, the newbie was tackled and wrestled to the ground. The platoon formed a circle and started the chant, "Nay-sal, Nay-sal!" And the poor kid—having no *clue* what was about to happen—would have a nasal trumpet shoved deep up his nose. Occasionally there was blood, sometimes tears. No one ever complained. When the next kid showed up to the unit, the previous victim was the loudest cheerer of the lot. I never watched, and heard about much of this later.

Recently, hazing jumped to the front pages of every publication, from the *Army Times* to the *Washington Post*. In November 2013, Miami Dolphins offensive lineman Richie Incognito's bullying behavior dominated sports and prime-time news for a few solid days. My own kids go to school in a place where students recite an "Anti-Bullying Pledge" that they all know by heart. Signs on hallway walls warn students to tell an adult if they witness bullying. Teachers and administrators wage a campaign replete with New York City–style "If you see something, say something" posters. Bullies are the new terrorists. Maybe it's a good thing, but it feels like (benevolent?) fascism to me. Look, bullying is awful—it can be a genuinely serious problem. So I apologize for making light of the topic. But what my guys were up to felt harmless, and made them forget the countdown to Iraq for just a few minutes. There are worse things.

### WAY HOTTER THAN IRAQ

FORT IRWIN, CALIFORNIA: 2006

In July 2006 our squadron took the twenty-hour bus ride to Southern California's Mojave Desert. Our destination—Fort Irwin, home of the National Training Center (NTC), for 3-61 CAV's culminating training event before deployment. NTC sits in San Bernardino County, about three hours west of Las Vegas and two and a half hours east of Los Angeles. Activated in 1980, NTC is the premier desert training center for the U.S. Army's brigade-size units (about three to five thousand soldiers). Like every unit en route to combat, we spent the next four weeks playing war in a simulated Iraqi province. NTC is huge, about 1,000 square miles of desert, mountains, valleys, and mock cities.[3] Even back in 2006, the training was pretty impressive. The bus ride was long, some might say awful, but I loved it. On the way there we headed south to New Mexico, then west through Arizona before crossing into California at the desert town of Needles. I felt as though we were retracing the steps of Steinbeck's Joad family.[4] I'd never seen the Southwest, and sunrise over the Mohave is spectacular.

My grandmother died four days into the training. It was sudden. She'd had emphysema, but I thought she had more time. My maternal grandparents meant the world to me. I'd spent much of my youth living in their house on Colony Avenue in Midland Beach. My parents were divorced and my mother worked nights, waitressing at various restaurants and clubs, so Mam and Pop—as I called them—were a major part of my life. Mary Elizabeth O'Brien—Mae—was a woman before her time. She married a bit later than usual and relied on my grandfather, Joe "Bubs" Peteley, for most of the housework. Pop was a decorated New York City firefighter and learned to cook on the job. Her kids jokingly called Mam an aristocrat, smoking cigarettes and reading the newspaper while Pop made dinner. She was an incredibly sharp woman. She'd finish the *New York Times* crossword puzzle in a few hours and could debate current events with any comers. In another time, she might have earned a master's degree and had a profession of her own. As it was, she never even drove a car. I learned about Mam's death just before our company entered the main training exercise at NTC. I asked my commander about the funeral, and while he didn't say *no*, he made it clear that my responsibilities were with the unit. I decided to stay. I rationalized that it was the selfless thing to do, that my platoon needed me, and this was our last training before the war. I've regretted it every day since. I don't remember much about what we did during the mock war in the desert. But I'll always remember my grandmother's straightforward wisdom and caustic wit. Mam doubted the war from the start. Though she rarely left her couch, perhaps she grasped some greater truths.

▇▇▇▇ That July was one of the most scorching on record, even for the hottest place in the country. Average daily highs were around 105 degrees with spikes up to 120. My platoon worked night shift patrols along the faux Iranian border, so we tried to sleep during the day. Our tents—back then—had little to no air conditioning. I can still hear Fuller's protests: "This shit ain't RIGHT, son. How we supposed to sleep in a mother-fuckin sauna, yo?" We didn't much. I'd wake up in a literal pool of my own sweat and have to dump the water out of my cot each afternoon. Halfway through the training, 2nd platoon switched to day shift. It was even hotter.

We'd mostly chase down pickup trucks full of "smugglers"—American soldiers dressed as Arabs—along the simulated border. One day the thermometer topped 120 Fahrenheit. Sergeant DeJane had the lead truck. Out from behind a sand dune popped a white Ford Ranger, and DJ's vehicle gave chase. We all followed. Problem was, training regulations set a 40 mph safety speed limit and these OPFOR (Opposing Forces, basically pretend enemies) didn't play fair. DJ pushed boundaries and hit almost 50 mph. Then, suddenly, his vehicle slowed to a crawl. My truck was following, and Smith had to slam on our brakes. Smoke started billowing from DJ's turret, and seconds later SPC Chris Shuman hopped out. As the truck rolled to a stop, DJ and Ford (his driver) jumped out their doors into the rocky sand. Flames literally trailed out DJ's door. Grabbing a fire extinguisher, some soldiers quickly put out the small blaze. Turned out the heat had literally *cooked* the vehicle's computer system and set it aflame. DJ and Ford laughed their asses off as we all stood around in amazement. Smith, our resident adrenaline junky, offered a hand

and pulled DJ up from the ground. "Yo, Sergeant DJ, That . . . Was . . . AWESOME. Can you do it again?!?" The sight of flames spewing from his still moving truck must have given DJ a thought. The idea for the new platoon nickname—Ghost Riders—was his.

### A LONG OVERDUE PROMOTION

Sometime during that awful month in the desert, Fuller pinned on his sergeant's stripes. You know, everyone has a backstory. But I think Fitzgerald got it wrong. Fuller was genuinely living his second act, in the army, and at the ripe old age of twenty. Over the next few months, he related some scattered details about his past life. He was born in New Bedford, Massachusetts, not exactly the most glamorous part of the Bay State. Along with nearby Fall River, New Bedford was a town past its prime, a once mighty manufacturing center left behind like countless other American cities. Early on, under circumstances he never discussed, his father had died. The Fuller family moved to Florida, and Alex—Al to his friends—bounced between Florida and Massachusetts. His mother, two older brothers, and sister were a less than stabilizing influence. He told me his mom used, his brothers sold drugs, and their friends ran with gangs. At least one ended up in prison. His sister, Katie, was serving time in a Florida state penitentiary for assault and battery. Fuller explained that hanging down in Florida would eventually get him killed or jailed. At fourteen he was already self-aware, always wanting better. That never really changed.

When he was fifteen, he met Anastacia (Stacey) Zinov at a local dance in the village of Centerville on Cape Cod. At age three, Stacey had emigrated along with her family from the Ukraine. Fuller, who had lived with a friend, eventually moved in with the Zinov family and spent less and less time in Florida. He did some high school, dropped out, and eventually earned a GED. It was hard to imagine this teenage boy living with his girlfriend's parents 1,000 miles away from his mother, but in a strange way, it was for the best. By the time I met him, Fuller had little contact with his own family. When I wrote to his sister cataloguing his success with the platoon, she quickly responded. Katie explained that she understood Alex might not be comfortable writing to her, since "she made a lot of mistakes to end up in here," but asked me to try and convince him to contact their mother. She included an address and phone number. The letter came from Lowell Correctional Institution in Ocala, Florida.

As a teenager, Fuller had worked at the Zinov family car dealership and local A&P supermarket. But that's not what he talked most about. He described other, more illicit activities, including extorting money from local debtors. I don't know the truth of this and I'm not sure it matters. Fuller swore by it. Overall, he was thankful for the comparably stable home life Stacey's parents provided. He boxed, played some football and lived for Boston sports. In June 2004, after completing his GED and in the midst of a deteriorating war, he enlisted.

Fuller was the heart of 2nd platoon. He was only a specialist, a rank just below sergeant, which meant he belonged to the undifferentiated mass of young Joes. But he was more. His peers called him "Specialist of the Army," a reference to the highest attainable enlisted grade—sergeant major of the army. He was a leader without any rank. He led by charisma, example, humor, and grit. On the fast track to sergeant, all he needed were a few more months in the service to meet the minimum for a waiver and an accelerated promotion. Long before that, we treated him like a sergeant and made him a team leader, a position normally reserved for noncommissioned officers.

No one mentored new soldiers the way Alex Fuller did. When a young kid walked into the platoon area, some guys were cold. Others were crude. A few were mean. A couple might be nice. Mostly it was social: new guys and old hands, cool kids vs. dorks. Just the usual *Lord of the Flies* high school stuff—with the added stress of a future deployment hanging over it all. You'd learn a lot about a person by watching how he treated the new guy. Fuller was firm but welcoming, and he could be inspirational. Some soldiers couldn't stand him. The lazy ones resented his can-do attitude and worried he'd make them look bad. But sometimes he won over even the hardest case. Whenever a new soldier got in trouble, he'd face weeks of extra duty—essentially additional work each evening and on weekends—usually performing menial, physical tasks. Fuller spent a lot of extra time at work, and, as the lieutenant, so did I. Sometimes I'd hear Fuller's unmistakable Boston accent engage the naughty soldiers gathered outside my office.

"Hey, yo, private, don't look so down man—you know something?

You're gonna be a god damn sergeant major someday. Man, I remember one time in Korea I got busted for underage drinking and over there they don't play, ya know. So they had me filling 'bout a thousand sand bags. And I'm just dying, ya know? Then my sergeant major comes by and he says, 'Private—you're gonna be a sergeant major someday. No one becomes a sergeant major without getting busted at least once.'"

Everyone heard Fuller's sergeant major story. A few times. It was part of his shtick, part of himself. I don't care if it was true. Storytelling was a big part of Fuller's identity—how he communicated big ideas.

In October 2004, right after basic training and just before heading for a one-year unaccompanied (sans spouse) tour of duty in South Korea, Alex Fuller married Stacey on Cape Cod. They were a combined thirty-six years old: Fuller, nineteen, to Stacey's seventeen.

After Korea, the couple transferred to Fort Carson, Colorado, one of the more desirable spots in the stateside army.[5] Colorado Springs, a medium-size city with an epic mountain skyline, was right out the base's north gate. Fuller and Stacey lived in a small apartment off post, the best they could afford on his soldier's pay, but all in all pretty decent for a married couple their age.

Fuller was my model soldier. I was so proud of everything he did. When we switched up the HMMWV crews, I took him on as gunner. Now he would spend countless hours in the tiny enclosed space of my truck. He'd prep the vehicle and fire the machine gun mounted in the turret. He was up for anything and everything. I held remedial physical training (PT) every Saturday at 11:00 a.m. for overweight and out of shape soldiers. I made remedial PT optional for the platoon's sergeants, and none ever came. No one wanted to waste even a few precious weekend hours, especially with a deployment hanging over our heads. Of course, Fuller showed up every week. He'd help me lead the training session and divide the soldiers into ability-based running groups. If a guy didn't show, Fuller would run over to the barracks and drag him out of bed. In the summer of 2006, Fuller finally had enough seniority for a waiver to sergeant. He made the rank faster than anyone in the company. The day we pinned his sergeant's stripes, the commander cited him as an example for all the other soldiers. Fuller overcame life's circumstances and did more than succeed—he excelled. He was the top young soldier in the company, if not the squadron. It was his day, and he took the opportunity to make a speech encouraging to the other troopers. Classic Fuller.

The thing is, he truly believed in the army. Not necessarily the war or the mission or all the everyday bullshit that came along with it, of course. Fuller was streetwise and cynical when it made sense to be. But he would tell anyone who would listen how great the army was.

"I'm telling you, man, the army is the greatest. I mean all you have to do is stay fit, work hard, and listen to the sergeant and LT, yo. The army will take care of you, give you a house, money, and let you shoot at some shit. You just do your thing and you can be a sergeant major, son."

As naive as that might sound, he wasn't all wrong. If you came from poverty, if you married young or needed a second chance, the army probably offered you a better life than any attainable job on the outside. Its meritocracy, while imperfect, was undeniable. Fuller knew he was lucky, and unlike many others, he didn't complain much. Forgive the cliché, but when he pinned sergeant I felt the proud father. Fuller gave me faith, made me want to believe. The army *could* be great. In some ways it is. Then came the war.

### THE GOOD, THE BAD, AND THE UGLY
#### OUR LAST DAYS IN COLORADO: 2006

My soldiers weren't angels. They were young men, with all the imperfections inherent in human nature. A white-washed depiction does them no justice. Sometimes they drove me crazy. Like when I heard Ford and Faulkner had started sharing prescription drugs. Just *days* before deployment, I heard through the grapevine that at least two of my guys were partaking in and maybe distributing some of Faulkner's prescribed painkillers. Furthermore, my informant implied that Sergeant DeJane, who lived in the barracks with the Joes—always a precarious situation—knew about this activity. I was pissed. Mostly because I was stressed about deployment and didn't need the hassle. Selfishly, I was more concerned about *that* than the long-term health of these guys. I assumed that they were just young and healthy "boys being boys." Besides, I didn't want them to get in trouble. If

I could prove these allegations, Ford, Faulkner, and potentially DJ could face serious legal action. I decided to handle it in-house.

We called them in one at a time and grilled each soldier in turn. Invoking my authority as an officer and protecting their constitutional rights, I began by reading them Miranda warnings. "You have the right to remain silent. . . ." DJ was genuinely offended—I'd treated him like a criminal—and he denied any knowledge of the drug sharing. The truth is we had nothing but hearsay, and I didn't think he had any truly nefarious intentions. At worst, he might have been protecting his buddies. Ford and Faulkner cracked as soon as I read them their rights. They admitted to sharing the drugs, but denied selling the pills. Faulkner cried. Both realized they could face legitimate charges and possibly jail time if I escalated the investigation. What they likely didn't know is that I really should have informed my troop commander and intensified the inquiry. But my guys were about to ship off to Iraq. Losing two or three soldiers would completely upset the platoon's balance. We were a team and needed to remain such to function effectively. So we punished them "in house." Life was rough for them the next few days, with extra hours cleaning the platoon area and doing exhausting calisthenics. But Ford and Falkner stayed in the platoon with a warning to clean up their acts and redouble their efforts. They did. Maybe I bent some rules by dealing with the incident on my level, but felt it was for the good of the platoon and my individual troopers.

DJ was extremely upset with me and Staff Sergeant South after the prescription drug drama. He didn't like our formal approach and resented the Miranda warning. But DJ—cheery spirit that he was— didn't hold it against us long, and besides, he wasn't someone we could stay mad at anyway. His contagious laughter and outrageous antics won everyone over eventually. A few nights later the three of us hit the Hatch Cover, a local Colorado Springs bar, for beer and wings. I liked the joint for its neighborhood-y vibe and twenty-four-ounce cans of Miller High Life—the champagne of beers. The buffalo wings were pretty solid, too. On the bottom of the menu was a wing-lovers' challenge—order and eat a full dozen "fire" hot wings—and get them for free. DJ just had to take the dare. Experience suggested to me this would not end well. Out came the wings and Damian and I each tried a bite—holy shit!—they were hot. I couldn't finish one. DJ tried a speed eating strategy and plowed through ten wings in about two minutes. With his mouth covered in sauce and smiling a toothy grin, he seemed all right for about . . . ten seconds. He reached for his beer, took a hurried gulp—spat it out—and ran full speed for the bathroom to vomit. Damian and I chased him into the stall, laughing our asses off the whole way. DJ was beat red, sweating profusely, and giggling through involuntary tears. Five minutes later, we were back on our bar stools joking about the shenanigans. Out of the bathroom walked Sergeant DeJane. He headed straight up to the bartender and ordered another batch. "I've got it this time; just one more try." A few days later, we left for Iraq.

# 4

# Doing More with Less

MADA'IN QADA, BAGHDAD DISTRICT : OCTOBER 2006

The majesty and burning of the child's death,
I shall not murder.
The mankind of her going with a grave truth . . .
After the first death, there is no other.
— DYLAN THOMAS, "A Refusal to Mourn the Death,
by Fire, of a Child in London"

This . . . thing, this ain't police work . . . . I mean, you call something
a war and pretty soon everybody gonna be running around acting like
warriors . . . running around on a damn crusade, storming corners,
slapping on cuffs, racking up body counts . . . pretty soon, damn near
everybody on every corner is your fucking enemy. And soon the
neighborhood that you're supposed to be policing, that's just occupied
territory.
— MAJOR "BUNNY" COLVIN, season three of the HBO series *The Wire*

Flying into a war zone is surreal. It takes one full day to get
from Colorado to Kuwait—our pit stop before entering Iraq—and
each step of the way another bit of normalcy disappears. First, you
drive from your apartment to unit headquarters. It's still dark—about
4:00 a.m. In the process, you've said good-bye to your bed, your car,
and all the comforts of the life you've built. Carrying two duffel bags
of gear, you draw your rifle from the armory and—wife, kids, or girl-
friends in tow—shuffle over to a large gymnasium. There you scan
your military ID card and wait in the bleachers for buses to arrive.
Someone yells out a two-minute warning and it's time for final fare-
wells. After several hours of hurry up and wait, both soldiers and
spouses are ready to end the protracted, exhausting process. It's al-

most a relief to board the bus. Next, you enter a plane at the Colorado Springs Airport. As you walk across the tarmac, a random one-star general—whom you've never met—shakes your hand and bids you good luck.

From Colorado we took a four-hour flight to New York and had about an hour layover at Kennedy Airport. I'd heard we might stop there and foolishly told my mom—Sue Peteley—about it. She made me promise I'd call her if we did. She just *had* to be the last one to see me. She tried to time it out, but we landed a bit early and our layover was shorter than expected. Realizing she'd never have enough time to park and get to me, she panicked and left her car beside the departures terminal. Running to the international terminal, she somehow found me. We got a total of three minutes together. We shared a hug, some tears, but there was also a strange look of satisfaction in her eyes. Of course, her car was towed and it turned into a long, expensive night. No matter. She'd gotten to me, and was the last mother in the entire squadron to see her son. That was enough.

After the quick stop in New York, it was about eight hours to Leipzig. The Germans corralled U.S. troops in a small holding area while the plane refueled, lest we mix with the German citizens. God forbid. The major central-European states (notably France and Germany) had little use for America's war. As a side note, I would say that there is one surefire way to know you might want to reassess your foreign policy decisions. If what you're doing unites the Germans and the French—historical enemies—against you, just maybe you've got some soul-searching to do. As NATO allies and economic partners, they tolerated our soldiers' transit needs. That was about it.

From Leipzig it was six more hours to Kuwait City. Landing at night, I was struck by the huge skyline of modern buildings. From 5,000 feet it could be Vegas. It's not. Our clients, the Kuwaiti emirs, relied on the U.S. military for independence and trade privileges. Not all Kuwaiti people were as supportive of the alliance. The first indicator of a problematic relationship: driving in charter buses with mandatory black curtains drawn to mask our identity. We didn't feel like trusted allies, but rather like contaminated cattle shuffled off to the slaughter. The lead and trail vehicle of our highway convoy to Camp Buehring were both armored HMMWVS. Nothing about our trip, thus far, had been very welcoming. This ought to have been a sign.

For nearly three weeks, we lived in a tent city in the barren desert of Kuwait. At Camp Buehring we received last-minute training, zeroed our rifles, and drew some new equipment. Kuwait is the flattest, hottest, most barren desert you could ever imagine. I actually kind of dug it. The place was fantastically exotic. One day, when we'd finished shooting on an ad hoc rifle range and just as we loaded buses to head back to camp, a group of Bedouins rode in on *camels*. They dismounted and started scooping up left-over brass from our M4 rounds—to melt down and sell. We allowed them to do it. Fencing off the vast desert expanse was impossible, and besides, it fueled Kuwait's shadow economy. No harm, no foul.

██████ A couple days before we flew into Baghdad, our squadron commander (a squadron is synonymous with battalion, or about four hundred soldiers and generally commanded by a lieutenant colonel) took all the officers—about thirty of us—on a long, slow, run. After we'd finished, he gathered us in a semicircle and spoke of the future. We were about to go to war, he said, and he expected the squadron to complete its assigned missions. But, he admitted, he'd just read Tom Rick's *Fiasco*—a brutal expose of the lies, omissions, and mistakes that had rendered Iraq a violent maelstrom since 2003. *Fiasco*, the commander said, had had an enormous effect on him, and he didn't plan to make stupid mistakes and refight the last three years of war all over again. He admitted that counterinsurgency would be difficult, and "victory," in the traditional sense, might elude us. The colonel ended on a positive note of teamwork and duty, but his tone never strayed from an uncharacteristic solemnity. This was the most I'd ever respected the man. Maybe it was the book; maybe the SCO (shorthand for squadron commander) was himself nervous about his upcoming responsibilities; perhaps both. A few days later, after an uncomfortable and nauseating flight in a C-130 cargo plane to Baghdad, followed by eastbound helicopter rides across the city, we found ourselves at Forward Operating Base (FOB) Rustamiyah. Here was the squadron's headquarters for the next year.

## DECEPTIVE NUMBERS

The 3-61 CAV had responsibility for the entire Mada'in Qada, a district of about 600 square miles and between 800,000 and 1.2 million people. The mission—provide safety, stability, economic growth, and political reconciliation for the people of Mada'in. Our resources—well, on paper, the squadron had 363 soldiers,[1] divided into four troops designated as A, B, C, and HHT (headquarters). But the squadron never had 363 soldiers under arms and available for patrols. The reality is it takes lots of support soldiers to facilitate one combat trooper's mission. For starters, 132 soldiers were in HHT. With a few exceptions, these were mostly staff members—supply, personnel, communications, and intelligence specialists. So, 363-132 = 231.

The real fighters—with the exception of the squadron commander's security platoon—came from A, B, and C troops.[2] Apache and Black Knight Troops each had an assigned strength of 75 men, and Cold Blood Troop had 81. This too is deceptive. Let's take the example of my unit, Black Knight Troop. The SCO divided the massive Mada'in Qada into three troop-size sectors. B Troop patrolled the southeastern segment of the district, including the largest city—Salman Pak. We had responsibility for more than 100 square miles and approximately 300,000 civilians. With 75 soldiers. Well, fewer, actually. The SCO needed a security platoon. His headquarters troop wasn't designed for counterinsurgency and thus didn't include one organically. He'd have to rob Peter to pay Paul. We were Peter. He took the mortar section of nine men from our troop.[3] 75-9 = 66.

Of course, two of our soldiers were supply specialists who worked on the FOB, so 66-2 = 64. And one was a communications specialist. So 64-1 = 63. Additionally, a few soldiers manned radios at the troop headquarters. Thus, 63-3 = 60. So on a perfect day we had 60 troopers. Only, perfect days didn't exist. At any given moment during our tour, slightly less than 10 percent of troopers were on EML (environmental and morale leave) for two weeks back in the States: 60-5 = 55. Day to day, that's about what we mustered: 55 soldiers, primarily grouped in three scout platoons, each led by a young lieutenant and a senior sergeant. One American for every 5,500 Iraqis. I didn't like the odds.

## THE FIRST PATROL, OR, "WHY ARE
## WE HARASSING THIS FAMILY?"

The 3-61 CAV took over for her sister unit, 1-61 CAV, of the 101st Airborne Division. The 1-61 had patrolled in the Mada'in Qada since late 2005. It was a rough time, a time of degeneration. They'd watched as the entire Baghdad region burst into explosive violence. The lieutenants in B/1-61 CAV spent the next few weeks familiarizing us with Salman Pak and the rest of our AO (area of operations). These LTs were exhausted. They had dirty uniforms, long hair, and abundant sarcasm. I didn't know *then* that we'd look exactly the same to *our* successors less than fifteen months later.

In response to the Sunni insurgency, Shia militias had formed across the city, including in Mada'in. The B/1-61 CAV quickly focused attention on dismantling these groups. A sniper, suspected to be a member of the Mahdi Army,[4] shot and killed a 1-61 CAV soldier in the city of Jisr Diyala. The B/1-61 CAV targeted the Mahdi Army and in order to focus on that, arranged informal truces with the region's Sunni tribal leaders. Sunni insurgents largely refrained from attacks, and B/1-61 mostly avoided the Sunni heartland south and east of Salman Pak. Divide and conquer is a tried and true strategy, perfected by British colonial forces over the course of centuries. And 1-61 CAV had their reasons, after all. Revenge, of course, is always a factor.

The 3-7 CAV, 1-61's preceding unit, fought hard to win the city back from Sunni insurgents. On 10 February 2005, Sunni insurgents overran the police station in Salman Pak, killing eighteen police, destroying ten cars, and blowing up the building.[5] For the next several months, 3-7 CAV slowly drove these Sunni groups out of the city and into farmland to southeast, in the "ball sack" peninsula. Miraculously, 3-7 accomplished this without the death of a single soldier, until late September. Then, Shia Mahdi Army militiamen detonated a sophisticated explosive formed penetrator (EFP) bomb on the road just north of Salman Pak. The deadly blast killed two troopers—decapitating the vehicle's gunner and instantly killing the driver.[6] The Mahdi Army quickly became public enemy number one, the most effective force fighting against 3-7 CAV in the region.

When 1-61 CAV took over a couple months later, they inherited the new priorities of 3-7 CAV. That's how things went. The 1-61 CAV had exactly the same combat power as my squadron, about 250 combat troops, divided between three separate troop AOs. Stretched to their limit, they couldn't afford a two-front war with Sunni nationalists and Shia militiamen. Unofficially, the officers in B Troop, 1-61 CAV, concentrated on the Mahdi Army. Meanwhile, Sunni insurgents bided their time, regrouped, and prepared to recapture Salman Pak. Nonetheless, with about 60 troopers available to secure the most violent section of the Mada'in Qada, it's hard to imagine a better strategy.

Unit swaps are tricky, dangerous times. In army lexicon, they're known as "Right seat/Left seat rides." Picture a car. When learning to drive you first sit in the passenger (right) seat and observe the driver. Only after practice and sufficient mastery do you enter the driver (left) seat. It's the same process in Iraq. Matters are complicated by an inevitable risk aversion on the part of the outgoing unit and the overlapping exit flights of soldiers from this squadron. Eventually, a tipping point is reached and vehicles and equipment are manned by the new unit's troopers. Leaders from the incoming unit must learn the terrain, the key powerbrokers, effective local tactics, and devise a working strategy, all in the two weeks before the experienced outgoing leadership departs—for good. It's a stressful time. By the last few days, both units are tired of each other. Every unit swap follows the same general pattern. Both commanders publicly praise the other unit, while privately disparaging their discipline, training, and inexperience. Incoming commanders swear never to let their troopers fall to such levels of indiscipline. Outgoing commanders secretly express concern for the safety of the incoming unit—how will these new guys *survive*, what with their inexperience and naiveté? A year passes and roles reverse. Like clockwork.

The transition with 1-61 CAV consisted of daily patrols led by their officers. We spent most of that time performing routine missions. Occasionally they would drive us around the entire expanse of the district, including the tiny rural villages of the southeast ball sack. You could tell the 1-61 CAV lieutenants didn't love driving down into the Sunni heartland. Only one (sort of) paved road, known as Route Crocodile, curved along the Tigris River south of Salman Pak. With tall grass and thick palm groves to the east and a steep riverbank to the west, our HMMWVs were extremely vulnerable to improvised explosive device (IED) attacks. Insurgents could lace Route Croc's sundry potholes with IEDs, run command wires into the foliage, and wait for our patrols. After detonating the device, insurgents could unleash an ambush of machine gun fire and then quickly retire on tiny "rat lines"—narrow paths that crisscrossed the entire ball sack. I could tell that the area southeast of Salman Pak—the villages of Duraya, Kanasa, and Al Lej—were under Sunni insurgent hegemony. We never saw a single military-aged male in town, and the locals were more suspicious and discourteous than elsewhere in the *qada*. Although 1-61 CAV took us on only a couple of patrols in this area, we knew the ball sack would be our troop's main challenge. We were only visitors in this region; once our patrol skipped town and the sun went down, the villages belonged to the powerful—that meant armed Sunni groups.

Most of the "right seat ride," however, was spent in and around Salman Pak, talking to local leaders and visiting Iraqi national police stations. Such routine errands, we learned, constituted the majority of a soldier's time during a counterinsurgency. My first mission off the FOB was a standard night patrol. The platoon I'd tagged along with was going to the house of a suspected Mahdi Army militia leader. We drove to the outskirts of Salman Pak, surrounded the farmhouse, and knocked on the door. An old woman let us in, and a few soldiers fanned out to search every room of the house. Only women, presumably the suspect's mother and sisters, were home. Through a translator, the lieutenant asked the old woman where her son was hiding. Where could they find him? Had he visited the house? Predictably, she had no idea. After the soldiers searched a few rooms and found nothing out of sorts, we prepared to leave. The lieutenant warned the woman they'd be back—just as they'd been to the house several times before—until she gave up her son.

I returned to the FOB with an uneasy feeling. I couldn't understand what it was we had just accomplished. How did hassling this family, storming into their home after dark and making threats, contribute in any way to defeating the militia or earning the loyalty and trust of Iraqi civilians? Sure, I was brand new, but the entire thing felt counterproductive. Let's assume the woman's son *was* Mahdi Army to the core. What does that matter? Without long-term surveillance or reliable intelligence placing him at the house, entering the premises and making threats only solidified the family's aversion to the U.S. Army. And what if we had gotten it wrong? If he was innocent, we'd potentially created a new family of insurgents. Those women must have felt like many African American families living under persistent police pressure in parts of New York, Baltimore, and Chicago. Even after countless incidents in Los Angeles, New York, and Ferguson, Missouri, it sounds outlandish to most affluent suburban dwellers that many impoverished communities see the police as their enemy. For most soldiers, it was equally unthinkable that some Iraqis saw all Americans in a negative light. I knew one thing: we were going to have to adjust our perceptions. And fast.

### POLITICAL MURDER: LONELY DEATHS
### ON A FORGOTTEN ROADSIDE

In early November, I led one of my first independent patrols. The 1-61 CAV was gone and Salman Pak was all ours. Driving south to the city that day, we heard a few faint gunshots off in the distance. Even to a green unit such as ours, this was nothing out of the ordinary. The mundane background noise of this country made the South Bronx seem serene. No one thought anything of it, registering just a cursory report from SSG South: "Ghost 1 [me] this is Ghost 2 [him], audible gunshot, south, over." But as we came over a slight rise, we could see significant commotion on the roadside ahead. Pulling over to a makeshift fuel station, we dismounted and saw our first scenes of bloodshed. They would not be the last.

Two teens lay prostrate—one moaning—on the roadside next to the gas cans they'd been peddling to passersby just minutes earlier. One of the young men had a bullet hole in the back of his head. His skull peeked through a bloody scalp of crimson soaked hair. Another groaning teen was bleeding from two bullet wounds to the chest and gasping for air with outstretched, flailing arms. Time seemed to slow, and basic communication grew difficult as the sounds from a growing crowd rose to a cacophony of shrieking voices. I tried to yell for our medic—Private First Class Joshua "Doc" Schrader, of Charleston, West Virginia—but he was already running to the wounded men. Before Doc could reach the headshot victim, some locals loaded the young man into the back of a taxicab, presumably to rush him north to the nearest hospital—15 miles away, in Baghdad proper. As they lifted the man's limbs, his unsupported neck swung toward the earth, and pieces of brain and skull fragment hit the pavement. I turned away in disgust, sure that he would die, and looked over at Doc kneeling next to the other wounded teen.

Schrader was a brand new private. He'd never been to combat, and never before treated a live trauma patient, let alone one shot in the chest and bleeding profusely from a gaping exit wound in the back. Besides a few months of training at Fort Sam Houston, he was no more prepared for this moment than any other new soldier. He froze. SFC Gass hollered at Doc to get going and *do* something for the dying man. Just then, Ford ran over and got things started. Ford's EMT experience must have kicked in, because he was smooth, calm, and efficient. His action steadied Doc, and the two began working together. As they did so, I called in a confused report to headquarters. All the while, Iraqi women swarmed around me yelling, wailing, and asking me questions in broken English: "Mister, you take him hospital?" they asked. "Jaysh al Mahdi! Jaysh al Mahdi,"[7] they screamed, identifying the suspected culprits. It was hard to focus.

Minutes later, SFC Gass was yelling for me to mount up. They'd loaded the wounded man into my backseat and we needed to roll. I still had no idea where. Not knowing what else to do, we zipped back north toward the FOB aid station. As we did, I called in my plan of action and was initially denied. The base's trauma unit was designated for U.S. troops, American civilians, and contracted employees—like interpreters. Doc—who was sitting in my backseat with the young man laid across his lap—yelled: "Sir, there's no WAY this guy's making it to a Baghdad hospital." I radioed base—I was taking the casualty in.

We raced north and I kept looking over my shoulder at the bloodied young man gasping for air in the backseat. Before we reached the base gate, he was gone. I helped carry the body into the aid station and they confirmed it—dead on arrival. As I left the building and re-entered the day's blinding sunlight, I noticed Doc puking beside the truck. His hands and forearms were covered in a stranger's blood—a young man who wheezed his last breaths on Doc's lap. Doc was a kid, not yet twenty-one years old. He was a good-natured guy, with half a dozen playful, punk-rockish tattoos. One, on his stomach, depicted a cartoon fire hydrant screaming out. Doc did well for his first day. I let him be. Ford, on the other hand, was a rock. He'd calmed the situation and taken charge. This was our first real indication that the kid who couldn't get to work on time or iron his uniform was actually legit. Who'd have thought? Our patrol might have ended right then but for one problem. In all the confusion, I'd never gotten an ID, a name, or any indication of where the young man was from. Come to think of it, I'm not sure I ever thought to check. So back we drove down to the scene of the crime. It didn't take long to find the young man's family. They seemed to know he was dead. It was at these moments I hated being in charge. I wished I were a private, driving a HMMWV, or carrying a radio. I'd have traded the pay and "prestige" to avoid telling this heartbroken father his son was dead. The distinguished looking, bearded old man broke into frenzied tears. I cried some along with him. We still had no idea who killed the boys. No one was ever caught or punished. Few ever were. The young men were just two among three thousand Iraqi civilians killed that November, most in a series of confused, brutal, unsolved murders.[8] Such was life.

This was where it ended, I thought to myself. All the grand revolutionary rhetoric in the world and the very best of intentions always seemed to find its way here—double murder on a forgotten roadside. Two young men—one just a teenager—shot at point blank range as they sold some fuel to make ends meet. Long ago, I'd found political rebellion romantic. Growing up in working-class, ethnic New York, I thought IRA gunmen fought the good fight against British imperialism.[9] No longer. Having seen—in spades—the output of organized violence, I'll forever question the efficacy of force. Too often it ends like this—two youths, dead in the street, simply because they were a different brand of Muslim. Or any other religion, creed, or ethnicity for that matter. It was Baghdad, November 2006. So it went.

### HUMAN INTERLUDE 1: POVERTY, HUNGER, AND ADORABLE KIDS BAGHDAD'S "SQUATTER-ZONE": 2007

When we patrolled on the outskirts of southeast Baghdad, one of our missions (and my personal favorite) was to distribute HA. That's humanitarian aid in military speak. HA drops varied.

Some were sacks of food in large bags that resembled the ones eco-conscious shoppers use and reuse in hip, affluent neighborhoods back home. Canned foods, rice, and other essentials were in each carefully packed bag. Another common item in the HA drops was a portable heater. Even though we never bothered to open a box and actually try one, these things looked pretty shitty to me. But on the street, they were like gold. I can think of a few reasons. Iraqis, like all people, ran a flourishing black market and sold half the stuff we gave out to them. Who could blame them? Besides, in November and December, it got pretty damn cold at night, even in famously sultry Mesopotamia. And the areas we patrolled and distributed HA in were the squatter zones.

████ A few million Iraqis had fled the ongoing civil war by 2006. Most headed to Syria or Jordan and lived in refugee camps. Hundreds of thousands more were internally displaced refugees, or IDPs. That's just another way of saying scared, often poor people, who fled their homes and eked out an existence in a different city, neighborhood, or in one of the growing slums on the outskirts of the capital. The barren fields of southeast Baghdad, not far from the massive garbage dump, became just such a place. I loved it there. It was safe. We were never, ever attacked in the squatter camps. No snipers, no mortars, and most important, no IEDs. The squatter zone was unreal. People lived however they could. It reminded me of the awful Caribbean shanty towns of Haiti or the Dominican Republic. But way worse and way more ad hoc. The people threw up whatever shelter was available. Tents, shacks, boxes, whatever. My favorite houses were made of stacked up tin cans, glued together with mud, and covered by scraps of sheet metal. The level of human ingenuity was staggering. You know what they say about necessity and invention. But it was awful. At night the place was pitch black. No power grid, no generators, no *heat*. They were cold. Some built fires, but doing so in a crowded refugee camp was potentially deadly. Our portable heaters were priceless on a cold night.

I always wished I had more to give out. There was never enough. My buddy Steve was our fire support officer and an amazing guy. Generally unable to perform his primary job—calling in artillery, because of the inevitability of civilian casualties in an urban setting—he was reassigned to a variety of other jobs. Artillery officers ran civil affairs, intelligence, political meetings, and humanitarian aid. Unlike some of his peers who resented the inglorious work and spent their time idling away on the computer at the FOB, Steve tried to make a difference. He became a jack-of-all-trades and the most valuable member of our unit. He was also my roommate, sounding board, confidant, cigarette smoking partner, and friend. Steve did everything he could to get me tons of HA, and he did a damn good job of it. The 2nd platoon always had the most. But it was never enough.

Steve Migliore had been my classmate at West Point. We were plebes (freshmen) in the same cadet company but didn't become close until we got assigned to the same troop at Fort Carson. Steve was from Eden, New York, a small town just outside of Buffalo. He loved fishing, reading, and occasional epic drinking bouts—he was just a good dude. Flash forward—this was a guy who would later wear a flaming sombrero, doused in kerosene, in my garage, after a booze-soaked night in Colorado Springs. He was an accomplished track runner at the military academy and very fit. It took Iraq to turn him into a smoker. One day, Steve got a shitload of children's shoes from unit supply. He knew I'd want to bring them on patrol. I took some shoes out one day and it was an absolute disaster. The people flooded our trucks and grabbed the shoes without regard to size or style. Steve solved the problem that night. He developed a board with the traced and shaded shapes of children's feet. Each shape corresponded to a shoe size. The next day, the kids lined up in an orderly fashion (with some help from my soldiers) and took turns sizing themselves on Steve's board. My driver, PFC James Smith, would then throw the correct size and color (pink for girls, blue for boys) down from the top of our HMMWV. Such fun.

When we'd pull up to a group of shacks, the people would swarm—especially the kids. We'd have to hide how much we had in our HMMW trunks in order to ration it out. It was a terrible amount of power to have—deciding who got sustenance and warmth. But I loved the thankfulness in their eyes when I handed stuff out. It was so pathetic, though. The people did what they had to. They knew our weaknesses. Parents sent their children to beg for supplies. You'd rarely see a grown man. One cute young girl, about eight, with piercing green eyes and a winning smile, would hold her fat baby brother up in her arms and whine, "Mister, please, look—baby, please, mister." She always got something from my private stocks. Then we would move on to another area until it was all gone.

There was one other kid I remember. About ten, he would have been a fourth or fifth grader here in the States. He drove an old wooden cart pulled by the saddest, oldest looking donkey I've ever seen. Every morning, he would drive to the side of the highway parallel to the squatter zone. There he'd wait, sometimes for hours, sometimes in vain, to see if my patrol would be on HA duty that day. If we were, he'd try to follow us. Of course, he was far too slow to keep up, but he had an old pair of binoculars and he'd watch us and do his best to pursue. All day he'd plod along, and sometimes he was able to catch up. Some of my soldiers found him irritating. He was. He had a weird confidence, a sense of entitlement, and a very annoying voice. But I always gave him something. I just had to. The way he argued, pleaded and made his case for the supplies plus the sheer *commitment* of this boy, earned my respect. And pity. Today, across America, a few million fourth grade boys will complain to their parents about some nonsense. Video games, television shows, boredom, you name it. I realize they don't know any better. Rationally, I can recognize that my love for the squatter kids shouldn't translate to a sometime hatred of these American children—but I often run on emotion, and memory. I think we all do.

# 5

# "These Dudes Are Trying to *Kill* Us"

SALMAN PAK : NOVEMBER TO DECEMBER 2006

Route Croc skirted the Tigris River from just south of Salman Pak to the end of the Mada'in Qada. The road traced the entire perimeter of the ball sack peninsula below the city. The road was so narrow; two HMMWVs couldn't comfortably pass each other along most sections of the route. On the south and west side of the road was the river, on the north and east stood thick vegetation, palm groves, and hundreds of perpendicular dirt paths and irrigation ditches. The concrete surface was in a state of utter disrepair, pocked with countless potholes. Large, exposed culverts ran under the roadway at several key junctures—perfect hiding places for massive IEDs. Unfortunately, Route Croc was the *only* paved, accessible road for our vehicles running south of Salman Pak. It was our only option. Insurgents knew our exact direction of travel, and given the cautious speeds we used to navigate the winding road, they had plenty of notice to set an ambush. Basically, Route Croc was a disaster—a death trap. Looking back, I'm staggered by our naivete. I literally can't imagine braving that road today. But those were different times. The newness of it all and our own ignorance rendered them so.

The villages south of Salman Pak: Duraya, Kanasa, and Al Lej sat sequentially along Route Croc. Small, dusty towns of a few dozen combination mud, stone, and brick dwellings, the villages were each surrounded by family farms and fishponds. A spider web of rat lines—dirt trails accessible to small cars, pickup trucks, and motorcycles, but not our HMMWVs—spread outward from the villages into the heart of the ball sack. The area was biblical. Driving two minutes south of Salman Pak—a city of some size, with multistory buildings—felt like traveling fifteen hundred years back in time. Mud homes, filthy, bearded old men, zero electricity, and no sanitation. It was another world down there. And it was Sunni country. A variety of insurgent groups operated in the ball sack villages—the secular, nationalist 1920 Revolution Brigades, local Islamists of Ansar al-Sunna, and mixed foreign and Iraqi fundamentalists of Al Qaeda in Iraq (AQI). When our squadron first took over, we weren't yet aware of the *extent* of insurgent infiltration and activity in the area. One of my platoon's first assignments was to explore, map, and study the southern villages. What we didn't fully realize then, but would soon learn, was that American and Iraqi government control of the ball sack, like much of Iraq, was an illusion.

So it was on 30 November 2006, when SSG South led the way, single file, down Route Croc. Our mission: circumnavigate the ball sack, stopping in each village to take pictures, give out humanitarian supplies, and gather census data. We made it about half-way. At the southern arc of the "sack," there's a long gap between the towns of Kanasa and Al Lej. A couple of kilometers in length, this stretch of road was the most isolated, densely vegetated, and eerily quiet portion of the entire route. We should have known better than to drive this road, alone, fifty minutes south of the nearest medical facility, without engineers to clear a path, or helicopters to reconnoiter. But resources were in short supply at the time, our squadron was dangerously overextended, and the truth is, we didn't know any better—yet.

As always, I was in the second vehicle. In a standard four-vehicle set, our scout platoons would travel with the senior scout (SSG South) in the lead, followed by the LT (me), the Bravo section sergeant (SSG Rittel), and trailed by the platoon sergeant (SFC Gass). Damian was moving at about 10 mph, scanning the road and calling up checkpoints. Without notice, his driver—PFC Jeremy Frunk, from Fort Smith, Arkansas—slammed on the brakes. Damian heard himself start to yell, "Frunk, what-the-FU . . ." when—*BOOM*—a deafening blast threw what seemed like the entire road straight into the air. Smith hit our brakes too, though we still almost rear-ended the lead truck. I called up the contact report to HQ—"Black X-ray, this is Ghost 1, contact—IED—Grid 1234 5678, over." Frunk, through some sort of redneck intuition, had seen an ever-so-faint line of dirt on the road ahead. Had he waited a split second to hit the brakes, his whole crew might have been killed. The IED was massive. The entire

51

center of the road was gone, replaced with a waist-deep crater about 6 feet across. Postblast analysis estimated that a few Chinese antitank mines had been stacked on top of each other under the roadway. The IED was command-detonated, meaning that a long wire ran from the bomb itself several dozen meters back to a "trigger-man" who manually timed and set off the explosion. As we swept the area, DJ found the spool of light blue wire leading from the blast site directly to the detonation point. It was an open and shut case. Obvious tire tracks led away down a narrow dirt path at the spool's end. A plastic grocery bag on the ground held a bottle of water and some half-eaten dates. The insurgent trigger-man had hung back at a safe distance in the foliage with a clear line of sight to Route Croc, munched on some snacks, and then tried to kill us. Afterward, he jumped in a pickup truck and got away. Too easy.

When it was all over, we snapped a bunch of pictures at the blast site. Both DJ and Sergeant John Pushard—of Corbin, Kentucky—took turns posing in the massive crater. Some of the new guys, myself included, I suppose, were proud to have "seen combat" and survived to tell the tale. The Route Croc IED was our closest call so far and the biggest bomb attack the squadron had yet encountered. Our immaturity in that moment strikes me, as I look back on it. Then again, hindsight brings clarity that none of us possessed on that day. As we rode back to the FOB that afternoon, Smith gabbed endlessly about how big the IED was, and how we need to go back down there and "find the fucks who did it." Fuller, up in the gun turret, yelled down: "I don't know, Sir, shit just got real. These dudes are really trying to *kill* us!" They were. And we wouldn't always be so lucky.

### THE DIRTY SECRET: "LOVING" COMBAT IN DECEMBER

Fuller was right. After our near miss on Route Croc, shit *had* gotten real. The next two weeks were a blur. November, all in all, had been quiet. At least for us, and by Iraq standards, that is. In the first week of December, everything changed. All three of our scout platoons—LT Mike Kovalsky's 1st PLT,[1] my 2nd PLT, and LT Scott Maclaren's 3rd PLT[2]—endured daily gun battles in Salman Pak and the sleepy village of Ja'ara, just north of the city. Ja'ara was once a mixed village, sitting as it did on the fault line between primarily Shia Jisr

Diyala on its north and Sunni Salman Pak to the south. That December, a revitalized Sunni insurgent alliance seized Ja'ara, displaced most residents, and used the village as a fortified base for attacks on Iraqi national police (NP) and American patrols. Ja'ara was perfectly situated for both. Set beside Route Wild, our main north-south artery in the district, Ja'ara dominated vehicular approach to southern Mada'in. Control of the village, and removal of its adjacent NP watchtower, would divide the two main police barracks of Salman Pak and Jisr Diyala.

Late one afternoon, driving down Route Wild, we heard the clatter of gunfire to our south. The closer we got to Ja'ara, the louder rose the din of approaching battle. Then—*BOOM*—a massive blast. We knew we were heading into a fight. Everyone checked weapons, adjusted body armor, and tried not to look scared. As we pulled up to Ja'ara, smoke and dust hovered across the roadway. The NP checkpoint tower, a tall concrete structure, was gone—blasted across the roadway. A few NPs had been killed, and the rest had sped away south to Salman Pak. A few scattered helmets were the only remaining evidence of police presence. Our HMMWVs came under sporadic machine gun fire from the east—from the village itself. We arrayed the trucks, returned fire from .50 caliber and M240B 7.62mm machine guns, and called for helicopter support. Fact: whenever our air support arrived, the insurgents melted away. Gunfire stopped, and it was almost embarrassing trying to convince the pilots we really *had* been under attack just a few seconds before. The pattern repeated itself dozens of times. The helicopter-induced lull bought time to reconfigure trucks, kick out some dismounted soldiers, and formulate plans to rush the village on foot.

Eighteen soldiers aren't very many when it's time to fight dismounted. Back in the Indian Wars of the American West, the rule of thumb for dismounted cavalrymen was that one in four troopers held the horses—leaving only 75 percent of effective combat power. HMMWVs were great for firepower, speed, and communications, but they inverted the old horse-holding ratio. You had to leave at least the driver and gunner on each of the four trucks, and at least two trucks needed a sergeant to command the mounted force and monitor radios. That's ten guys right there, leaving a maximum of eight for dismounted maneuver. Our platoon standard operating procedure (SOP) designated SFC Gass to stay with the trucks while Damian and I led dismount teams. We huddled behind my truck and planned an assault across the 50 or so yards of open terrain to the edge of Ja'ara. We planned to move under the helicopter umbrella until Smith yelled out the door—"Hey, Sir, Gunslinger (call sign for the helos) is peacing out and heading to another TIC" (troops in contact—code for an American unit under attack).

Within a minute of the birds' departure, we came back under fire. Nothing too intense, just enough to let us know they were still there. Our gunners let them have it, suppressing the rooftops, windows, and building corners in a hail of steel. As I huddled behind the truck, barking last-minute instructions over my dashboard radio, a few stray rounds smacked into Fuller's turret. "Aww . . . SHIT, son. Those mugs are close," he yelled and began firing wildly with one arm on his weapon, while ducking his head up and down—not exactly textbook gunnery. He sprayed at the insurgent positions screaming, "Yeah! Yeah! You see that shit? I set that shit on FIRE!" His rounds had, in fact, ignited a line of tall brush at the village edge. With the sun now setting, the flames glowed against the dark sky. It looked like something out of *Apocalypse Now*. Seconds later, our dismounts bounded forward. As the gunners provided suppressive fire we leapfrogged across successive canals in small teams. Most enemy fire seemed to cease. At the edge of Ja'ara, the irrigation ditches channeled us to one narrow entrance. Of course, this very area was ablaze, lit by the tracer fire from Fuller's wild rounds. One at a time, we jumped through the scattered flames and into Ja'ara. Then—nothing. The village was abandoned, except for one large house. After kicking in a derelict door, we rushed into the home. Screaming women wrapped each other close in their robes, yelling in Arabic and broken English: "No Al Qaeda, No Ali Baba!" Our interpreter calmed them and advised that they lie on the ground. In times since, I've tried to imagine that night through the women's eyes. Where were the men? Maybe their husbands were dead, or worked in Baghdad, or were the very ones shooting at us. Doesn't matter, really. Women remain war's—maybe life's—tragic victims. Men posture, fight, and die. It's the women who are left with all the consequences, picking up broken pieces in our wake.

Bounding from corner to corner, clearing houses, and yelling commands, it all felt like an intense training exercise. With about ten times the endorphin flow. We ran around corners, behind trucks, through buildings, and onto rooftops. But the insurgents were just one step too far away, melting away as soon as we applied pressure. It went on like that for about a week: daily gun battles in and around Ja'ara followed the same pattern. Ambush and retreat, helicopters and re-engagement. It reminded me of ritual forms of ancient warfare, full of posturing and bravado but short on serious destruction. The Ja'ara fights yielded few casualties but all the rush of combat. There were exciting moments. One day we decided to clear a house recently used by insurgents. Instead of rushing across the road or hopping the courtyard wall, I had Smith drive clear through the gate, taking down a chunk of wall along the way. You can bet he loved *that* shit. Out we hopped and rushed in the door—no enemy inside, but one hell of an adrenaline rush.

Sometimes the power went to our heads. After a brief fight in Ja'ara—probably the tenth in as many days—we drove south to gather some NPs. As we hit the traffic circle near the mosque—*BOOM*—an IED blew between Damian's truck and mine. It was a relatively small blast, but I lost my shit. Securing the area, we fanned out on foot to clear surrounding houses and alleys in search of a triggerman or intelligence. We'd had about five close calls by this point, and IED attacks were on the rise across the troop AO. That plus the rush of the day's fight must have set me off. I ran toward an older man standing across the street from the blast site. I demanded information. "Who placed the bomb? Did you see them? I know you did! This isn't that big of a town, mother fucker!" Mark, our "terp," tried to keep up with my rapid-fire questions/accusations. And then, instinctively, my pistol was out of its holster and in my hand, waving around as I gestured and yelled. "LT, calm down, man. This guy don't know shit," said Mark. The whole thing was childish. Looking back, I cringe at the image of myself gyrating in the street and intimidating this man. That was the first and last time my pistol left its holster, in Iraq *or* Afghanistan. You live and learn.

The unpleasant truth is, in those first weeks of December 2006, I, we, *liked* it all. I'd go back to the FOB to swap stories and lessons learned with LT Scott Maclaren from 3rd platoon. Other days, Scott would relieve us in the fight, or we'd maneuver the platoons together. Army life, at root, is a boy's game. What few people admit is the dirty little secret of combat: men *enjoy* it, at least a little. It produces a chemical high in the body that's hard to match. I remember enjoying showers back on the FOB, washing off the smell of gunpowder and carbon residue. It didn't seem real yet—no one on *our* side had died. Kind of felt like commuting to a regular job, a job where fighting and killing was the office norm. For a moment, ever so briefly, I *loved* it. It's a kid's game, but the fun only lasts so long. War remains inherently dangerous, and sooner or later it hurts those closest to us. Perhaps it's good that it does, for like whiskey without a hangover, we might not otherwise stop drinking it.

### GREETINGS FROM THE SALMAN PAK HOTEL: A POSTCARD FROM IRAQ

It was easy to forget that Salman Pak was once a resort town. Beautiful, massive, riverfront villas lined the Tigris on the west side of town. Saddam rewarded party loyalists with these tracts during his rule in the 1980s.[3] Close enough to Baghdad for convenience but sufficiently far to feel removed from the urban sprawl, Salman Pak was perfectly situated for tourism and leisure. Before the invasion, the Taq-i-Kasra arch and royal palace ruins were surrounded by lush gardens and palm groves. Because of destruction and the rerouting of the complex irrigation systems, they now sat on a barren piece of land. The ancient Sassanid capital had a history museum, a curator, and was once one of Iraq's most popular destinations. On the southwest edge of town stood the huge Salman Pak Hotel. Actually a series of buildings, it was better described as a resort village. It now served as headquarters for the Mada'in Qada's assigned national police brigade. Three years after the invasion, the place was a wreck. Ironically, the police commander and his wife had *honeymooned* at the hotel years earlier. He showed me an old postcard of the place. He mustn't have recognized it now, because I saw the sadness in his eyes as he showed me the crumpled photograph. It could have been a metaphor for his shattered country.

Salman Pak was devastated by the invasion, with U.S. Marines wrenching the city from stiff Fedayeen resistance in 2003.[4] When the insurgency kicked off, Salman Pak became an immediate stronghold, and the former luxury hotel served as a venue for grisly insurgent beheadings.[5] Because of the regularity and intensity of fighting in Ja'ara and the Pak, our commander started forward positioning platoons (on rotation) 24/7 at the hotel. This allowed us to respond rapidly to attacks, fostered joint operations with the NPs, and would presumably deter violence. All things considered, it wasn't such a bad gig. The hotel was relatively secure—guarded by a couple hundred NPs—so the guys could strip off their vests and chill on the trucks between missions. We also had access to some creature comforts. The police had a small sundries shop in the former hotel lobby, and we'd buy Miami brand cigarettes and potent Arab energy drinks.[6]

I spent most of my time, along with Damian, and my interpreter—"Mark"—in the NP commander's office. He had comfortable chairs and we'd sit around watching Egyptian soap operas or Syrian music videos on his television set. The colonel couldn't be bothered with talk of military operations. He rarely wore a uniform, but rather a bright green Iraqi national soccer team track suit. He'd lounge back in his recliner, press out his huge belly, and talk endlessly about politics, movies, religion, or women. Sometimes he'd remark on my boyish looks. The soldiers used to joke that they could make a fortune selling me off—sexually, I presume—to the NP colonel. There we'd sit, night after night, getting "chaied up"—drinking enough chai tea to hit a wild sugar high—and smoking cigarettes. Sometimes we'd respond to gunfire or local intelligence. Occasionally, a small firefight would result. Every few hours we'd conduct a mounted or foot patrol across the city to gather information, search for weapons caches, and basically show the colors.

One night the NPs cooked us a big meal. We all stood around the table (there were almost never chairs in Arab homes) and ate from family style platters with bare hands. Needless to say, most of the NPs didn't adhere to American hand-washing standards. I didn't care. The food was actually delicious. I'd taken to eating local cuisine at every opportunity, and most days I didn't touch any army-issued rations. Not all my soldiers were as enthusiastic. The platoon sergeant, SFC Gass, wasn't much interested in interacting with the locals. He'd had a rough tour in Ramadi in 2004 to 2005 and hadn't gotten over a visceral distrust of most Iraqis. Other guys were on the fence. There was far too much food for the half-dozen of us present, so I sent a runner to bring over some Joes to join the feast. Ford, Smith, Fuller, Longton, and Frunk shuffled in. Everyone cautiously grabbed some meat and rice and took a few heaping bites. I guess I should have warned them. Ford thanked the NP commander for the delicious food and asked what kind of meat we were having. "Lamb lung," the colonel said, through our interpreter. Fuller started spitting out some half chewed meat and dry heaving on the floor. "Yo, count me out next time, Ford. LT's gone all native—but I don't play that shit." We had a good laugh, the NPs included.

December in Iraq is colder than you'd think, especially at night. Some guys slept in HMMWVs with the heat on, and others wrapped up in a poncho liner on the ground. One squad had to man an observation post (OP) on the hotel roof all night. We'd rotate the position, but it was the coldest spot in town. The wind whipped off the Tigris and none of us had taken sleeping bags, not expecting the quick overnight temperature drops. On the coldest evening, I climbed several stories up the gutted hotel staircase to spend the night with the rooftop squad. We shivered together, unable to get any sleep, until about 3:00 a.m. Finally I relented and let them break regulation to make a small fire. We scrounged wood wherever we could find it. The guys pulled panels off doorways, frames from the walls, and anything else they could find. Here we were, literally stripping apart a once majestic resort on the Tigris. It was cold. Such was life at the Salman Pak Hotel.

### A FITTING PLACE TO DIE
#### SALMAN PAK GRAVEYARD: 9 DECEMBER 2006

A few days later, the troop conducted a joint operation with the national police in Ja'ara. As missions often do, the Ja'ara attack quickly shifted to something completely different. Scott's 3rd platoon, covering the troop's southern flank, came under significant fire from a Salman Pak graveyard, on the north end of the Bali peninsula. The 3rd platoon maneuvered aggressively into an attack but came face to face with about a dozen insurgents, better armed and organized than usual. These insurgents took cover, fired well-aimed shots, and—uncharacteristically—stood their ground. Our troop commander, unthinking and impetuous, sped off with his two headquarters trucks to join the fight. The commander tried to envelop the insurgents' east flank while 3rd platoon pushed northward. Unfortunately, the west side of Salman Pak—like most of the area—quickly turns into an impassable line of small trails and irrigation ditches. His HMMWVs quickly reached their limit of advance.

Fearing the insurgents would once more slip away, he ordered my platoon to disengage from Ja'ara and head southwest to his position. In the interim, he impulsively sent a comically small dismount team to charge forward and pin down the insurgent flank. The headquarters section isn't meant to maneuver independently. Rather, its purpose is command and control of the three subordinate scout platoons. The only dismounted soldiers in the backseat of the two trucks were LT Steve Migliore, his hefty but competent fire support sergeant, and a random HUMINT (human intelligence) specialist attached to our troop for the day. *Three guys.* Nevertheless, intent on trapping the enemy, the commander ordered them forward.

Steve and company made it a few dozen yards under intense fire before getting pinned down behind a large dirt mound. A few minutes later, my platoon arrived and quickly stacked up on the canal road behind the troop commander. I hastily grabbed my eight dismounts and sprinted forward to the commander's vehicle—whose gunner was blasting away wildly. Upon hearing that the captain had sent dismounts forward, we bounded west across the canal. I can still hear my corny voice yelling, "I'm coming, Steve!" Years later it seems laughable, but at the time it was all so epic and sincere. Truth be told, by this point the insurgent fire had slowed to scattered bursts and we had no issue reaching the dirt mound. When we did, Steve lifted his head and managed a playful smile that I'll never forget. It suited him. Fuller (who wasn't in the gunner's spot that day), Damian, Ford, Faulkner, SGT DJ, Doc, and SGT Pushard returned fire at the enemy positions. To our south, 3rd platoon had shifted the momentum. Maneuvering into better firing positions, the "Bastards" (3rd platoon's nickname) pinned down a few insurgents, forced the rest into retreat, and hit at least one fleeing toward an escape van. I coordinated with Scott and he shifted his fire west so my dismounts could sweep the field, hoping to cut off the remaining enemy fighters.

With all enemy fire ceased, we slowly traversed the graveyard. Despite the lull, we moved cautiously, knowing that a few insurgents were supposedly pinned down between us and 3rd platoon. Crossing a small path, we found the first body. A heavyset, middle-aged man with a bald head, wearing a black "man dress," was sprawled on his back across the trail. Shot in the chest, shoulder, and face, he appeared lifeless. Doc checked his vitals—dead. Here was our first "kill," though the honor likely belonged to 3rd platoon. We continued southwest, now wading into waist-high grass, methodically measuring each step. As I reached down for my radio, I heard Fuller's screaming voice behind me:

"Oh, fuck yo! Mother-fucker, I GOT one."

[He kicked wildly at the grass.]

"Get out of there, son; motherfucker, get OUT. Help me out, yo, there's a fuckin DUDE down here."

We ran over and sure enough, a man was huddled in the grass, grasping an AK-47. We'd all walked right by him. My path passed so close that I could have literally stepped on him. Fuller kicked wildly at the guy's body and rifle. In a mixture of fear, panic, and good sense, he tried to get the AK-47 away and also gave the guy a few swift kicks to the abdomen. We calmed Fuller down and began searching the prisoner.

Unlike his dead comrade, the prisoner was dressed in modern attire and had a well-trimmed beard. Maybe it's the movies that do it, but everyone I talk to seems to envision all Iraqi insurgents as kufiya-clad, dress-wearing jihadists. Not the case. Many wore Western clothing. This guy sported a velour soccer track suit like some sort of Arab Paulie "Walnuts" off *The Sopranos*. Another thing: most insurgents weren't suicidal fanatics. Americans imagine the Iraqis as profoundly different from us, as lunatics trapped in the eighth century, wielding the zealous sword of Islam no matter the cost. Usually, they weren't. This guy had a loaded, operational AK-47 and I walked right by him. He could have killed me and a few others before we got to him, but he didn't. That's just it. Like most human beings, he didn't want to die.

Despite what you hear, only a tiny minority of insurgents fought with that brand of suicidal fervor. The majority wanted to attack, win, and *live*. Just like this guy. He didn't sacrifice his life for the eternal jihad. Instead, Arab "Paulie Walnuts" was headed to jail.

We took pictures of the prisoners with the illegal weaponry found in their possession. This aided in future Iraqi government prosecutions of the accused. Snapshots of the dead were also common practice, in order to run the faces against wanted lists. We were always trying to understand the insurgent hierarchy, leadership, and organization. Not that we ever fully did. We had a few terps with us that day. Mark hated when we took pictures of dead bodies. On the truck ride back to the hotel, he explained why. Although the deceased was a Sunni insurgent, and despite the long history of repression Mark's Shia people had suffered at Sunni hands, the man remained a *human being*—one of God's creatures. I myself was conflicted. Excited by the knowledge we'd finally killed the enemy, I was also surprisingly dismayed by the sight of the body itself. Perhaps Mark and I shared something different from most other participants in the day's graveyard fight. Or maybe we were just more open about it.

"Bob" was working with another platoon that day. An animated and popular interpreter, Bob was angry and excitable. He'd helped to interrogate the prisoner,[7] yelling aggressively in the man's face and trying to gather intelligence. A few weeks later, Bob was dead.

# 6

# Indispensable Friends
## Mark and the Interpreters

Because you're kind—and it's in your nature.
— Jody to Fergus in dialogue from *The Crying Game* (1993)

Like a stormy ocean tide, the war washed up all kinds. One hears a lot about the cruel sociopaths empowered by chaotic violence. Without a doubt, I met many of those individuals—Iraqi as well as American. But the war also coughed up the best among us. Not just the brave, charismatic, or noble. Sure, there was some of that, but not in the cinematic ways you might imagine. No, I was drawn to another type of human being—the kind. Ever so rarely the war yielded a gentle soul who shone like a beam of reason and benevolence in a dark place. Mark—my favorite interpreter—was one of these.

His name wasn't actually Mark, of course. He was Iraqi after all. Local linguists chose code names in order to hide their identities. Working as an interpreter in the pay of American forces was a dangerous business. But you could tell a lot by the name an interpreter chose. Some fancied themselves as warriors alongside their American masters—and took names like Saif (Arabic: "sword") or Asad ("lion"). Others craved acceptance and camaraderie—they might be dubbed Bob, Jimmy, or Steve. Still another group worshipped Western culture. These terps (as we called them) went by slick monikers such as Big Easy or Slim Shady. Mark didn't neatly fit any of these categories. His real name was Akeel Ali Jasim.[1] A fitting title: Akeel means "wise" in Arabic. A young man in his late twenties, Mark was short, maybe five-foot-six, with relatively broad shoulders on an otherwise thin frame. He had longish, messy, dark hair and a sympathetic smile. His thin wire glasses never left his eyes and lent him a fitting air of bookishness. I liked his face.

We received interpreters on a rotation system. They were not, at that time, permanently assigned to a platoon. Rather, all the Iraqi linguists on duty gathered in a small "terp-shack," waiting to be picked for a patrol. The terps knew nothing of the day's mission—its length, location, purpose, or time. They weren't trusted with such information. They showed up to the FOB and waited in the shack while a designated sergeant assigned them to the day's upcoming patrols like a taxi dispatcher. I worked with many terps during my tour and remember few names and almost no personal details. In fact, I can hardly conjure a face unless captured in a photograph. But I think of Mark all the time. He spoke clear, crisp, English—more of a rarity among the terps than one might assume. We shook hands—his were soft but firm—and he introduced himself in a courteous manner. I think he saw something in me too, because he seemed pleased to be coming along with us.

Our drive down to Salman Pak took about thirty minutes, and we didn't run into any trouble. I don't remember anything about the day's mission, but do recall the conversation. I'm not sure how it began, but I complimented his English and it was off to the races from there. We talked about books, religion, education, history, and politics. Mark was amazing. He had read and could expound at length upon Western Arabist authors such as Bernard Lewis, Edward Said, and Gilles Kepel. He understood U.S. politics and current events. He possessed an avid interest in both Judaism and Christianity. He quoted the Torah, the New Testament, and the Koran. I was blown away. I learned that Mark possessed two degrees from the University of Baghdad, one in English and one in German Studies—a mixture of language, culture, and history. He was trilingual. He was brilliant.

Mark hailed from a large, poor family in the Shiite ghetto of Sadr City. This infamously destitute and violent neighborhood would claim the lives of perhaps a hundred U.S. troops. "Sadr City" was once called Revolution City and then renamed Saddam City. It was built in the late 1950s on the northeast side of Baghdad and consisted of a huge, rectangular, densely packed grid system of narrow streets with multistory and low-rise apartments. Initially built to alleviate severe housing shortages in the growing city, the area rapidly filled with primarily impoverished Shia families. The Sunnis, though a minority, dominated Iraq's central government and Sadr City—as it was often unofficially known—developed into a crowded slum.[2] The neighborhood gained its nickname from the populist Shia religious leader Imam Mohammed Al-Sadr. Sadr was killed in 1999 after infuriating Saddam Hussein with his political and religious defiance. Most suspected that the shooters were direct employees of the Hussein regime. Mohammed Sadr's son, Moktada, went on to form the Mahdi Army and contest the U.S. occupation.[3] By 2006 probably more than a million people lived in the squalor of Sadr City—Mark was just one.

He loved his family and his people. Mark lived with both parents, eight brothers, and two sisters. He adored his youngest sister in particular. They all shared a small home in a rough area of town. His father operated as a small bread vendor, and Mark often helped in the family shop. This was his cover—and his "day job." The real money came from his work with us. Terps received pretty solid pay— at least for the Iraqi economy—of about $1,500 a month, and Mark gave nearly all of it to his parents. He saved only a few dollars for himself in hope of someday making it to the United States. On occasion, he slipped a few dollars to his favorite sister. The rest kept the family afloat. It was blood money. Being an interpreter for the U.S. military was an enormously dangerous venture. They served on pain of death.

Consider a day in the life of a terp. Leaving their local neighborhoods once the city's curfew had lifted (curfew start times varied throughout the war between 8:00 and 11:00 p.m.), they drove shitty cars through dense traffic to an American FOB. Before starting their cars, they would first check the underside for signs of tampering or a booby trap. As they drove, they would nervously stare in the rearview mirror to be sure they weren't followed. Upon arrival, the terps lined up in a holding area for searching. Although they were indispensable to the mission, the terps were never fully trusted. This was understandable from a rational perspective but difficult for some of them to swallow. Once patted down and waved with a handheld metal-detecting wand, they would enter the base and report for work. Within a few minutes or a few hours, they'd draw a mission. The thing is, they never knew how long they would be out. Some terps got in the habit of bringing extra clothes. They never knew whether the mission would be a routine four-hour mounted patrol or a several-day-long air assault. The terp would meet his patrol leader, usually a lieutenant, get a quick once-over of the general plan, and then hop in a HMMWV. Some of the terps didn't even tell their families what they did. To do so would put their loved ones at risk. Others didn't even trust their own parents. These were nasty times, and it was a dirty game.

The terps wore a variety of clothing. Most dressed in some hybrid combo of outdated U.S. military fatigues and assorted civilian attire. Some terps were quite a sight. A common ensemble included a Desert Storm–era desert fatigue blouse, ill-fitting off-brand blue jeans, and hand-me-down American combat boots. The terps often filled their camouflage tops with assorted patches, pins, and other flair given to them by successive units. You see, the terps were kind of the one constant in the ever-changing world of the FOB. Units came and went, but the terps kept working for one group after another. Sometimes they knew more about the neighborhoods, the roads, and even the enemy situation than even the most seasoned U.S. soldier. Some terps livened their get-ups with aviator sunglasses, "Tupac-style" bandanas, black leather jackets, and all kinds of other chic accessories. Most wore a mask. Some tied a Wild West–looking bandana around their face, but most went with dark balaclavas that lent them the air of Irish Republican Army gunmen. They looked intense; they looked shady. But damn if they didn't have their reasons. The terps were mostly *from* Baghdad or the surrounding area. They tried to work with units that didn't regularly patrol their neighborhoods, but they just never knew. By late 2008, more than three hundred interpreters had been killed for working with the Americans.[4] A terp could run into someone he knew, and that person might inform the local militia. That's all it took. Guys were tortured to death for less. A terp once told me (they loved American cinema) that after working with us, he could understand the stress Johnny Depp's character felt operating undercover in *Donnie Brasco*.

One can imagine the collective anger and frustration of the terps when the U.S. military outlawed the use of masks in 2008. As violence dropped across the capital, the military changed its policy. A senior spokesman for the U.S. military, explained the new guidelines: "We are a professional army and professional units don't conceal their identity by wearing masks," he wrote in an e-mail. He said that those dissatisfied with the new policy "can seek alternative employment."[5] Some did, but most were desperate for the money within an Iraqi economy plagued by unemployment. Terps had little choice. Mark was interviewed by an American newspaper about the decision to ban the masks. Needless to say, like most terps, he abhorred the policy change. When the article came out, the battalion commander called Mark into his office. The colonel warned him not to give any more critical interviews or he'd be fired. Sometimes our ideals don't match reality. We rarely see the hypocrisy—but others do.

When we patrolled Salman Pak, Mark did so sans mask. His home turf of Sadr City was a fair distance from the area, and he didn't know anyone down there. Mark never wore any military fatigues. He always dressed like a bookish, young grad student—blue jeans or khakis and a checkered button-up shirt. Mark wasn't there to play soldier. It wasn't his style. Though well read and intelligent, he was no secular humanist either. Other terps tended to take on the habits and style of the young enlisted soldiers. They watched trashy porn on their cell phones, cursed like sailors, and horsed around with the American kids. Mark never fit in with most of the other terps. He abhorred violence, never used a cuss word, and shrank from any, even verbal, confrontation. His innocence ran deep and his authenticity was endearing. Mark abhorred pornography and remained a virgin. He cringed when the guys made crude remarks about women. Instead, he longed for love and companionate marriage.

He had been in love once. One night he told me about the experience. It was the late 1990s; he was in his teens and fell for the girl next door. Literally. She lived across the narrow alley separating their homes. Stand in that space and you could touch your arms to both apartments. These were tenements in the poorest of Baghdad slums, after all. The two teens were so close yet so far. A few years his junior, the girl was a Feyli Kurd. The Kurds, of course, were a non-Arab ethnic minority that predominated in the north of Iraq. They had a long history of persecution by the central authorities in Baghdad, including poison gas attacks ordered by Saddam Hussein. The Feyli, unlike most of the Kurds, were Shia—hence the girl's family living in Shia Sadr City. Mark could still recall her beauty. Inas—Arabic for "friendliness"—had light skin and yellow eyes. Like many Kurdish girls, she wore Western-style clothes. It was love at first sight for Mark—her eyes captivated him. Years later he couldn't explain why she had so enchanted him, except that she was his first love. A powerful force, indeed.

Desperate for a way to talk with her, Mark bought a small pigeon coop for his rooftop. He didn't particularly care for birds, but she spent a lot of time on her own roof, especially in the sweltering summer heat. He'd tend to the pigeons as an excuse to stare at her and eventually strike up a conversation. They became dear friends and he fell deeply in love. Despite their profound connection, the two never even kissed. Mostly they just watched one another through their windows and talked endlessly across the alley from their rooftops.

Then her family suddenly moved. They were heading south to the city of Najaf. Even though there were no Kurds in the region, Najaf had cheap housing and her destitute family hoped to buy a bigger place. In Baghdad, the Feyli were second- or even third-class citizens. They bore the double stain of being both Kurdish *and* Shia in a state dominated by Sunni Arabs. In the 1970s and '80s Saddam expelled thousands of the Feyli—branding them as Iranian Persians—despite their long roots in Iraq.[6] Violence and expulsions continued for years afterward. Perhaps her family sought a better, safer life in the south. Mark never saw her again.

I craved any and all knowledge about Iraq—obsession is in my nature. Mark was my tutor. He spent countless hours on patrol, on the FOB, or at various combat outposts lecturing about Arab history and Iraqi culture. He bought a few children's school books and used them to teach me rudimentary Arabic. A demanding instructor, he quizzed me constantly on my vocabulary. Within a few months, I was carrying on respectable conversations in precise Baghdad-dialect Arabic. People on the streets were surprised by my skills, and I'd catch a smile on Mark's face—I was his prized (albeit only) student.

He was a devout Shia Muslim, deeply conservative, and dedicated to his faith. Many Americans associate Islam with a number of "isms": fundamentalism, extremism, terrorism. They don't acknowledge its capacity for tolerance, nor do they realize how closely related it is to the other core monotheistic faiths of Christianity and Judaism. Mark taught me all about religion, history, and culture, but mostly about *tolerance*—as much through his daily actions as his informal lessons. A rather pious man himself, Mark didn't subscribe to exclusionary religious beliefs. He respected moral people from any and all creeds. Poor, fanatical young men, whether motivated by faith, country, or ethnicity, will lead a society toward violent implosion. He often recalled the euphoria in his neighborhood of Sadr City in the wake of the U.S. invasion back in '03, and how quickly the jubilation turned to dejection and violence. War bred chaos, chaos led to radicalism, then to intolerance and bloodshed. For Mark, that was the lesson of his country. One he wouldn't soon forget.

An unknown number of terps died while serving with U.S. forces. Some estimates range as high as one thousand.[7] They shared our trucks, thus they shared our dangers. Many were killed by the same IEDs that targeted our troops. Others met a more horrid fate. Whereas American soldiers faced the most danger while on patrol, many terps feared going home even more. Hundreds were kidnapped, tortured, murdered, and mutilated by militiamen, insurgents, or criminal gangs. Some simply disappeared. One of our popular translators, "Bob"—a friend of Mark's—was abducted and murdered by the Mahdi Army in his own Baghdad neighborhood. No one knew the details of his death, but his close friend, "Jimmy," received a call on his cell phone from the killers. They took credit for Bob's murder and informed him he'd be next. Jimmy never returned to work and eventually left the country. He now lives in the Netherlands.

Before 2007, any real program for the immigration of Iraqi translators to the United States was nonexistent.[8] Every single platoon patrolled with a terp. Over the years, tens of thousands served with our troops. After 2007, 839 Iraqi translators finally received a visa. Some 777 of those came in fiscal year 2007 or 2008. Once we began pulling out, the numbers plummeted. Many of these men and women, who risked everything to work with us, were left behind. As 2009 turned to 2010 and as Iraq faded ever further from the headlines, the number of interpreter visas nosedived. There were 30 in '09, just 12 in 2010. When the combat troops left in December 2011, most terps had to stay. In 2011 only 8 left, then 6, then just 5 by 2013.[9] Thanks for your service.

I spent my last night in Iraq on FOB Loyalty in east-central Baghdad. While our unit waited for helicopter flights to Baghdad airport,

I stood near the smoking pit,[10] talking with Mark. I gave him a copy of a letter of recommendation I'd worked up in his behalf. I hoped it would help him with the process of getting a visa. He'd been on a wait list for months and held little hope. "LT, only the terps working for the generals in the Green Zone get a visa these days," he'd tell me.[11] Nevertheless, he appreciated my letter. The choppers started to come in. My time was short. We embraced. I think we both cried—I'm sure I did. Just like that, I was gone. My time in Iraq was done. And Mark, like so many others, was left behind—tomorrow he'd begin work with a new unit. This was the terp life—continuity was their charter.

### HUMAN INTERLUDE 2: MJ IN SALMAN PAK

Sometimes Iraq seemed so far from home. It could feel distant in both space and time. When I'd patrol down in the ball sack and hit villages like Duraya and Al Lej, I felt a long way from the States. Down there hygiene was awful, some of the people lived in mud huts, and the level of poverty was shocking. It was like a time warp. But Iraq didn't always feel that way. Salman Pak itself was much more modern. There were a few hours of electricity, some impressive mansions, and for the most part all the structures looked less archaic. The best way to describe the architecture is to imagine a place where all time stopped in about 1974. Because of international sanctions and a crippling war with Iran, nothing much got built in Iraq after the '70s. Salman Pak, and Baghdad in general, bore a strange resemblance to Atlantic City, New Jersey, and some of the older towns along Route 209 in the Pocono Mountains of Pennsylvania, or really any one of a million places in America that have that sense of being trapped in the mid-1970s. But the villages to the southeast (which were only a *few miles* away) looked like 1370 instead of 1970—so it's all relative.

Many of my memories are bizarre and seemingly arbitrary. We were patrolling on the south side of Salman Pak, behind an old abandoned elementary school. As a side note, no one was attending school in the city during 2006. Period. Military occupation, civil war, and the effects of societal collapse roll downhill. Children suffer. I can't remember what we were doing except showing presence and providing "security," but at any rate, I look up at the backside of some storefront and what do I see? A full-size mural—pretty well done, too—of

Michael Jackson, the King of Pop himself. There he was—right hand on the brim of his tipped fedora, left leg cocked up and bent at the knee. You know the pose.

I had to ask. "Mark, what the fuck? Is that seriously Michael Jackson?"

Mark had the dual role of translating both Arabic and the idiosyncrasies of Iraqi culture for me. He rather matter-of-factly answered that the mural *of course* depicted MJ. "LT," he said, "these people love Michael Jackson so very much. He is such a great dancer and his voice has such soul." Some of the more extreme Islamic elements in the city—and I must state that they were a small minority—believed that any artistic depiction of the human form was punishable by death. And here in the same town was Joe Jackson's sensitive, tragic son—painted on the wall. Salman Pak didn't feel so far from home that day.

Baghdad proper was downright cosmopolitan by comparison.[12] Once, we were assigned to "pull security" in the vicinity of Mustansiriyah University in east-central Baghdad. So there we sat in our HMMWV on a corner near the academic buildings, basically glad we had caught a safe and relatively easy mission that day. My crew watched the students and hoped to see some "fine Hajji ass." Smith, in particular, was always on the lookout. Most Americans might be surprised to know that Iraqi women attend college. Even at the height of a sectarian civil war and Iraq's revived conservatism, many still did. So we sat watching as a few classes let out for the afternoon. Walking down the road came three girls, maybe about twenty years old, holding their books and chatting away. They were clearly friends. The girl on the far left wore a full head-to-toe burka with only an eye slit exposed to the 100-degree sunlight. In the middle, an average-dressed Iraqi girl—long slacks, long sleeves, and a colorful hijab covering the back half of her head. On the far right was the third friend. She had blonde highlights in her hair, a too-small purple shirt that could have been from the Limited Too, and a pink miniskirt. It was surreal. But that was Baghdad. Mark and the other terps told me that before the invasion and its subsequent chaos, women and men went on public dates and drank alcohol in outdoor cafes. There were no morality police or sectarian killers. Styles of dress and moral codes were determined by one's parents. Not all that different from here in the USA.

I watched the girls walk past our truck. I thought back to the MJ mural and I smiled. There was a mixture of bemusement and anger in my grin. I remembered President Bush, Vice President Cheney, and company. They had told us the Iraqis "hated us for our freedoms."[13] Did they? I sat there and recalled a photo of Don Rumsfeld meeting with Saddam Hussein in the 1980s. Back then, we supported the regime with intelligence and military hardware for its war with Iran. At that time, Saddam's Iraq was the relatively "open" and secular alternative to the Islamic Republic next door. American arms and American culture seeped in. It pretty much always does. I suppose that's why Michael Jackson made it onto the wall in Salman Pak, and why some female students wore outdated, skimpy, American-style clothes. The 1980s produced the Iran-Iraq War and about a million deaths. But it also produced *Thriller*.

# 7

# Breaking Point
## Fear, Loss, and Defeat

DECEMBER 2006

All luck runs out eventually. By mid-December, we'd patrolled Mada'in for about forty-five days. Despite dozens of firefights and several IED attacks, the troop sustained no serious injuries or deaths. Some of it was blind chance—the bomb that blew a second too soon, or the bullet that ricocheted left instead of right. But there was something else. I had the distinct feeling that both sides—ours and the enemy—had spent the last month groping blindly for opportunities. The insurgents, especially the growing Sunni elements, were feeling us out, probing for weaknesses. Perhaps that explained their tendency to fire and retreat in the Ja'ara gun battles.

The graveyard fight, however, was something new. The insurgents fought well, holding ground and maneuvering with a degree of tactical prowess. Hindsight tells me we should have seen it all coming, but in the moment, everything felt normal. Normal for Iraq, that is.

Our platoon's day in the hotel rotation was 14 December. We swapped out with 1st platoon about midday and settled into our routine of patrols, chai, food, smokes, and more patrols. About 4:00 p.m., the shooting began. It started out faint but quickly rose to a new level of uproar. NP radios blared with frenzied Arabic voices, and the police commander ran out to my truck with a panicked report. The southernmost NP checkpoint in Salman Pak, at the corner of routes Wild and Croc, was under intense attack and in danger of being overrun. This checkpoint represented the furthest reach of Iraqi government authority in the region. Except for ever-so-brief U.S. patrols, the villages in the ball sack belonged to the insurgents. They owned the night and most of the day. Like St. Louis in the early nineteenth century, the checkpoint was the last permanent outpost before entering "Indian Country." The NPs, naturally, worried for the position's security. Just then we heard the first mortar rounds explode to the south. This was for real.

We mounted up, checked weapons, and rolled out of the hotel at full speed. It took only about three minutes to reach the checkpoint. The NPs were hunkered down and wildly returning fire into the tall grass along the canal lines to their east. Some NPs were pointing over the barriers to indicate the enemy's direction. This intensity of fire was something we hadn't yet seen. Suddenly, four men with AK-47s darted out of an irrigation ditch and down the canal line—indicated on our maps as Route Blue Jays. The insurgents were exposed for only a second and sprinted down the trail before our gunners could return accurate fire. "Route" Blue Jays was really just a narrow canal road with an irrigation ditch on either side. It ran east to west, and sat about halfway between Salman Pak and the village of Duraya. We'd never been down Blue Jays before, neither mounted nor on foot, but it was a bit wider than the usual canal road. So I took a chance.

Sending my platoon down Route Blue Jays that day, from a tactical standpoint, was a textbook bad decision. Plain and simple. The responsibility, and guilt, is mine alone. Here are the facts: I had no idea about the route's trafficability, no sense of what was in front us, zero concept of the enemy situation, and worst of all, I'd arrayed heavy HMMWVs in single file down a narrow path with essentially zero turnaround ability. I ordered us down the canal because for once we could see the enemy; because we were fired up and wanted to take aggressive offensive action; mostly, though, because in the moment, I didn't stop to think. It was all over in about thirty seconds. Down the route we went.

We rolled in five trucks that day. Damian had the lead down, followed by SGT Pushard. I was in the middle, trailed by SSG Rittel and SFC Gass, respectively. About 50 meters down Route Blue Jays, the fire began. We hit an unnamed perpendicular route with a dilapidated farmhouse at the intersection. Insurgents with AK-47s and Russian PKM machine guns started hitting our trucks from the east, farther down Route Blue Jays, and from the south from behind the farmhouse and beyond. It was pretty intense. Mortars were still flying overhead and landing back by the NP checkpoint. At this point, all of our gunners fired simultaneously in the two directions. I sent Damian and Pushard south about 40 meters on the unnamed trail. They took up positions and suppressed groups of insurgents maneuvering in the canals. Placing my own vehicle at the hinge of our position—where I could keep visual with Damian—I sent SSG Rittel about 30 meters farther east on Route Blue Jay. Within a minute of splitting the platoon, the enemy fire intensified. This was a firefight unlike any others we had experienced. Anywhere between twenty and fifty insurgents maneuvered around our platoon, popping up to fire and taking cover before the gunners could adjust their sights. The problem lay in the terrain. With grass between waist and shoulder height on all sides, and deep irrigation ditches running parallel to all the paths, the insurgents could move around our positions with the security of ad hoc trench lines.

It got nuts pretty fast. Both SFC Gass and I sent frantic and increasingly frenzied reports to headquarters and requested immediate air support. In the interim, insurgents maneuvered undetected down the irrigation ditches and started popping up to the left of and *behind* my truck. SPC Matt Singleton, my new gunner—he'd replaced Fuller a few days earlier when we promoted Al to dismount team leader—couldn't depress the .50 caliber machine gun low enough to return fire. Besides, the .50 had been jamming for the last few rounds. Cursing at the machine gun, Singleton grabbed his M4 rifle and started firing down into the ditch. He claimed he hit one insurgent, who tumbled backward into the tall grass. In the meantime, all the windows on our HMMWV were taking direct hits. The bullet-proof glass held, but spider webs of splintered glass made vision increasingly tough. Furthermore, it indicated that the insurgent fire was both close and accurate. I heard myself yell out to the crew: "Fellas, we're in the fight of our *lives*." I wanted that one back immediately—corny as ever. I'd clearly seen too many movies. Smith, our in-house adrenaline junky, *begged* me to let him dismount and fight on foot. He hated driving, since he rarely got to fire his weapon or dismount. He kept grabbing at his rifle and putting his hand on the door latch. I had to literally order him to stay put.

For all our troubles, SSG Rittel and SFC Gass took the brunt of it.

Insurgents swarmed on their position from the north and southeast. Suddenly and without warning, DJ—his adrenaline pumping and desperate to support Ducks with some supporting fire—hopped out of Rittel's backseat and took aim with his rifle. He popped off a few well-aimed shots before SFC Gass screamed at him to remount. It was too late. DJ turned to do so, ducked down a bit, faced toward the truck, and was struck in the back by a round from an AK-47. He hit the ground. I saw him fall and heard it simultaneously hit the radio waves—"Ghost 6 is *DOWN!*" DJ tried to get up—couldn't—and knew something was desperately wrong. It was 4:48 p.m.

Just as DJ was hit, two vehicles pulled out of adjacent canal roads to the east of SSG Rittel's lead truck. One was a van that kicked out a few more dismounted insurgents. The other, a modified pickup with a 12.7 mm DShK heavy machine gun mounted to a tripod on the truck bed. Both groups opened fire on our trucks. Seeing our casualty and correctly sensing vulnerability, the insurgents struck hard. It was becoming clear that the enemy had *planned* this thing. They'd attacked the checkpoint to lure our platoon to the area and baited us to rush down an inhospitable canal road. Observing and learning from us in the Ja'ara fights, and seeing our aggressiveness in the graveyard attack, they had counted on a similar response from whichever platoon was on duty that day. I played into their hands.

Ford and Gass both jumped out as soon as DJ was hit. They moved through a hail of bullets, grabbed DJ, and dragged him back a few meters until he was adjacent to Gass's vehicle. Doc dismounted, and he and Ford went to work. Gass returned fire in an effort to protect them. He quickly took a grazing bullet to the helmet and had to take cover. The fire was getting worse. DJ's helmet was left farther down the path, and Ford—without a thought for his own safety—took off his own and placed it under DJ's head for protection. He also propped up DJ's Kevlar vest to form an improvised shield while they treated his wounds. The vest blocked a few rounds almost immediately. DJ was verbal, said he was hit and couldn't feel his legs. He felt no pain. Turning him over, Ford and Doc realized that the bullet had entered DJ's back, tumbled around, and likely done some internal damage. DJ's breathing became labored and he soon stopped speaking. The last thing he remembered was pulling the chewing tobacco from his mouth. Another round pierced Ford's boot heel, just missing his ankle. With Gass's truck blocking fire from only one direction, and needing to stabilize DJ before moving him off site, something had to give. And fast. It was Ducks's moment.

▬▬▬ Ducks was a genuinely nice, lower-middle-class kid from Gage Park in southwest Chicago. It's a district of mostly working-class Irish and Eastern European Catholics, and Ducks grew up in one of the neighborhood's ubiquitous bungalows. His early childhood was a blur, and that's probably for the best. His twin sister, born three months premature to a mother suffering from neurofibromatosis type I tumor disorder, inherited that affliction, as well as mild retardation. Ducks was underdeveloped for quite some time but grew into a healthy, normal child. His mother died within a year, and he never met his father. Ducks bounced among two or three foster families before being taken in permanently by his adoptive parents. He was two and half. His adoptive father spent forty years unloading trucks at a warehouse, while his mother worked in the insurance business and also as a professional clown. Ducks's parents raised him in a wholesome, loving environment and encouraged him to be himself. He was sheltered and different, plain and simple. In Chicago schools, that posed a challenge.

Ever since grade school, Ducks had been a target for bullies and rampant teasing. He played ice hockey in a private league, but also enjoyed chess and drama club in high school. Always a stellar student, Ducks loved to read but never really needed to study to pull solid grades. Academic success rarely translates into popularity, and boys being boys, some of them pounced. Ducks fought back and was even suspended a few times for a series of physical altercations. Ducks's granddad had served with Patton in Europe, and that plus a fascination with old war movies attracted him to the military. He was the kind of boy who had his whole life planned out by his early teens: join the army, do twenty years, retire, teach history, and someday pull two pensions. His parents always joked that he was fifteen going on fifty. Mostly, though, he was a quiet, smart, well-mannered kid.

That was part of the problem. He lacked the crude speech and edgy temperament of his peers in the army. First stationed in South

Korea, he preferred to read or play videogames in his room rather than drink or whore around the many red light districts surrounding U.S. bases. His assignment to the intelligence section during much of his first Iraq tour didn't help his case, and Ducks confronted some mean-spirited torment. He also shouldered another affliction—night terrors. He'd had them since he could remember, and they got worse after the first deployment. In any other profession that would have stayed private—maybe only a spouse would know. But in the army, you sleep countless nights in close quarters. The platoon sergeant kept Ducks isolated at the far end of our platoon tent, but he'd still wake us all with ear-splitting, shrill screams. I'd never heard anything like it.

■■■■■■ The kid with night terrors, who'd struggled endlessly for respect, was gunning on the lead—and most exposed—vehicle. Ducks's turret was getting peppered with bullets. A fragment slammed into his ammunition belt, jumped up and hit his face. Blood dripped into his eyes and obscured his vision. Unfazed, he pulled the hot metal from his face and continued firing. Angry and aware of the critical situation, Ducks trained his sights, lifted his head, and unleashed accurate bursts of fire. With all the measured control of a training range, Ducks hit the pickup truck, disabled its engine, and killed the mounted machine gunner. Suppressing the adjacent dismounts, he slowed the enemy momentum just enough to allow Gass and company to move DJ. Meanwhile, another insurgent hopped onto the pickup truck's mounted machine gun. Ducks shifted fire and killed him too. By the end of the fight, Ducks had fired more than fifteen hundred rounds from his M240B machine gun. On the other canal, SPC Brian Longton and SGT Caleb Holloway, both gunners, continued to suppress and eventually pin down the enemy. Longton eventually "went black on"—almost ran out of—ammunition. SSG South's cool efforts and the controlled fire of the gunners kept our south flank from being enveloped.

I knew we had to get off the canal and back on Route Wild as soon as possible. I'd coordinated to hand off the fight to 3rd platoon—which was speeding south at that very moment—and needed to get DJ to the hospital. I decided to leave the truck, fearing it'd get stuck or further block the narrow path if we moved forward, and move on foot to DJ's position. As I grabbed for the door's latch, another bullet smacked into my passenger window. I froze. I'm not sure for how long, maybe thirty seconds, but it felt like forever. Every moment I hesitated was dangerous for DJ, but I couldn't move. This was the first time since landing in Iraq that I was truly, dreadfully afraid. I breathed in, closed my eyes, and flung open the door. Running forward, I saw and *felt* a few rounds skip by me across the dirt path. I genuinely expected to be hit. Reaching SFC Gass, I said the obvious—"Sergeant, we gotta go, NOW!" As if he didn't know that. Gass already had a plan. DJ was loaded into the truck and we literally backed out—in reverse—down the canal road, Ducks providing covering fire the whole way.

Once we hit Route Wild, the platoon sped north. The commander of C Troop had set up an LZ (landing zone) north of Salman Pak. The plan was to use this secure site, wait for a MEDEVAC helicopter, and further stabilize DJ. On the way, SFC Gass's HMMWV shit out. His engine had been shot up pretty good and we had to tow him the rest of the way, which slowed us down by a few extra minutes. At 5:19 p.m. we hit the LZ. The guys lifted DJ out of the truck and onto a stretcher laid in the middle of a field. The sun had set, and the medics needed light to work. I stood over them and shone the flashlight from my rifle over DJ. My hands shook with fear, nerves, shock—or something—and I actually struggled to keep the light source steady. The hole in DJ's back was huge, and his condition was worsening. Doc kept his legs raised to increase blood flow, started an IV to help with the blood loss, and used five needle decompressions in his chest.[1] Needle decompression involved sticking a large-gauge needle into a trauma victim's chest to allow the escape of air from that cavity to reinflate the lungs.

Ford worked with a calm and competence I'll forever admire. When he pulled out the nasal trumpet—the old platoon *initiation* device—I knew DJ's condition was serious. At 5:32 p.m., the helicopter landed. As DJ was loaded onto the bird, I was sure he'd die. I tried to light a cigarette but couldn't. My hands shook and I paced around alone with the distinct feeling that this had all been my fault. It was. C Troop's commander, a former Army Ranger who had served three previous combat tours, walked over and steadied me. I didn't know him that well. In fact, we never got close—though we did run into each other years later in Kandahar, Afghanistan—but I respected the hell out of the guy. He had kind words and consoled me, explaining that he too knew what it was like to lose a soldier. The captain was calm, composed, and totally in control that night. I was emotional and exhausted. His demeanor stabilized me, and I gathered the strength to assemble and steady my platoon.

The fight down south was far from over. Scott took over the battle and engaged in sporadic skirmishes for about an hour. At 5:37 p.m., our requested air support arrived in the form of fixed-wing aircraft. The pilots observed fourteen insurgents firing on Scott's position and shuttling a rocket launcher to the front. The fighter planes engaged that group at 5:48 p.m. A few were killed and the rest fled. I'm not sure how many insurgents we (mostly Ducks) and the planes killed. The enemy generally carried off their dead, so it was always hard to tell. Later that evening, C Troop headed south and swept the area. They found only two bodies.

DJ almost didn't make it. He flat-lined twice that night—basically, died—once on the helicopter when his heart stopped beating, and later in the hospital. DJ was terribly wounded. The bullet that hit his back had tumbled about inside of him, took out half a lung, and nicked his spine. That spinal injury left him paralyzed from the waist down. SFC Gass and I got to visit DJ before he left Baghdad Hospital. The squadron commander saved us two seats on his ground convoy to the Combat Support Hospital—CSH, pronounced CASH—in Baghdad's "Green Zone." Later popularized in the original series Baghdad ER, the CSH handled the single largest number of our wounded among all the military hospitals. When DJ was shot, the CSH was treating around 300 trauma patients per month.[2] The 28th Combat Support Hospital—the unit responsible for the CSH during our fifteen-month tour—dealt with a staggering number of wounded. All told, the 28th handled 6,152 casualties and conducted 14,253 surgical procedures—in one tour.[3] As we entered the main lobby that day, I was immediately struck by the level of frantic activity. This had to be one of the busiest hospitals in the world. And yet, despite the MEDEVAC helicopters landing outside with horribly wounded trauma victims and the record-breaking patient flows, it still seemed like a peaceful environment. As I watched the nurses and doctors rush around, and saw the sheer number of wounded in the clean, well-kept facility, I thought, *this* is the noblest job in the whole war effort. For a moment I was jealous. No moral qualms here, nor any killing; just a single-minded, life-saving mission.

We headed upstairs to DJ's room, and I remember thinking how recently he'd been injured. It had been less than twenty hours since he was hit. He was a rough sight. Tubes everywhere, monitors beeping, and his shriveled-looking body lifeless on the bed. He was unconscious and under close supervision. On his chest was a Purple Heart Medal, pinned there by our brigade commander. DJ hadn't stirred. No one knows what to say in those moments. Things get pretty silent and slightly awkward. Gass and I quietly asked some nurses about his condition. The squadron commander thanked the medical staff. Mostly we stood around, knowing DJ wouldn't speak, and wondered how long we should stay. By this point I was drowning in guilt. I suspected everyone in the room—my platoon sergeant, the SCO, even the *nurses*—of judging me and my decisions. Looking back, I doubt that was the case. At the time, though, I couldn't shake the feeling. Seeing DJ lying there, I felt some tears creeping under my eyes but held them back for fear they'd expose my guilt. It was a tough day.

After the visit, we had a few minutes to kill before our patrol returned to FOB Rustamiyah. This was my first time in the Green Zone: Baghdad's international zone and home to the U.S. military headquarters, the embassy, and thousands of civilian federal employees. The place was surreal. Only a few hours out of our last firefight, my uniform was filthy and still carried the smell of Salman Pak. Here I was, though, watching female State Department officers jogging by in short-shorts and tank tops. Then I saw the embassy pool and an enormous food court, replete with Burger King and Pizza Hut. I felt like a stranger. As a twenty-three-year-old insecure and exhausted lieutenant, the place made me angry. Seven years later, while understanding the diverse purposes of the Green Zone, the memory still makes me furious.

The battle on Route Blue Jays was the talk of the squadron for quite some time. In fact, in terms of sheer intensity and number of enemy engaged, it was the most serious firefight of the unit's deployment. I spent the next few days writing citations, and eventually SFC Gass, SSG Rittel, Ducks, Ford, and Doc Schrader all received valor awards for their actions in the battle. No one ever saw Ducks the same way. His accurate fire, cool demeanor, and ability to fight through his wound earned him a whole new level of respect. After December 14, everyone in the platoon looked at him in a different light. You could see this infusion of confidence in Ducks's step as he strolled about the barracks. After our brief Green Zone visit, we drove back to the FOB and prepped for another patrol. We got that one day off but the next morning headed back to the Pak.

▬▬▬ DJ faced a long road. Over the course of numerous surgeries and moves from one facility to another, his heart stopped three separate times—he's been *thrice* dead. The first time was during surgery in the CSH when they removed his entire right lung. After leaving the Baghdad CSH, he flew to the U.S. Army hospital in Landstuhl, Germany. This stopover facility was meant to stabilize patients before risking a long transatlantic flight to the States. Midflight, DJ's heart stopped again; the plane turned around and headed back to Germany. Finally, after some more stabilization, DJ flew to Walter Reed Medical Center in Washington, DC. At Walter Reed his heart stopped a *third* time—this time the doctors' only explanation was that "too much trauma" had caused his body to shut down. The docs got him pumping again, and DJ was finally through the worst of it.

It was in Walter Reed that DJ first came to. He'd been in a medically induced coma for *weeks*. When he awoke, the sight of tubes and monitors indicated immediately that something was terribly wrong. Besides, he *couldn't feel his legs*—nothing at all from the waist down. After a few weeks, DJ ended up in Albuquerque's New Mexico Veteran Affairs Medical Center. The hospital specialized in spinal injuries, and there DJ underwent terribly difficult physical therapy, learning to do even the simplest things over again: brush his teeth, feed himself, and lift his body into a wheelchair. That last task was particularly difficult, especially after he'd lost 55 pounds from a 180-pound frame.[4] DJ was still DJ, though. He never lost his cutting sense of humor. When New Mexico's governor and future U.S. commerce secretary Bill Richardson came to visit, DJ told him with a grin, "I'd stand up . . . but I can't."[5] DJ had a long road ahead of him, and his prospects for ever walking again remained uncertain. But on Thursday, 15 March 2007, three months and a day after he was shot, he took a cell phone video of himself wiggling his toes for the first time. Baby steps, but still progress.

### THE POWER OF SELF-DOUBT: REFLECTIONS ON COURAGE

There is always a philosophy for lack of courage.
— ALBERT CAMUS

After DJ was wounded, I endlessly questioned my own actions, courage, and general performance under fire. Up until then, I had been confident in my leadership and personal behavior during our many firefights. But 14 December was the first time I'd felt genuinely scared. Moreover, it was then I first realized that my actions could *actually* lead to a soldier's death or critical injury. Worse still, I was unaware things were about to get worse. From that day forward, everything always seemed so deadly serious. They have ever since.

People ask me all the time whether I was scared in Iraq or Afghanistan. They'll inquire about courage, valor, and cowardice among the troops. Civilians seem to have the sense that everyone in the army is somehow inherently braver than the population at large, by virtue of self-selecting for military service. Were that it was so simple. Courage and cowardice are not binary functions. Fear and valor aren't contradictory and usually coexist within the same soldier. Almost nobody is *always* brave or *always* cowardly. Reality is far less consistent. Soldiers perform selfless, daring actions one day, and freeze up on others. Some days I had the confidence to move from position to position in a firefight, and on the next I'd cower at length behind cover. At the margins, some men regularly crack under fire and others are somehow always courageous. But they represent the minority. Most men, myself included, faced a new challenge every single day, waking up and waging an internal battle to remain steady in the harrowing circumstances to come. Uncertainty bred more fear than the fighting itself. The vast majority of soldiers, who served legitimate combat duty in Iraq, know deep down that their internal fortitude weathered both good and bad days. You hoped each day that cour-age wouldn't be a problem—but you never really knew. I mostly just hoped.

Individual instances of valor or cowardice often made little logical sense. I'd run through open fields of fire in Ja'ara and the graveyard, but momentarily froze on Route Blue Jays. Sometimes "courage" bor-dered on recklessness, without any sensible rationale. Our platoon found many IEDs, especially on Route Wild, during the last months of 2006. When we'd see a suspicious device, pile of rocks, or disturbed earth—anything that might contain an IED—we had to follow a stan-dard, protracted process. We'd call in a descriptive report to head-quarters and request an explosive ordnance disposal team (EOD) to investigate, and if necessary, destroy the IED. Unfortunately, this could take hours, especially farther south in the sector. We'd have to pause our mission, cordon off the area, and wait. Just wait. The 2nd platoon probably babysat real and suspected IEDs for some one hun-dred odd hours during the tour. We'll never get back those four *days* of our lives.

Once we found a dirt trail on Route Croc near the village of Du-raya. The suspicious dirt led off the east side of the road to a large hole that dipped under the roadway. Damian—who first spotted it—was about 80 percent sure it was a bomb. But then again, Route Croc, in chronic disrepair, was full of patches and potholes. As this suspected IED was south of Salman Pak, we knew we'd wait at least a few hours for EOD. It had been a long day already, and we were supposed to swap out and get back on the FOB in time for dinner. Besides, it was getting dark. The prospect of sitting there all night was a nightmare. My knees bounced impatiently in my truck as I sat and thought about it. "Fuck this," I said to Smith as I jumped out of the vehicle. I walked forward and knocked on Damian's window. "Hey, what do you say you and me just go check this fuckin thing out?" I asked. "Sure, let's do it," Damian instantly answered.

Why I decided to take him with me and put another life in dan-ger, I can't exactly say. Probably had something to do with strength in numbers and group think. Like two idiots, we strolled over to the suspected device. We crept along carefully—as if slowly approach-ing would save us from a blast—until we could peer into the hole.

Damian shone his rifle's flashlight down and *sure enough*, there sat a few antitank mines, all wired-up to blow. "Oh Fuck," we yelled and scattered back toward his truck, laughing the whole way. We'd risked our lives to try and make it back in time for stir-fry night at the mess hall. And it seemed totally reasonable at the time. When we got to his truck, Damian grabbed the radio and reported, "Yeah, Black X-Ray (HQ call sign), we're *definitely* gonna need that EOD support." Then he dropped the hand mic and we smoked a couple cigarettes as the sun set over the Tigris.

A few months later, Steve and I were lifting weights at the FOB gym. Our base, Camp Rustamiyah, was for a time the most mortared FOB in Iraq. Rusty—dubbed "Mortaritaville"—came under fire every day, and even took some casualties. One military police soldier was killed by a direct mortar hit on his way to Thanksgiving dinner. Mostly, though, we didn't worry much about the mortars and went about our routine business. It was Steve's turn on the bench press. As a side note, the gym's televisions were dominated by news of former Pakistani prime minister Benazir Bhutto's death at the hands of suicide bombers. Perhaps the best hope for democracy in Pakistan, a nuclear power, and she was dead. The region, I remember thinking, was truly going to shit. It kind of still is, but I digress. So Steve's got maybe 250 pounds on the bench, and he only weighs about 175. We'd been bulking up in our free time and throwing around some heavy weight. I gave him a lift off and he put up the bar once . . . twice . . . *BOOM, BOOM*—mortars coming in, and close! Like any good friend, I panicked and *took off.* I instinctively ran toward the door and left the heavy bar on his chest. Steve needed all his might to press the bar onto the rack, and then took off after me. When he reached the bunker outside, I didn't give him a chance to say anything. "Sorry, dude that was fucked up." Like I said: Good days and bad.

### CATASTROPHE AND COLLAPSE
### OPERATION DOLPHIN: 23 DECEMBER 2006

Things changed after DJ's injury. A series of successive firefights and an increasing number of IEDs around Salman Pak finally convinced squadron headquarters that the ball sack was effectively under AQI control. By mid-December the squadron commander had designated Route Croc as black, meaning impassable for military convoys unless specifically cleared by engineer assets. We spent the next few days holding defensive positions to the southeast of Salman Pak and engaging in small skirmishes to keep insurgents from infiltrating the city. Meanwhile, the commander prudently requested reinforcements to clear out the ball sack. We'd need to cordon off and search the villages for weapons caches, IED-making materials, and high-ranking insurgent leaders. A fine enough plan, but manpower was short all across Iraq. All but one U.S. brigade were committed to sectors of their own. One reserve brigade reinforced needy units across the entire country—an area larger than California—so they too were stretched to capacity. Occupation duty and active counterinsurgency are enormous manpower drains. Extra troops were just hard to come by. Against all odds, the squadron commander secured a full Stryker infantry unit, 2nd Battalion, 3rd Infantry (about seven hundred men) from the theater reserve brigade. They'd be attached to us in just one week, but we'd get them for only three short days—one for planning and two for operations—max. Still, the infantry battalion increased our combat power several times over.

The plan—dubbed Operation Dolphin—was simple. Apache Troop (our sister element in the same squadron), with an attached National Guard platoon from E/1-125 Infantry (nicknamed the Hooligans, this element primarily trained local Iraqi police—it wasn't uncommon for active-duty units to have such attachments), would move southeast along Route Pluto, then maneuver due south on Route Crazy to seal off the ball sack and prevent insurgent escape. Our troop broke up and interspersed with the Stryker battalion to help direct them, since after all, it was *our* sector and unreasonable to teach them the geography with just one planning day. The squadron received one dedicated engineer route clearance team to slowly proof and clear the entirety of Route Croc. As the engineers cleared the road, the Stryker battalion would follow to search each successive village and its surrounding area for bomb or weapons caches, and capture or kill any resisters.

Given the limited time and resources available, it wasn't such a bad plan. On paper, that is. But there were some significant problems. Without dedicated air support—helicopters—to lift the infantrymen into the center of the ball sack, the element of surprise was essentially gone. The danger of Route Croc, and the fact that it was the *only* traffic-able route in the region, meant that we were slaves to the road. Engineer clearance is a painfully slow process—by design. That gave all the momentum to the insurgents. They'd see the huge force buildup, realize we were coming, know which *way* we'd have to travel, and prepare accordingly. We weren't surprising *anyone*. In such a deliberate operation, we placed the ball squarely in the insurgents' court. They could choose to fight or not. All they'd have to do is activate their IEDs and wait. Any caches could be moved, covered up, or destroyed while they watched our vehicles slowly plod south. Then there was the issue of resources. The squadron had just one engineer clearance team, which meant that only Route Croc could be deliberately swept for IEDs. Apache Troop and the Hooligan platoon would have to brave Route Crazy—aptly named, since you had to be a lunatic to drive it—with nothing but their eyes and intuition to detect roadside bombs. After some impressive rehearsals coordinated by the squadron staff—specifically our exceptional executive and operations officers—OP Dolphin was to kick off early on 23 December. But there was another problem—the weather. A rare storm passed through Mada'in that morning, bringing rain and wind along with it.

The SCO faced a tough decision. By dawn on 23 December, it was obvious the skies wouldn't clear. Low cloud ceilings, sporadic bursts of rain, and wind gusts meant that helicopters—including critical MEDEVAC flights—would be spotty all day. Helicopters are incredible assets on the battlefield, but like all technology, they're vulnerable to war's inherent friction and environmental constraints. Flight status for army helicopters was categorized in one of three ways: Green, Red, and Black. Green status meant no restrictions to flight; black essentially grounded all aircraft and thus brought most ground operations to a halt—for fear wounded soldiers could not be evacuated in a timely manner. As a rule of thumb, medical professionals spoke of a "golden hour," the imperative for severely wounded soldiers to reach the CSH within one hour of injury. So long as he received sufficient on-site buddy aid and reached the hospital—by air or ground evacuation—within that allotted time, a casualty's chance of survival increased exponentially. Army doctors first developed the concept during the Korean War, as statistics indicated that over 90 percent of combat deaths occurred in the hour preceding treatment in a dedicated medical facility.[6] We were trained to expedite our wounded out and always adhere to the golden hour. Red air status, however, was a grey area. Aircraft might or might not be available to fly and would require emergency, senior officer approval for most missions. Under red conditions, it was the commander's call to halt or proceed with ground operations. Typically, the decision was based on proximity of the operation to medical facilities, likelihood of danger, and necessity of the mission. On 23 December, air stayed "red" for most of the day.

The night before the main attack, I'd bunked down in a Stryker combat vehicle with one of the company commanders in 2-3 Infantry. I'd gone to West Point with his younger brother. My job was to help lead him to the target villages and advise on enemy tactics in the area. The next morning, I heard over the net that air status was red and hoped the operation would be delayed. The ball sack was highly volatile and casualties were likely. Furthermore, it was more than a forty-minute drive (if you floored it) to FOB Rustamiyah and another fifteen to thirty (traffic dependent) to the Green Zone CSH. Bottom line, southern Mada'in was critically distant from proper medical attention—it was textbook Air MEDEVAC territory. Nevertheless, the squadron commander decided to proceed.

When I heard about the decision, I was livid. At the time, I was *certain* the commander had made his choice solely to win points with the brigade commander and impress higher headquarters with his aggressiveness. Looking back, I realize that the commander's decision—while still unwise—was far more complex than I'd given him credit for. He had his reasons. The ball sack *was* extremely dangerous, littered with AQI insurgents who weren't going anywhere. And we owned the AO—meaning that our underequipped squadron would have to deal with them at some point or another. The inevitable fight would likely result in casualties. Most important, the huge troop increase 2-3 Infantry brought to the fight was temporary. They'd only be with us for another twenty-four hours. Besides, 3-61 CAV needed a win—at least the commander seemed to feel we did—and this was our best chance. For better or worse, Operation Dolphin was on.

For a few hours, everything proceeded as planned, if quite slowly. The engineers were extremely cautious and crawled south on Route

Croc. Knowing the road's reputation, the clearance team took it slow. By midmorning, the Stryker battalion had begun clearing the houses, farms, and canals around the village of Duraya. They found nothing. Apache Troop, with its Hooligan platoon attachments, moved down Route Crazy to cut off the insurgent escape route. It was 12:20 p.m. Seconds later, everything fell apart. A massive bomb, buried deep under the asphalt of Route Crazy, detonated directly below a Hooligan HMMWV. The result was catastrophic. Lieutenant Keith Marfione, from Reading, Massachusetts—a West Point classmate, and the Apache Troop FSO—was one of the first to respond to the blast. What he witnessed was unforgettable. He and several other soldiers tried to make sense of the dreadful scene. The first radio report, at 12:30 p.m., listed two U.S. soldiers and one Iraqi interpreter dead, another soldier wounded, and one *unaccounted for*. They literally couldn't find the guy. It took thirty minutes of searching through the scattered wreckage to update that initial report.

The scene was gruesome beyond any explanation. The blast left shards of twisted metal and pieces of human flesh dotting the landscape for a hundred meters in all directions. There wasn't much left. Keith and a few other sergeants kept most of the soldiers away from the horrible sight and began personally collecting the remains in body bags. Eventually they realized that the missing soldier had been simply blown so unrecognizably apart that he couldn't initially be identified. At 1:00 p.m. they classified the soldier as KIA—killed in action. Surveying the damage to the vehicle, it was amazing that anyone had survived. The final count on Route Crazy was four dead and one—remarkably not very seriously—wounded. Apache Troop spent the rest of the day skirmishing with insurgents and recovering the vehicle wreckage. Later estimates placed the bomb at up to *300 pounds* of explosives.

Everyone's heart sank when reports of the Route Crazy blast hit the radio. Some of us had feared this would happen, and we now worried about follow-on ambushes. The SCO's instincts kicked in. Upon hearing the report and its dire aftermath, he ordered his security platoon down to the blast site. *What?!?* I thought. He's going to *pass* route clearance and drive several *kilometers* down an *unclear* black status road—Route Croc! I honestly couldn't believe what I was hearing. This just wasn't done. The engineers were in place specifi-cally because the route was deemed impassable. I pulled off my head-set in disgust, turned to the 2-3 Infantry captain in the vehicle, and declared: "They're gonna hit an IED." Within minutes—*BOOM*—an audible blast to the south. The captain stared back at me with wonder. The command security platoon's lead vehicle had hit a one-hundred-pound deeply buried bomb. It was 12:58 p.m., just twenty-eight min-utes after the Route Crazy attack. All five soldiers in the HMMWV were wounded, three critically—one, SPC Elias, of Glendora, California, was urgent—and the vehicle was catastrophically damaged.

The commander was stuck between two bad options: zip north for FOB Rustamiyah—at least a forty-minute affair—or set up an LZ and hope to hell a bird could reach them. He chose the latter. But air had been red off and on all day. It took forty-one minutes after the blast until a MEDEVAC helicopter was cleared for take-off from distant FOB Kalsu—several miles to our southwest. All told, an hour elapsed before the MEDEVAC arrived and took off with the casualties. They didn't land at the CSH until 2:10 p.m., seventy-two minutes after the attack—just outside the prescribed golden hour. Ten minutes later, Elias was pronounced dead.

Operation Dolphin ended right then and there. For all intents and purposes, it became one large recovery operation, removing vehicle wreckage and friendly casualties from the battlefield. Insurgents harassed us with some scattered firefights but mostly just watched as we limped off the field. The mission was disastrous. On our side: five dead and five wounded. As for the insurgents: zero dead, wounded, or captured. We'd searched a few square kilometers of the northwest ball sack—only a tiny percentage of the planned area—and found exactly *one* illegal weapon, a basic AK-47 with an attached scope. Worse still, we'd left the field under insurgent control—they held every village south of Duraya—and Route Croc remained black: im-passible without engineer support, which we'd rarely be able to get. By Christmas Day 2-3 Infantry was gone and it was just us again. After 23 December, we recognized our inherent limitations and essentially ceded the area to Sunni insurgents. So ended Operation Dolphin—an enemy victory.

At the time, I—and the vast majority of my peers—judged the SCO's actions quite harshly. We blamed his poor judgment on careerism and lack of knowledge about the terrain or enemy. His decision, I'd felt, was unforgivable. Then again, my own decisions, just nine days earlier, had gotten DJ shot and paralyzed—perhaps for life. Maybe my own guilt fed this unforgiving assessment. That was probably the case. With hindsight and experience, I'm still sure that the commander's decision to rush past the engineers was a poor one. Nevertheless, my judgment has since softened and I've generated a great deal of sympathy for my old commander. The SCO felt responsible for the hundreds of troops in his charge. When the bomb hit Hooligan platoon on Route Crazy, his only thought was to get to his wounded boys and help out. That turned out to be a bad call. But Iraq was full of confusion—the famed "fog of war" popularized by Prussian military theorist Clausewitz—and no commander possesses perfect information or an ability to predict the future. Contingency—the unending series of events that may or may not occur, affecting each subsequent episode—drives the process we call history.

I've since had some awful commanders. Looking back, I realize that the SCO was—generally—one of the better ones. He had real courage—who else would brave Route Croc under those conditions?—and his intentions were pure. He cared for his men and had a strong, deeply human conscience. In times since I've worked for genuine sociopaths, who wasted lives for professional gain and were incapable of human empathy. Our squadron commander wasn't that sort of leader. Not by a long shot. He was plagued—like all of us who made life and death decisions—with guilt and self-doubt. And in subsequent days, he wasn't afraid to admit it. As commander, he probably made fifty good decisions for every bad one. He was a competent professional directing violence in a horrific, complex combination of civil war and counterinsurgency. Later in the deployment, as we moved up into downtown Baghdad, the SCO would drop by our troop patrol base, strip down to his undershirt, and smoke cigarettes with the lieutenants. I know now how truly rare that is. Sometimes I wish I could go back and tell my angry twenty-three-year-old self to reserve judgment. The guy was a pretty solid commander. More important, he was a good man.

## HOLDING THE LINE: KILLING TIME
## AT THE ANCIENT RUINS

In the aftermath of Dolphin, operations stagnated. The squadron was back to its original size and had to continue securing the entire, massive district. The ball sack belonged to the Sunni insurgents—for now—and in the short term we hoped to just hold on to Salman Pak itself. In those trying days after Dolphin, we legitimately feared that AQI elements would infiltrate parts of the city and utterly destabilize the region. B Troop had to work overtime to hold the line. From then on, two of three scout platoons were forward positioned 24/7, generally arrayed along a defensive line from the ancient ruins on the Tigris River stretching east to the north end of Route Blue Jays. This long-term, static observation position protected the south and east end of Salman Pak from infiltration out of the ball sack. Those were long days. We'd work forty-eight hours on and twenty-four off, sleeping in our trucks or on the ground during these two-day shifts. We'd detach sections to do mounted or foot patrols in the city, then return to our established defensive perimeter. Occasionally we'd get in small firefights, but typically the insurgents resorted to mortar attacks. Most important, none of our guys were hurt in the barrage. Nonetheless, I remember thinking what a tragedy it would be if an errant mortar round damaged the fourteen-hundred-year-old Sassanid ruins standing *right behind* our trucks.

The ruins themselves were quite a sight. The two main buildings were remnants of the once great Sassanid (Persian) capital of Ctesiphon. First, the main portico of the palace audience hall, dated from the reign of Khosrau III in the early seventh century. About 120 feet tall and nearly as wide, the structure stood above all other buildings in Salman Pak, with one exception: the famed Taq-i-Kasra arch. The arch was part of the grand palace complex and the largest freestanding brick arch in the world.

It was a time of anger; it was a time of boredom. The Operation Dolphin debacle exhausted all my remaining enthusiasm for the war. And we'd only been there two months! Perhaps good soldiering requires more conviction, but, alas, I fear I wasn't such an outstanding soldier. Then or now. My thoughts at the time can best be summarized as hopeless. *How*, I wondered, could we win? What would victory even *mean?* If after three and a half years of occupation we still hadn't secured even marginal control of a district less than 20 miles from the capital city, how many years would it *take?* And with a few thousand American deaths already on the books, how many more lives would securing all those places cost? Was it worth it? Did enough Iraqis *want* to live under a central, Baghdad-based regime? And if the Sunnis and Shia were killing each other in a sectarian civil war, what did that say about the viability of an Iraqi state clumsily formed by European colonial powers a century earlier? Would Sunnis *ever* accept a Shia-dominated, Iran-aligned government? On Christmas Eve, 2006—as I jotted a few angry pages in my journal—those were some of the questions on my mind. But perhaps, most of all this: how does an officer balance personal opposition to a war with his duty to serve and lead a combat platoon? I'd spend the next year, and another one in Afghanistan, living in the shadow of that question. I'm not sure I've yet found the answer.

Mostly, though, I tried to compartmentalize those deeper concerns and just focus on being a solid platoon leader—protecting my guys and making sound tactical decisions. Excruciating boredom and thousands of mindless, intratruck conversations eased the process. Sitting in a small vehicle for forty-eight straight hours with the same three people can drive you mad. Imagine spending that much time a couple of feet from your wife and kids—divorce rates and murder-suicides would skyrocket. But, at that moment in my life, listening to the crew's endless banter was exceptionally soothing. It literally helped me sleep.

My crew was hilarious. Smith and Singleton were best buds and two certifiable lunatics. They kept me laughing each and every day. On Christmas, I walked out to the truck, ready to give my patrol briefing, and noticed a shit-eating grin on Smith's face. He'd taped a snowman to the front hood of the HMMWV and wanted to see me freak out about it. I didn't. We rolled with "Frosty" all the way to Salman Pak. With my crew, every patrol was an adventure. Back then, Smith—in classic twenty-year-old dude fashion—flirted with all the female soldiers on gate guard duty. The girls would walk up to my window, so I could sign out on the manifest roster, and chat incessantly—across my body—with Smith. He'd be like: "Yo girl, fancy seeing you on this fine day," or "Hey, babe, you come here often?" You haven't lived till you've seen two people wearing bullet-proof vests flirt with each other. It's like spring break in postapocalyptic Cancun. After a while, of course, Smith's assorted ugly gate-girls started finding out about each other. Shit changed quickly. The next day, as we rolled out the gate, the old scene repeated itself. I grabbed the manifest, and Smith yelled across: "What's up, girl?" This time her body language was completely different, and she fired back: "Fuck you, Smith, you dirty mother-fucker." The gate opened, Smith pressed hard on the gas, and shrugged: "Don't hate the playa, hate the game, ladies."

Smith was a solid driver. Aggressive, fearless, and steady at the wheel. He and Singleton were also responsible for prepping the truck. Topping off fuel, checking the engine, loading up ammo, and cleaning the machine gun were basic daily tasks. Essentially, lieutenants are the aristocrats of the crew. Sure, I'd plan missions and handle the radio on patrols, but my "horse" was always ready the moment I wanted to roll out. Overall, we were a good team. Except for two things: Smith (a) was a slob, and (b) *never* packed the right supplies. Generally, your crew cleans out the trash, food, and expended ammo from your HMMWV after each mission. And had Smith driven for any of the *sergeants*, they would have smoked his ass for not doing so. But I was a softy about that kind of stuff, and the fellas *knew it*. Sometimes, I think they'd let a thick layer of rubbish form at my feet just to see how far they could push it. They also liked to watch me eventually crack and throw one of my epic temper tantrums. Then they'd try not to smile, shrug, and say: "Sorry, Sir."

I'd also told Smith we needed about fifty bottles of water for our two-day missions and at least a dozen should be on ice in the cooler. "Roger, Sir," he'd say. The next day I'd open it up looking for a nice, cold water and yep—*all Red Bulls!* Smith would barter with the Iraqis for cases and cases of the off-brand, Arab energy drinks and then stack the whole cooler with them. He lived on the stuff, literally bouncing around in his seat all—damn—day. I'd lose my shit! He'd try not smile. Oh but we do cherish our routines.

████ James was always James—fearless, impulsive, and tender-hearted. It was fitting that he drove our HMMWV. He'd gotten an early start. At just past two years old, baby James had walked out the house, climbed into the family's truck-bed, crawled through the back window, and somehow shifted the pickup into neutral. As the vehicle rolled down the driveway, his mother, Susan, yelled out and gave chase. After the truck came to rest against the opposite curb, he told his mother, "I was just backing up, mama." On one of many family camping trips, just after he'd learned to walk, James decided to cross a busy road to reach a nearby lake. Rather than wait for traffic to pass, he waddled into the middle of the road, rose up his hand, motioned the cars to stop, and crossed at his leisure. As his father, David, remembers, "That's how he went through life—expecting the cars to stop for him. Thing is, they always did." Raising a boy like James was unique. If other parents received a report that their son had damaged a neighbor's property, they might say: "Not my kid." The Smiths, well, they'd just wonder how James managed it.

He started everything early. James caught his first fish at two years old. He shot a deer at eight, and by age twelve he would traipse off alone into the woods to hunt before first light. But James's big heart and sensitivity were legendary. An avid hunter and fisherman, he also loved all the neighborhood dogs and never wanted to hurt an animal. On one fishing trip, he asked Susan if "they should really be doing this—mustn't the hook hurt the fish?" She had to explain that she thought the fish didn't feel the same way we do. He went on to catch seventy that day. Susan lost count of the times James picked her flowers or shiny rocks from neighborhood flower gardens. Ever affectionate, he just had that knack for making everyone feel like they were number one.

Sadey was James's niece. James and his sister Candace were always close—even after she got married and moved to a new city. Although the distance posed some challenges, Sadey's birth brought them closer than ever. Things weren't always easy in the Smith home. James and Candace clashed with their parents and both moved out of the house as teenagers. With only nineteen months separating them, James and Candace maintained a deep connection and met each other's needs. Candace was the good listener, full of tough love and candid advice. James just wanted everyone to be smiling all the time, and worked hard to make her happy. He always did.

Susan Smith liked to refer to Sara Bench as James's "other mother." She met James during an AG-class (agricultural) during freshman year at Grapevine High School. I suppose we all craft an image and then display it for the world. James played the rough-around-the-edges cowboy type, complete with a bold "Don't Mess with Texas" belt buckle that some found ironic. After all, he came from a middle-class suburb in the Dallas area. Texas being Texas, sports—especially football—were everything. James played a couple of years of football but found his wiry frame was better suited to wrestling, and he developed into one of the best in the state, finishing second in Texas for his weight class.

James navigated high school with a tight group of about ten friends. They were an inseparable clique of boys and girls, but no one actually dated within the circle. They did what kids do: drinking at Daren's house because his parents were cool with it, hitting Sonic after school, and attending country music concerts at Lone Star Park. Some of the guys liked to tie one on, and James was a notorious whiskey drinker—even back then—but they mostly stayed out of trouble. Thanks to Sara, that is. The girls in the group kept things just on the right side of the line, and when James—impulsive to the core—would start a fight or try to get behind the wheel of a car, only Sara could talk him down. "Come on, James, forget it—just come with me and let's have a beer," she'd say, and for some reason he listened. Sara never had a brother, and James quickly filled that void. They protected each other. He'd boost her confidence after a tough breakup—"No one's good enough for you anyway, Sara"—and she probably saved James from himself a few dozen times. We find the people we need; life's like that.

James was a freshman at Grapevine High when the towers came down in New York. He'd always been interested in the military, but 9/11 settled it. He was going to be a soldier. No one, least of all Sara, was surprised when James enlisted after graduation. The group took a senior trip soon after, but James couldn't get off work and missed out. To make up for it, Sara and the gang threw him a sendoff party just days before he left for Fort Knox and basic training. James stripped off his T-shirt and everyone took turns shaving some of his hair off. The army was going to do it anyway, so why not have his friends do the honor?

Smith *was* impetuous, reckless even. He joined 2nd platoon in January 2006 and immediately made a name for himself. He was fun as hell to be around, and super motivated, but he didn't always know how to channel his energy. For reasons I don't remember, we switched drivers and Smith came over to my crew. Now we spent lots of time cooped up together in the HMMWV. I had a front-row seat to his personality—the "Smith show." Every time he passed me in the troop area he'd start grinning 20 feet out, wait a few seconds, salute, and shout, "Scouts Eat the Dead, Sir"—his personal greeting for me. I kind of liked it. One day I held a section on section platoon football game. Smith showed up late (no surprise there) in a full getup. While most of us wore sweatpants, sneakers, and a T-shirt, he was rocking a skin-tight Under Armour shirt, football pants, and legit cleats. He was a damn good athlete too, running the option and scrambling as his team's quarterback. Then, he didn't like a call made by our refereeing sergeant. After some heated arguing, Smith labeled the game "bush league" and walked off the field. Honestly, it was ridiculous and unnecessary. At the time I was pissed off, but whenever I think back on it, I smile. Just classic Smith: living moment to moment and getting spun up about *everything*.

That September, just a few weeks before we left for Iraq, the whole unit got two weeks' leave. Back home in New York, I got a call from Texas. Smith was in jail. He'd been speeding down a Lubbock street with another guy from our HMMWV crew—Matt Singleton—after the Texas Tech football game. Stopped by a local cop, he was booked for reckless driving and DUI as a minor (he was not yet twenty-one).[7] Great. Less than thirty days before deployment and my driver was in city lockup. True to form, Smith spent a couple of nights in jail before finally breaking down to call his father for bail. He knew, of course, that to wait any longer would mean missing formation and being designated AWOL (absent without leave—a criminal offense under the Uniform Code of Military Justice, and a big deal in our world). Problem was, he now had a pending court date that would fall *after* our unit's departure for Iraq. Long story short, I spent a few hours on the phone with the police and local district attorney. I had to explain the Servicemen's Civil Relief Act (SCRA) and fax over some paperwork with a signed memorandum. SCRA "is intended to postpone or suspend certain civil obligations to enable service members to devote full attention to duty and relieve stress on the family members of those deployed service members."[8] Examples of protected obligations are outstanding credit card debt, taxes, termination of lease, and pending trials.

When Smith got back to Fort Carson, I didn't have the heart to yell. Just glad he was home, I promoted him a few days later. Fast cars and a stint in jail made him who he was. A few months later he chose me as his re-enlistment officer. After everything he'd been through, all the combat and hardship—he signed on for another stretch in the army. Re-enlistees can decide the place, time, and style of the ceremony. It's a tradition. Smith did it at the Baghdad squadron headquarters behind two gargantuan flags hung off the balcony—the stars and stripes and the Lone Star state flag. I looked up at the comically large flags, smiled, and began the oath: "Repeat after me: I, [James David Smith], do solemnly swear, to support and defend the constitution . . ." Like his state of birth, James did everything big.

▨▨▨▨ By tradition, conversations in the HMMWV are notoriously dirty. Smith and Singleton were besties, but they ragged on each other incessantly, about anything, really. Every argument ended the same way though. Here's a tip. If you want to win any dispute, there's a simple retort that trumps all others, and Smith had mastered it. Singleton would hassle Smith endlessly about one thing or the other: ugly girls he used to date, his country music, and the fact that he had to drive while Singleton got the sexy gunner's job—you name it. Smith would take it all in, wait patiently, and then drop it on him: "True, true, but yo—I fucked your wife!" Argument over. The best part is Singleton never really got mad, and they'd *laugh about it* moments later. The best part of the day was my front-row seat to the "James and Matt show." Never a dull moment.

Interpreter Mark was the straight man in the truck. Perennially conservative, he'd silently listen to awful banter about porn, booze, wife-fucking, and the like until he couldn't take it anymore. "Matthew, James (he *insisted* on using their first names), you are just horrible, simply horrible!" Of course, Mark absolutely adored both of them, and they laughed their asses off every time he chastised their morals.

Smith and Singleton would have died for Mark—he was our terp, our guy—and they were nothing if not loyal. I don't think it crossed my mind until just now that all three of the men in that truck were named after Gospel authors. And while I wish it were, I'm fairly certain that is not a significant fact. However, "Mark"—Akeel—the Muslim in our midst, was most certainly the conscience of the crew, the most prudish and conservative, no doubt, but also the most kind and genuinely innocent. They, we, were all so young. Sitting for endless hours, day and night, in that confined space, we got to know each other's life stories, strange habits, sleeping rituals, hopes, fears, and dreams. We lived on cigarettes, dip, energy drinks, and mindless chitchat. We had each other, and it was comforting. Two weeks later, on 10 January 2007, President Bush surprised everyone. He ignored a midterm election defeat in Congress, as well as vocal opposition to the war, and announced the deployment of thirty thousand more U.S. troops to Iraq. The Surge had begun.

### HUMAN INTERLUDE 3:
### THE MUTANT CHILDREN OF MADA'IN

At the southernmost end of Salman Pak, where Route Wild bent east and became Route Croc, lived the famed "spider boy" of Mada'in. I'm not sure I ever got his name, but the spider boy was about ten years old and lived in a house along the roadside. He spent every day from sunup to sunset on the curb outside his front door. Afflicted with a rare deformity, his legs bent horizontally outward and operated more like another set of arms. Unable to stand upright, he walked on all fours, his head arched in the air from between hunched shoulder blades. Mostly, though, he pushed himself back and forth on a homemade skateboard—really just a flat piece of plywood with some wheels attached—all day long. Each time our patrol passed, he'd rock back and forth excitedly, let out an undecipherable sound, and wave his arms . . . or legs . . . or whatever they were. He was kind of a platoon mascot, and oddly enough we always felt better when he was outside—sure that even the insurgents wouldn't dare place a bomb close to the poor kid. Maybe he was their mascot too.

Come to think of it, there were a *lot* of deformed and mentally challenged—I think the proper term these days is "special needs"—people,

especially children, in the Salman Pak area. A shocking amount. After
a while we just had to ask. Local people had no qualms discussing
the subject and provided a simple explanation for the high rate of
deformities—al Tuwaitha. The Tuwaitha Nuclear Research Center
was a large, dilapidated complex on the Tigris River just a few miles
north of Salman Pak. Built in 1977 by Saddam's regime, the French-
designed facility had an interesting backstory. Although it had been
intended for civilian energy purposes, Israeli intelligence suspected
that it fronted for a nuclear weapons program and bombed Tuwaitha
in 1981.[9] Better safe than sorry, U.S. warplanes again leveled the complex during the First Persian Gulf War.

After the regime collapsed in April 2003, several hundred local
Iraqis looted Tuwaitha and stole several barrels of "Yellowcake"—
uranium concentrate powder—and took them back to nearby villages.
The barrels were emptied and used *to store food* and other household
items.[10] Invading marines found the complex and believed they'd discovered Saddam's reputed WMD facility. However, experts quickly
ruled that out, finding only natural uranium—unenriched and therefore not weapons grade.[11] Years later, researchers from Texas Tech
University took hundreds of samples in the local villages and found
some elevated levels of radioactive contamination. Polluted or not,
Tuwaitha had a few remaining buildings, a tall dirt berm wall surrounding the complex, and was centrally located. Our C Troop turned
the site into a combat outpost and lived there for several months.
Cancer be damned.

The Texas Tech researchers did find some contamination in surrounding villages, but on nowhere near the scale of some early media
reports. But myths die hard, and the people of Mada'in were *convinced* that Tuwaitha was the source of all their health woes. It reminded me of my father's friend. This guy had been a grunt in Vietnam during the late '60s. For years afterward he'd complain about
his health. "I've got the Agent Orange," he'd say. So my dad would
ask, "Yeah, man, I get it. So maybe you were exposed to the chemical, but what are your *symptoms*, you know, like what's *wrong*?" "I
don't know, man, I just got Agent Orange!" he'd exclaim—as if Agent
Orange *was* the disease. Well, down in Salman Pak there were a lot of
kids suffering from "Tuwaitha." Thing is, most of us kind of bought

into it too. That partly reflects the morbid, cynical side of soldiers—we like to believe we're always being fucked over and exposed to all kinds of harmful things as a matter of course. Well, sometimes we are.

In this instance though, I think the problem lay somewhere else. There were genuinely a lot of disabled kids—and adults for that matter—wandering the streets of Salman Pak. Once we got up to Baghdad, though, things were the same way. We blamed it on the Tuwaitha fallout, but in all actuality, the volume of disabled kids probably just reflected different societal values toward the deformed and mentally ill. Salman Pak didn't even have an operational *school*, let alone a special education program or long-term facility for kids with special needs. The city had *one* doctor willing to work in town, and he had essentially no staff. Advanced procedures, plastic surgery, behavioral medication, or physical therapy? Nonexistent. Disabled children just burdened poor families trying to survive a brutal civil war. For the most part, these kids were left to fend for themselves—rolling to and fro on a makeshift skateboard.

Sometimes the United States seemed like a damn fine place. I know some academics are uncomfortable with applications of any strand of "modernization" theory. According to such relativist philosophy, judging Iraqi behavior is just another form of cultural and racial ethnocentrism, to be avoided at all cost. Look, I'm generally sympathetic to such notions. That said, if you saw the mutant children of Mada'in, and the way the disabled were dealt with during the war—you too might gain new appreciation for "modern" medicine, social relations, and Western-style special education. The 2003 invasion shattered the state structure: hospitals, nursing homes, clinics, and government support offices shuttered overnight. Looting, violence, and fear kept most facilities shut down for years. The wave of communal conflict breaks hardest upon the weakest among us—poor, female, young, and vulnerable. Some children in Salman Pak were all of the above. And the war was getting worse.

The "Original" Ghost Riders; 2nd platoon, B Troop, 3-61 CAV. Kuwait, October 2006.

The LTs (*left to right*): Steve Migliore, the author, Keith Marfione, Ken Blewett, Scott Maclaren, Luke Periera.

B Troop leadership, including the three platoon sergeants: SFC Malcolm Gass (*bottom left*), SFC Terry Kennedy (*bottom middle*), SFC Chris Lyons (*top left*).

Taq-i-Kasra arch, ancient Salman Pak ruins.

Salman Pak ruins of the Sassanid empire.

Sergeant Alexander Fuller of New Bedford, Massachusetts. Dismounted team leader.

Sergeant Ty DeJane of Salem, Ohio. Call sign, Ghost 6.

SPC Jeremy Frunk (*left*) of Arkansas and SPC Ed Faulkner of Elon, North Carolina.

SPC Edsel Ford, our unofficial medic and lifesaver, eating some lamb with the author at the Salman Pak Hotel.

Staff Sergeant Damian South of Panama City, Florida. Our "senior scout."

My driver, SPC James Smith of Hurst, Texas. Back home on leave, 2006.

The author, re-enlisting James Smith in front of his enormous Texas Flag. April 2007.

Akeel Ali Jasim, "Mark." My interpreter and friend at home in Sadr City, Baghdad.

Incredible poverty. Makeshift shack just north of Salman Pak.

SGT Biederman, our platoon fire support specialist, posing with makeshift shacks in the east Baghdad squatter district.

Damian gives out candy to the kids. Salman Pak market, 2006.

Kids trying on our shoes. East Baghdad, 2007.

My favorite kid with his new shoes. East Baghdad, 2007.

The author patrolling the Salman Pak market. Note the interpreter's covered face.

The author with the national police battalion commander. East Baghdad, January 2007.

The author does his best to juggle radios and computer screens in the HMMWV.

The crew (*left to right*): Gunner SPC Matt Singleton, FO SGT Biederman, Driver SPC James Smith.

SGT John Pushard of Corbin, Kentucky, stands in the crater left by an IED that just missed Damian's truck. Route Crocodile, Salman Pak, November 2006.

Civil war: aftermath of a sectarian store bombing. Salman Pak market, 2006.

Destroyed HMMWV on Route Crazy. Operation Dolphin, December 2006.

A child holds a toy *zanjeer zani*, chains affixed with blades used in self-flagellation rituals for Shia Ashura celebrations.

Arab Paulie Walnuts—track suit and all—captured after Salman Pak graveyard fight.

One of many bunkers constructed for village defense during the civil war. Ja'ara, 2006.

Wires as tangled as the war itself. East Baghdad, 2007.

His sense of humor remains: Ty DeJane dressed as LT Dan from *Forrest Gump*. Halloween, 2008.

Sadey visits Uncle James's grave.

Akeel—"Mark"—finally in America.
Visiting the White House.

Home for good. Damian and his wife,
Melissa South.

The author and his wife, Kate.
West Point, New York, July 2012.

The author and family (*left to right*): Kate, Brady, Danny, Ryan, AJ.

# 8

# Sunni versus Shia
## The Anatomy of Sectarian Civil War

We rush to a foreign land in a deluge of embattled sympathy, we give
away clothing, cigarettes, our rations . . . we do everything in our power
to proclaim our good intentions, our nobility of purpose, our loftiness of
soul . . . and all because we think we're too good for the rest of the world.
. . . We can't be bothered with the sordid details, the actualities of human
motivation. We stubbornly, sublimely refuse to see man as he is . . . we're
so damned certain about how he ought to be. We know how he ought to
be—he ought to be American.

— ANTON MYRER, *Once an Eagle*

Things fall apart. Unintended consequences multiply. In Iraq,
our invasion had about the same effect as feeding a wet gremlin after
midnight. By 2006, an ugly civil war consumed much of the country. Iraqis killed one another wholesale in a largely uncoordinated
but widespread campaign of ethnic cleansing. A concurrent nationalist insurgency—waged by both Sunni *and* Shia groups—attacked
U.S. soldiers. From 32 daily attacks on U.S. forces in October 2003,
numbers rose to 61 in October '04, 100 in the same month of '05, and
peaked at 180 when we arrived in October 2006.[1] By then it was hard
to keep up. Civil strife blended with insurgent attacks and further
fused with common crime, until no one knew who was battling whom
or why. The best explanation lay within deep fissures in Iraqi society:
Sunni vs. Shia.

Dynastic succession is a bitch. Back in the seventh century, when
the prophet Mohammed, founder of the Muslim faith, died without
a male heir, a power struggle ensued. His companions (think Christian apostles) couldn't agree on the prophet's preferred successor.
A powerful majority agreed that Abu Bakr, Mohammed's friend and

101

father-in-law, should inherit Arab leadership. Believing that a successor must only follow the prophet's teachings—or *sunna*—they became known as Sunnis. Others believed strongly that the prophet's kin should succeed him. They backed Ali, Mohammed's cousin and son-in-law. They were called Shias, a contraction of *shiaat* Ali—partisans of Ali.[2] After years of sometimes violent struggle, Sunni armies prevailed, massacring Ali's son, Hussein, and his small band in the battle of Karbala (AD 680) in modern-day Iraq. From that day forward, Shias retreated into the shadows and generally lived under Sunni-ruled regimes. Today about 80 percent of the Muslim world is Sunni. A quick note on context: most Americans wrongly assume that Sunnis and Shias have engaged in perpetual civil war for the last millennium. Periods of violence and repression certainly punctuated the Islamic sectarian divide. Nonetheless, Muslims never clashed on anywhere near the scale of Europe's great sixteenth- and seventeenth-century religious wars between Protestants and Catholics.[3] Shia populations generally chose introspection over resistance and a tenuous stasis took hold.

Here's the problem: Iraq was a synthetic creation of British colonialism. Once the center of the Sumerian and Babylonian kingdoms in what was dubbed "the cradle of civilization," modern-day Iraq hadn't been an independent entity for about twenty-six hundred years. Division and foreign rule were the norm. First Persians, then Greeks, Seleucids, Romans, Parthians, Sassanids, Arabs, Mongols, and eventually Ottoman Turks—among others—conquered and governed the region. The Ottoman was the last Islamic empire to rule. Then the Turks chose the losing side in World War I—a bad call. Defeated along with Germany, the Ottoman Empire was dissolved and divided up between the British and French. France took modern-day Syria and Lebanon, and the British grabbed Palestine. The Brits also pieced together the three separate Ottoman provinces of Mosul, Baghdad, and Basra into a new colony—euphemistically called a "mandate"—known as Iraq. The Mosul district held a Kurdish majority, Basra was overwhelmingly Shia, and Baghdad province was mixed but held a Sunni plurality.[4] The British, following long-standing colonial tactics of divide and rule, allied with and empowered the Sunnis. In 1920, Iraq's Shia population rose in revolt and had to be suppressed by

British arms. Literally importing an Arabian king, Faisal, to the area, the Brits hoped to unite Iraq's disparate parts into a coherent whole. It never really took. The broke and overstretched British granted independence in 1932, and Iraq, despite a Shia plurality, was ruled from its inception by a Sunni minority. Saddam Hussein was only the latest, and most brutal, kingpin in a line of Sunni regimes.[5]

The place was a tinderbox. Saddam utterly suppressed any inkling of Shia independence, and the Shia bore the scars not only of his rule but of fifteen hundred years of repression and disappointment. The Sunnis, like all minority regimes, were fully cognizant of their vulnerable position and lived in utter fear of the Shias. They were like the wealthy planters of the antebellum American South, anxiously anticipating the day when black slaves would suddenly rise up in murderous fury. Kurds wanted only to separate into an autonomous ethnic state in the north. When the U.S. Army invaded, the rubber band snapped. Out came fifteen hundred years of angst, fear, ambition, and eventually—violence. Not that the different sects *couldn't ever* coexist—in fact they often had—but the combination of chaos, fear, poverty, and a power vacuum pushed identity politics to the forefront. It happens—democracy can be messy.

When the Sunnis lost their grip on power, they faced one major problem. Iraq's Sunnis *have no oil*. All of Iraq's lucrative reserves rest in the Shia south and Kurdish north. The landlocked Sunnis of west and central Iraq had no natural resources. They were playing with a losing hand. So they did what they had to. Sunnis grabbed guns and bombs and doubled down. They'd play their weak hand out to the bitter end. Of course, President Bush, his advisors, and most of the soldiers closing in on Baghdad in 2003 hadn't the slightest inkling of all this. We were in for a surprise.

The problem ran deeper, even, than sectarian division. After the Gulf War in 1991, crippling sanctions remained in place. The hope was that the tightened noose of economic hardship would eventually bring down Saddam's regime. That was not to be the case. For one thing, the people didn't blame Saddam—they blamed the United States. Numerous building materials, medical supplies, and critical natural resources populated the list of prohibited imports—an attempt to weaken Saddam's grip on power, which both backfired and shifted the suffering onto innocent civilians. Depending on the report you believe, sanctions-induced malnutrition and heightened infant death-rates resulted in the death of anywhere between 100,000 and 500,000 Iraqi children. Those kinds of numbers, unsurprisingly, caused some bad press. In 1998, Pope John Paul II sent New Year's greetings out to "our brothers and sisters in Iraq, living under a pitiless embargo."[6] Later the same year, the UN humanitarian coordinator for Iraq resigned, citing that he "no longer wished to be part of a situation in which sanctions were starving to death 6,000 Iraqi infants every month."[7]

Had these children's deaths resulted in Saddam's downfall, maybe, just maybe, one could argue the merits of the embargo. But the opposite occurred. In 2003, Saddam Hussein still reigned in Baghdad. The sanctions had actually reinforced his hold on power while concurrently ruining Iraq's infrastructure, health care, and public services. The U.S. Army War College's official publication, *Parameters*, ran an essay shortly after 9/11 concluding that the sanctions had "strengthened the Iraqi government's control of the economy, increased poverty . . . and triggered emigration of the professional classes."[8] Not to mention "intensifying anger throughout the Middle East" and undoubtedly deepening Iraqi distrust of American motives when the 2003 invasion finally began. Thus, when U.S. troops toppled that statue of Saddam in central Baghdad, they had entered a traumatized nation, crippled with poverty, starvation, and a shattered infrastructure. As Colin Powell reportedly warned President Bush prior to the invasion: if we broke Iraq, we'd have to buy it. Turns out the place was broken long before we ever arrived. Some of the fault, at least, was our own.

Growing sectarian violence was a problem throughout 2004, and increased during 2005. Matters exploded, however, on 22 February 2006, when suspected AQI operatives dressed up in Iraqi Special Forces uniforms and bombed the Askariya shrine in the city of Samarra. Also known as the Golden Mosque, it held the remains of two Shia imams including Hassan al-Askari, father of the "hidden imam," Mohammed al-Mahdi. Messianic "Twelver" Shia—the majority of Iraqi Shia—believe that the twelfth and last imam, Mohammed al-Mahdi—son of al-Askari—will someday reappear along with Jesus

Christ to bring peace, justice, and Islam to the world.[9] Moktada Al-Sadr's militia—the Mahdi Army—took its name from this last, messianic imam. Most U.S. officials believe AQI's leader, Abu Musab al-Zarqawi, instigated the bombing to trigger a sectarian civil war and thereby render Iraq ungovernable. It worked like a charm. Immediately after the bombing, millions of Iraqis left work, shuttered their shops, armed themselves, and awaited an explosion of violence. It was almost immediate. Estimates vary, but probably a few hundred people died in the day following the bombing, and within a week Baghdad's morgue had a backlog of about a thousand bodies.[10] Most official Shia and Sunni leaders urged restraint, but the orgy of violence gathered a momentum of its own. Communal violence played itself out to the logical extreme for more than a year.

Not that senior American military or political leaders would admit it. In early March—despite reports by *thousands* of U.S. patrols discovering bodies—Defense Secretary Rumsfeld sought damage control. Media reports of Iraqi civilian deaths were "exaggerated," said Rumsfeld. Attacking journalists' motives, he further asserted: "Interestingly, all of the exaggerations seem to be on one side . . . the steady stream of errors all seem to be of a nature to inflame the situation . . . give heart to the terrorists and to discourage those who hope for success in Iraq."[11] Question the war, he implied, and you're essentially working for the "terrorists." Fear not, Rumsfeld assured the public, Iraqi Security Forces (ISF) had "taken the lead in controlling the situation," providing "a calming effect."[12] The top U.S. general in Iraq, George Casey, told reporters that "the country is not awash in sectarian violence," and, as for the prospects of a civil war: "I don't see it happening, certainly [not] anytime in the near term." In all fairness, defining just what constitutes "civil war" is a slippery business, and General Casey was inundated with thousands of conflicting, complex reports in the weeks following the Samarra bombing.

That said, Bush administration officials went to great lengths throughout early 2006 to dispel the notion of an all-out sectarian war in Iraq. Ironically, this was precisely the case on the ground. In 2010, WikiLeaks data revealed the extent to which military and civilian officials knew about the mass killings in the aftermath of the Samarra bombing. That September, *Washington Post* correspondent Ellen

Knickmeyer, one of the very reporters criticized at the time by Secretary Rumsfeld, published an array of tactical reports by U.S. patrols depicting horrific violence on an immense scale. The Iraq Body Count Project estimates 1,570 civilian deaths in February 2006.[13] In response to Knickmeyer's 2010 article, Pentagon spokesmen released their own graph that showed civilian deaths topping 2,500 for the same month.[14] February was only the beginning; violence and body counts would steadily rise month after month. It was going to be a bad year in Baghdad. Why had so many high-ranking officials in the Bush administration downplayed these reports for so long and desperately avoided the term "civil war"? Easy. The year 2006 was a midterm election year, and everyone knew the Democrats were running on an antiwar platform. To confess that things were as bad in Baghdad as they actually *were*, would have all but admitted that the administration's pet project in Iraq had become a quagmire. Besides, no one was hurt by a bit of semantic manipulation anyway—no one, that is, except the Iraqi people.

Americans may have been squeamish about uttering "civil war" out loud. But ask an Iraqi in 2006 or 2007, and they had *no hesitation* using the term. They lived the reality of Baghdad's streets. It wasn't some semantic exercise for average Iraqis. They knew what they saw, and it was civil war. Down in Salman Pak, everyone knew *everybody*. It was one of those medium-size cities—you know the type here in the States—where families all know just a bit about one another and anonymity is nearly impossible. In Mada'in the war was truly *civil* and people *knew* their killers. Salman Pak was big enough to field large gangs of opposing fighters but too small to have isolated, homogenous neighborhood enclaves. Sunni and Shia were neighbors. When the civil war came to the city, it did so in dramatic and intimately violent fashion.

Salman Pak, and Iraq more generally, became a bizarre, dystopic world. Neighbors who once sent their children to the same school now fought for control of their own blocks. Integrated, peaceful communities slipped into shocking violence as the old social contract disintegrated. We responded to explosion after explosion when militiamen threw satchel charges into neighboring homes. Roofs caved in on sleeping families; fathers were shot at point blank range walking to the market; teenage boys were abducted at militia checkpoints—never to be heard from again. We, the soldiers, had only limited control. Restricted by our small numbers, we couldn't possibly be everywhere at once. Besides, sometimes talking to us was a dangerous proposition. A young, intelligent female teacher was beheaded and placed on public display for simply speaking at length—not even about military matters—with one of our patrols. The insurgents severed her head not at the neck but rather across the mouth, with obvious symbolic implications.

In the new world that military occupation, state collapse, and sectarian chaos wrought, almost *anything* could get you killed. Sunnis and Shia were hard to tell apart, as they *look* exactly the same. Thus, it was a world in which names—given first names—mattered. It could mean life or death. Just as an ethnic Italian-American mother in New York would name her son Anthony, Shia women across Iraq call their boys Ali. They also like Hassan or Hussein—names derived from among the Shia imams. Sunni parents favor Omar, Abu Bakr, or Yazid—opponents of the Shia imams and early Sunni caliphs.

Names defined religious affiliation. Religious affiliation meant everything. At illegal checkpoints across Baghdad, Sunni insurgents and Shia gangs literally checked IDs and murdered more than a few Alis and Omars, solely based on their given name. American soldiers and Iraqi policemen discovered the aftermath in the fields, alleys, and streets of Iraq. In Salman Pak and later on in Baghdad, we'd find discarded bodies as a near daily matter of course. So did a few hundred other American platoons across the country. Some victims were bound and shot in the back of the head. Others bore signs of torture. Power drills were used to bore holes in kneecaps and elbows—a Mahdi Army (Shia militia) favorite. Sunni insurgents liked to behead their victims and leave bodies in public spaces—often with politico-religious manifestos pinned to the corpse. They were a more theatrical lot. But most Iraqis just tried to hunker down and survive. Some learned to leave ID cards at home and give false names at checkpoints. Names mattered in fanatic communal warfare.

The tide of war washed up reckless, derisible figures and placed them in positions of power. Violent, criminal, thuggish men—otherwise of little value or respect—emerged as valued protectors of their communities. Frightened people placed their trust in dangerous, uncultivated killers. It's a story as old as time. On a macrolevel, national leaders rose in much the same fashion. Moktada al-Sadr, a younger son of the venerated Shia cleric and community leader Mohammed Sadiq al-Sadr, wasn't always regarded as a serious figure. Despite a fine family pedigree, he never completed the religious education and degree required to earn the title *mujtahid* (senior religious scholar). A rotund and lazy young boy, he was derisively nicknamed "Mullah Atari" because of his preference for video games over the serious business of Shia law and theology.[15]

Saddam killed his father and older brothers in 1999, and then the invasion changed everything. Sadr seized the moment and established himself as a leader of the newly empowered, impoverished, urban Shia millions—distributing food and social services in Sadr City during a period when the rest of Iraq lacked the bureaucratic capability to do so. He also quickly established nationalist credentials by calling for an early end to the American occupation. Ironically, of course, it was only the American invasion and removal of Saddam Hussein that rendered Sadr *capable* of such an esteemed leadership position. Regardless, Sadr's militia—the Mahdi Army—grew rapidly and by 2004 engaged in attacks on both U.S. forces and Sunni militants. As Iraq slid toward outright sectarian war, the Mahdi Army increasingly shifted its attacks to Sunni civilians. War's chaos spurred the worst among us to power. On the streets and at the top.

Fear, hatred, religious fervor, enigmatic leaders—any of these alone might not have been enough to fuel the orgy of violence. Together they were a powerful brew, but the formula required one more thing: guns. Iraq was awash in weapons. To put it in context, one must understand the absolute uncanny proliferation of firearms and bizarre rules regarding their ownership. In 2006 and 2007, every Iraqi household was allowed one AK-47 *assault rifle*. Seriously. The U.S. military respected Iraqi national law in this area, probably to avoid tension and respect local traditions. We searched lots of houses and apartments—thousands by my platoon alone—and every time we found an AK-47, which was always, we simply handed it back over. You can imagine how a military-grade rifle in every home might make combating an insurgency difficult. Literally *anyone* could be a civilian by day and guerrilla by night. These weren't the eighteenth-century muskets of our forebears at Lexington and Concord. No, an insurgent with an AK could legitimately *kill* an American soldier. Iraq was an NRA (National Rifle Association) paradise but a real life *disaster*. Make no mistake, universal assault rifle ownership may appeal in theory to gun enthusiasts, but in practice it complicated absolutely everything. Besides aiding in attacks on U.S. Army patrols, abundant rifles rendered conditions *ripe* for civil war.

Here's where it got weird: AK-47s, A-Okay; pistols—totally illegal. Search a house and find a pistol and you could cart the owner off to jail. Pistols were associated—psychologically, and thus legally—with murder. Assault rifles, by contrast, represented self-defense. The whole bizarre situation fused the worst aspects of New York City and Florida gun laws. Pack a pistol and you'd do time as quick as New York Giants wide receiver Plaxico Burress. Keep an AK-47 under your bed and you're just preparing to "stand your ground"—George Zimmerman style. None of it made much sense. Regardless, Iraq was a country absolutely full of assault rifles in 2006. When sectarian conflict erupted, overcrowding and copious guns were a recipe for disaster.

Iraq's fledgling, inept, and often corrupt criminal justice system didn't help matters any. War, especially civil war, tends to dredge up communal rivalries and provide new outlets for old conflict. Sometimes it wasn't even about religion, really. Lawless chaos created opportunities for violent score settling. It was like the argument for New York City–style "broken windows" policing. Criminologists claim that lawlessness flourishes when petty crimes, vandalism, and filthy streets become the norm. So goes the theory: when people sense that small crime is acceptable, they're more likely to commit a serious illegal act. When shootings and bombings spread across Iraq, many citizens began to see *that* as the relative norm and escalated their own quarrels accordingly. Land disputes, interfamily squabbles, and deep-rooted animosities exploded in ferocious bloodshed. Hatfield and McCoy–like gang wars raged in towns and cities across the country. Everyone involved tried to use the Americans to their advantage. We became pawns in an old, dirty game. Our own desperation to identify and capture insurgents early in the war led to a dangerous prosecution system. In order to arrest a man on charges of violence or militia membership, all we needed were our own notions of "probable cause" and two sworn statements from local Iraqis. That's it. Predictably, plenty of people stepped forward to rat out their rivals on trumped up charges. Thing is, most Shias were released by the government within a few days. Sunnis, on the other hand, might languish in prison for months or years awaiting a legal hearing. That sort of disparity fed Sunni mistrust of the new government's institutions.

Problems were further exacerbated by amateurish, biased, and unethical policemen. It's important to remember that the Iraqi government was only a few years old at the time of the al-Askari mosque bombing. National and local policemen were almost exclusively Shia and were by and large inexperienced and unprofessional. Many were diligent and well intentioned, but a significant minority sympathized—actively and passively—with the Mahdi Army. It only took a portion of the government security forces to devastate public trust, especially in the Sunni community. By 2006, and in the eyes of many Iraqis, the police no longer represented the *law*, but rather just another sectarian militia. With that threshold crossed, society broke down.

### FU#K THE POLICE!: OPERATION LION DAWN AND THE MAKINGS OF A STILLBORN WAR CRIME

If American soldiers were ever going to leave Iraq, local security forces (army and national police) would need to step up and take over. Down in Salman Pak in 2006, they had a long way to go. The 3-61 CAV partnered with an Iraqi NP brigade to stabilize the Mada'in Qada. Don't be fooled by the term "police." Make no mistake, the NPs were *soldiers*, not your local beat cops. They wore camouflage fatigues, Kevlar helmets (when they felt like it), flak jackets (if they had them), and carried AK-47 assault rifles. The NP cruised around town in modified green or brown pickup trucks, often with PKM machine guns mounted on the back bed. They operated like soldiers too, conducting raids (sometimes) and checkpoints (all the time). They didn't fight common crime and had zero training in forensics, evidence collection, or the intricacies of criminal law. U.S. Army officers and NCOs trained the NPs and unsurprisingly they reflected our martial values. One more thing about the police—they were nearly *all*

*Shias.* They had some Kurds too and a couple token Sunnis, but much like the new Iraqi Army, this was a Shia institution representing an increasingly Shia dominated government. In parts of Salman Pak and its southern environs—Sunni country—this presented problems. The NP faced a legitimacy crisis.

The backstory to all this is well reported. The Bush administration appointed hundreds of politically loyal neoconservative bureaucrats to run postwar Iraq, including the top civilian official—L. Paul Bremer. Bremer, heavily influenced by Iraqi exiles like Ahmed Chalabi and supported by Vice President Dick Cheney, implemented a policy of de-Baathification. De-Baathification aimed to cleanse the Iraqi government of Saddam supporters and members of his official Baath Party. The term derived from de-Nazification, the removal and prosecution of Adolf Hitler's henchmen after World War II. As a rule of thumb: whenever someone invokes a Hitler analogy—be immediately suspicious! Hitler, the Munich crisis, Nazi Germany, and World War II in general form perhaps the most prolifically and imprudently used analogy in history. Saddam Hussein was a brutal dictator. He was not, however, Adolf Hitler. The Baath Party was neo-fascist in its ideology, but they were no Nazis. Details matter. Nazi Germany fought a worldwide campaign of conquest and genocide that rendered tens of millions dead. They presented a genuine threat to global peace. The Saddam-as-Hitler analogy is both deceptive and dangerous. If Saddam is Hitler, he *must* be destroyed immediately. But wait. After he invaded Kuwait in the First Persian Gulf War and was subsequently defeated by American arms, we let Saddam stay in power. Can you imagine the Allies allowing Hitler to remain Fuhrer once they liberated France? Or furthermore, allowing him to keep tanks and helicopters operational in order to ruthlessly suppress a domestic rebellion—exactly what we allowed Saddam to do in 1991? That's the problem with the Hitler/Nazi analogy. It never works. The Third Reich and its war of conquest were so terribly exceptional as to be all but useless as a comparative tool. Unless one intends to make an awful mistake, that is. So, of course, we did just that.

On 16 April 2003, Bremer, against the advice of Colin Powell's State Department and the Central Intelligence Agency, disbanded the Iraqi Army.[16] This seemingly simple decision placed a few hundred thousand unemployed young men back on the street with no effective reintegration strategy. Although many of the rank and file were Shia conscripts, many of the elite soldiers and nearly all the officers were Sunnis. The army was Saddam's and the Sunni minority's prize institution. Eliminating the force sent many Sunnis a message—you are not welcome in the new Iraqi state. Most units just evaporated, shedding uniforms and taking their weapons home, thus sowing the seeds of a nationalist Sunni insurgency.

Over the next three years, reconstituting a new Iraqi army became one of the biggest challenges for the United States. Almost all the initial recruits were young Shia men. Desperate for a paycheck and excited by the prospect of serving a new "democratic" government—which the Shia majority would presumably control—Shia youths joined the army and police in droves. The NP, in particular, became infamous for their sectarian character.[17] A U.S. House of Representatives report from July 2006 summarized as follows: "Since its inception in 2004, the National Police (NP) have been riddled with corruption and sectarian influence, and members have participated in illegal activities."[18] Sunnis would never accept the national police in their neighborhoods. They considered the NP an extension of Shia militias like the Mahdi Army. Our primary local partners, the ticket to leaving Iraq, were completely illegitimate in the eyes of 50 percent of Salman Pak's population. Not a good start.

Iraq had a unique governmental structure. Its three key leaders were purposefully divided along sectarian lines. The president—largely a figurehead—was a Kurd. The most powerful, the prime minister—Nouri al-Maliki—a Shia. Maliki controlled the Ministry of the Interior (MOI), the agency in charge of the national police. He was also a lifelong member of the Islamic Dawa Party, a Shia-based, anti-Saddam group with close ties to Iran. Maliki himself spent 1979 to 2003 living in exile; many Sunnis considered him a traitor, having lived in Iran during the vicious Iran-Iraq War (1980 to 1988). The vice president—Tarik al-Hashemi—was a Sunni. All three figures tended to guard the interests of their own religious and ethnic communities.

This was the situation on 24 December 2006, when Vice President al-Hashemi sent a frantic letter to General George Casey, the senior American commander in Iraq at the time. Al-Hashemi alleged that our partnered NP brigade had kept food and humanitarian supplies from the Sunni residents of Salman Pak, aided militiamen, and even took part in illegal killings. The vice president claimed that Salman Pak's Sunnis were "victims of a scheme aiming to restore this district to be under Persian Iranian predominance."[19] Some of this was probably exaggerated. But deep down we knew much of it was true. Nevertheless, for the vice president of Iraq to reference Salman Pak and our NP partners was indicative of a larger problem.

We'd heard countless accusations that NP checkpoints were allying with militiamen to kidnap young Sunni men. One day an elderly man handed me a typed Arabic letter, addressed "to U.S. forces," and asking for help finding his kidnapped son. The letter alleged that the police—working with militiamen—were behind the kidnapping. We'd also witnessed firsthand the evidence—in the form of badly battered faces—of rampant detainee abuse among the police. On a recent occasion, the squadron commander had even ordered the NP to hand over abused prisoners and had our forces safeguard them to a U.S. holding facility. The Sunnis had no trust in government institutions. Worse still, they believed us to be allied to that government and, by extension, to various Shia sectarian militias.

It was in this climate that our squadron conducted Operation Lion Dawn, a major joint clearance operation meant to highlight the revamped skills of the national police and put an "Iraqi face" on our operations. The small village of Ja'ara had been a disaster for months. In the last few weeks it had become a major sectarian battleground, Sunni insurgent foothold, and—after a few dozen gun battles—a virtual ghost town. Ja'ara was to be the NP brigade's first test. Each of our platoons partnered with an NP company—in other words, about fifteen of us to every seventy-five or so of them. The plan was—by necessity—extremely simple: pull up all our vehicles in one long line on Route Wild and, staying in designated lanes, help the NPs clear each house from west to east through Ja'ara. I split up and partnered each of my squads with an NP platoon and instructed our scouts to stay to the rear and supervise. This was all in accordance with the squadron commander's intent to keep the Iraqis in the lead. Everything started out just fine. That lasted five minutes.

As soon as the NPs entered Ja'ara, all hell broke loose. Not firefights—any insurgents had gotten out of Dodge as soon as they saw a couple dozen vehicles roll their way. Besides, because of our increased permanent presence in Salman Pak after Operation Dolphin, the insurgents had generally shifted operations out of Ja'ara and into the south. That was part of the reason we chose Ja'ara. It was an easy target—a warm-up round—for the national police to take the lead. My element walked with the NP company commander—a captain— during the clearance operation. He seemed like an okay guy at first. Then we entered the village. It was like a switch was flipped. NPs swarmed wildly in all directions firing weapons in the air, kicking in doors, shooting dogs, and yelling. They tossed houses and scared the shit out of the few destitute residents left in the village. I'm not sure why they responded this way, but I think its genesis lay in the dangerous intersection between religious bias, fear, and power-mad group think. One gaggle of NPs to my front started shooting wildly into a window—I heard a woman's voice screaming—and I decided to shut it down.

Freaking the fuck out, I screamed in the captain's face, Mark struggling to keep up, and told him to get control of his men. "This isn't how we search a village, motherfucker!" The NP commander seemed perplexed and didn't respond. I jogged over to one of his policemen— who was walking out of a house with some rolled up rugs—looting— and literally threw him into a wall. I was out of control. Fuller ran over and pulled us apart, saying, "Yo Sir, I'm with you. I'm with you, but hey yo, there's like five of them for each of us!" I calmed down quick, apologized to the NP, and called off the operation after we'd cleared less than half our sector. No one was killed—except a couple of dogs— but things could have been much worse. Lion Dawn had all the makings of a war crime. Only American soldiers had stood in the way.

The NPs were scared, pumped up, and angry. They were almost all Shia and saw Ja'ara as a Sunni, al-Qaeda haven. After the incident I tried to sit down with the captain to understand what he'd been thinking, how he could deviate so far from the carefully briefed plan. Thing is, he *genuinely* seemed confused about what had upset me. "They're all Al-Qaeda," he told Mark. "This is how we do operation." Caught in the middle of this mess were a few hundred thousand Iraqi civilians. The police didn't trust the people. The people didn't trust us, the police, or the militias. Some area villages began digging trenches and building bunkers to defend themselves—from *everyone*. These earthworks were shockingly sophisticated and resembled a micro-version of the Western Front in World War I. Who could blame them?

### SHOVELING SHIT AGAINST THE TIDE: SCENES FROM THE SALMAN PAK HEALTH CLINIC FALL 2006

Salman Pak once had a first-rate hospital. Just three and a half years earlier, the facility had seventy patient beds, a hematology laboratory, surgical room, birthing center, male and female patient accommodations, a café, and emergency services.[20] By December 2006, the place was a shell of its former self. The NP took over much of the heavily looted hospital and used it as a barracks. The remaining facility—which we called the health clinic—was pathetic. Few residents even *used* the place for major medical concerns, preferring to brave the 20 mile drive north to Baghdad. That was a long way, given that Route Wild was a veritable gauntlet of bombs and militia checkpoints.

Nevertheless, I took an interest in the health clinic for two reasons. For one, I enjoyed missions that benefited the civilians in some small way. I'd lost almost all faith in our ability to defeat the local insurgency and preferred, whenever possible, to distribute humanitarian aid. Sometimes we'd throw together ad hoc "health days"—grab an extra medic or two and set up a day-long clinic—and treat minor ailments in the community. Second, I'd been having trouble making sense of the *scale* of sectarian violence in the city. Basically, we suspected that the civil war was a more serious problem than initially thought and sought a rudimentary way to count the dead. Morbid, sure, but I thought it essential to know the true extent of the carnage. In late December we spent a whole day at the clinic. The one doctor—his name, unfortunately, is lost to me—had sad eyes and the fatalistic realism of one totally resigned to incessant violence. He was the last doctor willing to work in the facility, but even he could make it only a few days a week, since he commuted from the refugee community in Baghdad. He no longer had even one permanent, trained nurse; rather, he relied on an assortment of local volunteers to help out around the clinic.

This doctor faced such abundant obstacles that one wondered why he bothered. Salman Pak had only a few hours of sporadic electricity each day on the Baghdad power grid. This was a nationwide problem, but rather more severe outside the city center. Without a reliable generator—a few had been stolen, sold, and destroyed—the clinic was without lights or electrical energy sources for ten to twelve hours a day. Minimum. Imagine trying to run a hospital, conduct surgery, take an X-ray, or just see your patients without any power. The bottom line is that none of those more serious medical functions really happened anymore. The place looked like a scene out of *Mad Max* or *Road Warrior.*

I complimented the doctor and was ready to leave when he asked me if I'd like to see his inpatient data. Uh, *yes!* In the midst of technical and personnel constraints that would have discouraged even the finest of physicians, this guy kept the most meticulous, professional, hand-written records I'd ever seen. Although most severely injured victims braved the drive to Baghdad hospitals, the Salman Pak clinic *did* see a lot of minor wounds and dead on arrivals. The doctor had a log for each one—name, father's name, village, sex, age, and so forth. Jackpot. Mark and I pored over the documents for hours, translating, photographing, and copying the data. The result was a disheartening summary of hundreds of attacks, wounds, and deaths among the civilian populace of just one city. The medical logs painted a gloomy portrait of Iraqi life in late 2006 and helped us to chart the *extent* of sheer violence and disruption wrought by civil war.

More shockingly, the statistics were incomplete. Many victims traveled to Baghdad for treatment. Here too, the medical system became embroiled in the maelstrom of communal war. In 2006 and 2007, hospitals became one part of an increasingly political Baghdad geography. A victim was not necessarily safe upon entering a medical facility. Every neighborhood became sectarian in character, and the local militias policed community infrastructure—including the hospitals. Should a victim from a rival sect enter the wrong treatment center, he could bet on militiamen waiting outside upon his discharge. People were shot in the lobbies, walking to cars, and even in their rooms. Such stories brought to mind the scene in the *Godfather* in which Michael (Al Pacino) has to guard his father (Marlon

Brando) from rival mobsters sent to assassinate him in his hospital bed. Baghdad became *The Godfather* on a grand scale, a world with Sunni and Shia *hospitals*. These were dark times.

As a postscript, in February 2008 our replacement unit finally got the Salman Pak hospital back open. It was now five years since it last operated at anything near normal capacity. Even then, most doctors, nurses, and patients were wary of returning. It still had a long way to go. And that was *before* ISIS.

### SALMAN "THE PERSIAN" ROLLS
### IN HIS GRAVE WINTER 2006

The large, beautiful, Salman al-Taher mosque—located as it was on a broad traffic circle at the city's heart—was central to life in Salman Pak. Named for and containing the remains of Salman Farsi—Salman the Persian—one of the prophet Mohammed's prominent companions, the mosque held great spiritual and cultural significance for both Sunnis and Shia. The mosque quickly became a flashpoint for sectarian conflict. Salman the Persian is best understood by Western readers as somewhat akin to one of Jesus Christ's apostles. He's an important figure in the Koran and, while the details of his life are somewhat contested, the basics are as follows: Salman was born somewhere in present-day Iran—hence the "Persian" moniker. As a youth he converted to Christianity and then set off on a religious quest through Syria and eventually on to Arabia. Along the way he was captured and sold into slavery. He met the prophet Mohammed in the Arabian city of Medina, and with his help purchased freedom.[21] Subsequently, Salman converted to Islam, fought early military battles for the faith, and became a dedicated companion of the prophet. Some traditions state that Salman was the first Persian convert to Islam; others assert that he was Mohammed's barber—gaining the nickname Salman "Pak" (Salman the clean).[22]

Salman the Persian is revered by most Muslims. The mosque bearing his name and his tomb was a contested place. Sunnis and Shia alike claimed the mantle of Salman and the al-Taher mosque. The city, of course, is an ancient one—once capital of a proud Persian empire—and Salman's grave only added to the historic gravity of the place. Shia, in particular, considered Salman one of their own—the first Shiite. Iran is the largest Shia Muslim country, and not surprisingly, Salman is a national hero in Tehran. Both groups were desperate to control the mosque, which traditionally had been under Sunni control. While much of the northern Mada'in Qada is Shia, the city of Salman Pak and its southern environs were majority Sunni. In 2003, everything changed. Shiites were now Iraq's largest group and had control of the prime minister as well as the army and police. Furthermore, many Sunnis left the city and were living on the run or in mobile insurgent bands. The balance was shifting.

Months before our squadron arrived, Mahdi Army militiamen—in response to the murder of Shiite civilians in the northern Mada'in town of Nahrwan—seized control of the Salman al-Taher mosque. The NP brigade in the city looked the other way, which infuriated Sunnis and validated their long-standing distrust of the police. Soon after, Sunni insurgents ambushed and killed an NP colonel in the city. Troopers from 1-61 CAV intervened, killed the attackers, and inadvertently confirmed Sunni suspicions that the Americans favored the Shia.[23] This was the atmosphere that 3-61 CAV inherited. Things only got worse. The local Sunni imam of the mosque petitioned the police to force the Mahdi Army gang to vacate. The NP sided with the militiamen. Area Sunnis complained to us that the NP were nothing more than another militia—"they fly Shiite flags from their base," they'd tell us. It was true—Shia people loved their flags. Sunnis gave up on the police, the government, and by extension the U.S. Army. When Al Qaeda elements infiltrated the city, the Sunnis threw their lot in with AQI.[24] Perhaps *they* would do something about it.

Sectarian disputes were fueled by powerful religious zeal. That much is indisputable. Nonetheless, it was also a *political* dispute. In order to understand the violence, one must understand the intersections of religion, resources, and money. The Salman Pak mosque was a classic example. Al-Taher had once been a Sunni mosque. The mosque's *waqf* (endowment) was one of the largest landowners in the city (much like the Catholic Church in medieval Europe). Many residents and shopkeepers actually rented homes and businesses from the mosque. The land deeds were held within the building, thus control of the structure meant influence over a lot of real estate, money, and power. As one might expect, control of the mosque became a central concern among Salman Pak's citizens. Sunnis feared Shia control would mean eviction from homes and places of business. The city's Sassanid ruins, proof the city was once capital of a great Persian—read *Iranian*—empire, fed Sunni insecurity. Many naively, but seriously, worried that Shia control of the mosque portended a return to Iranian influence and control in the region. Beyond a simple theological dispute, sectarian conflict became an existential crisis in Salman Pak.

There was more. In al-Hashemi's letter, Iraq's vice president alleged that the NP had taken control of the Salman al-Taher mosque and converted it into "an abattoir to slaughter innocent human beings on a sectarian basis."[25] As Americans, by army regulations, we couldn't enter the mosque, so it was difficult to determine the truth behind such accusations. However, by early January 2007, enough people repeated the story to warrant action. The city's residents—mostly the Sunnis—told us that Mahdi Army militiamen maintained a 24/7 armed guard in the mosque and used it as a gang armory, replete with weapons and explosives. A few days later, the commander requested an Iraqi Army Special Forces unit, replete with U.S. Green Beret advisors, to raid the mosque. He wisely used an external army unit, since the NPs were neither trustworthy nor impartial. They were kept in the dark about the operation. Our platoon formed an outer cordon to isolate the area, and in the middle of the night, Iraqi Special Forces troops cleared the mosque. The small militia element was taken by surprise and offered zero resistance. Inside, the troops uncovered a veritable arsenal: AK-47s, PKM machine guns, RPG launchers, explosives, and thousands of rounds of assorted ammunition. In a bizarre twist, they also found a few British colonial-era Lee Enfield rifles!

After the raid, we temporarily closed the mosque to both Sunnis and Shia. Better that no side dominate the land deeds and spiritual sanctuary until a full bipartisan settlement could be reached. Within a month, though, the Iraqi government's ministry for religious affairs had returned the mosque to Shia rule.[26] It might surprise some to know just how truly feeble our position often was, but empowering the new government—no matter how Shia dominated—was our charter and ticket out of Iraq. The case of the Salman al-Taher mosque illustrated the underlying weakness of the Iraqi state and its (continuing) intractable sectarian problems. A sectarian, Shia-directed government capable of such decisions will *always* face a legitimacy crisis. Perhaps this begins to explain later Sunni support for ISIS in western Iraq.

Vice President Hashemi stayed in government for five more years. A staunch opponent of President Maliki's coalition, Hashemi used his rather limited influence to campaign for increased Sunni participation in government. Perhaps the VP was himself a sectarian lobbyist for his own community, but he did have significant support among secular, as well as Sunni, parties. And he *was* vice president. Nevertheless, on 19 December 2011—just *days* after the final U.S. troop withdrawal—Maliki issued an arrest warrant for al-Hashemi. Charging Hashemi with orchestrating bombings and assassinations of Shia officials, the Maliki government released confessional videos by Hashemi's bodyguards that implicated the VP in the alleged murders.[27] Hashemi denied the charges immediately and accused Maliki of orchestrating a witch hunt against political opponents. Events went from strange to preposterous rather quickly. Iraq's president, Barzani—a Kurd and relative figurehead—refused to extradite Hashemi from the Kurdish city of Irbil, where the VP had been at the time of the arrest warrant. Imagine a similar situation here in the States: President Obama refusing to extradite Vice President Biden from New York to Washington, DC, at the request of House Speaker John Boehner. Not a perfect analogy—but *still*.

The inherently unstable quality of the Iraqi government was on full display when Maliki's courts tried and sentenced the country's vice president to death in absentia. Hashemi, meanwhile—by now a refugee on the run in Turkey—was still received as Iraq's serving vice president by diplomats in Sunni states such as Qatar, Saudi Arabia, and of course Turkey. Inside Iraq, the Sunni population viewed the whole scandal as a sectarian attack meant to sideline opponents and exclude Sunnis from a power sharing government. One of Iraq's main Sunni tribal leaders, Sheikh Talal Hussain al-Mutar maintained, "The whole thing from the beginning was a conspiracy against the Sunnis," and "The whole investigation and courts were fake and controlled by the government."[28] Turkey refused to extradite Hashemi. Years after sectarian killings significantly dropped, that was still the state of

Iraqi "democracy." A vice president on the lam, Sunnis unreconciled to Shia dominance, and a sectarian prime minister forging a new autocracy around his own political loyalists.

Given the condition of Iraq's nascent republic, why were we surprised to see Sunni tribesmen join once again with radical ISIS elements in early 2014? Many Iraqi Sunnis didn't believe in most tenets of the ISIS brand of Salafi Islam. They did, however, sense in ISIS the means and opportunity to challenge a Shia-dominated federal government that had no legitimacy in the Sunni communities of northern and western Iraq. The events of the "Surge era," and those of the last few years, convinced many moderate Sunnis that the government in Baghdad served only one sect. Yet not until mid-2014 were American policy-makers leveling any real pressure on the Maliki government to share power or step down. Fewer still were willing to ask whether such pressure was too little, too late, or outside the scope of U.S. power and responsibility.

### A CLASSIC EUPHEMISM: "GATED COMMUNITIES" AND THE CONCRETE BONANZA BAGHDAD: SPRING 2007

In 2007, VBIEDs—vehicle-borne improvised explosive devices (car bombs)—were the bane of the Shia community. They still are. Markets, mosques, and gathering places became the target of hundreds of lethal explosions. Shia militiamen mastered the bullet-to-the-head, but the Sunni tool of choice was indiscriminate bombing. Thousands of Shia civilians died in these attacks. Terror was the bombers' intent, and terror is what they achieved. In Baghdad proper—where our squadron would soon relocate—the car bombs were a daily occurrence. The sound of blasts throughout the city became as ubiquitous as the clock striking noon in a small town square. We'd shrug and speculate about which neighborhood had gotten hit. Outside our gates, Iraqis cringed and wondered when the horror might end.

American troops searched for a solution, but car bombs were hard to stop. They blend in with every other vehicle—there were *millions* on the roads—and in the byzantine streets of Baghdad it was nearly impossible to control traffic flow. In early 2007 a fresh strategy, supported by the newly instated U.S. commander David Petraeus, filtered across the city. We began walling off key markets and eventually entire neighborhoods to protect from the car bombs. Tall, concrete "T-walls" (so named for their upside-down "T" appearance) soon littered the city, creating mazes of stone and a massive urban eyesore. The walls bore the names of U.S. states, based on their relative size. The 20-foot-high Alaska walls were the tallest; Texas T-walls were 12 feet; and the most common, Jersey barriers, were just under 3 feet tall and used to channel traffic into checkpoints. The walls each cost the American taxpayers between $800 and $1000 dollars, and by midyear literally *millions* blanketed the city. It was a concrete bonanza.

The problem was these walls actually *discouraged* sectional mixing; walling off neighborhoods only further partitioned the city into Sunni and Shia fiefdoms. But these were desperate times, and the U.S. Army was willing to try anything to decrease the violence. The bombings and shootings did eventually lessen, though whether the walls were really responsible we'll never know. I tend to doubt it. Surrounding neighborhoods with concrete was, unsurprisingly, controversial and required a good deal of explaining. And, of course, the strategy needed a name. So senior commanders dubbed these sectional bastions with the embarrassing euphemism "gated communities."[29] Sure. Minus the private swimming pool, financial stability, and basic sense of safety. A classically American phrase: lifeless, insincere, and self-consciously suburban.

Our unit spent weeks guarding wall construction around the famous Palestine Street market in our new sector, the east-central Baghdad neighborhood of Rusafa. We basically babysat the Iraqi contractors emplacing the walls. It was long, boring business, interrupted only by the chance to buy some treats in local shops. One day in June, Sergeant Eric Snell—of Trenton, New Jersey—was on foot and pulling security along Palestine Street. An extremely popular soldier, Snell was in his mid-thirties and had lived an entire life before joining the army. Drafted by the Cleveland Indians out of high school, Snell had declined the offer in order to attend college. After earning his degree, he pursued a number of interesting careers as a truck driver, Wall Street bicycle messenger, advertising executive, and model. Then in 2005 he decided to join the army.[30] Everyone in his platoon—actually the entire troop—respected and looked up to the mature, dedicated, and mild-mannered sergeant. In the gym, his strength was legendary. Nevertheless, a lone sniper's bullet extinguished his life in a flash. Snell was powerful and, honestly, beautiful. I wasn't there the day he died, but those who were spoke with disbelief about how such a formidable man could be struck down in an instant.

Sergeant Snell died guarding concrete, concrete meant to protect innocent Iraqis and ostensibly pave a path to democracy. He'd been conducting dismounted security while local contractors emplaced concrete barriers around the local market. A single shot rang out and Snell was gone. We never identified the gunman. It usually went that way. Explaining our purpose could get tricky. We were a long way from fighting Nazis or liberating France. Not everyone in the unit was enthusiastic about the Palestine Market barrier mission, and after Snell's death, most guys just stayed in the truck.

Many Iraqis hated the walls. They destroyed local aesthetics, turning a neighborhood into an ugly postapocalyptic mess. One angry man screamed in my face: "You Americans tell us you make democracy—all you bring is walls." We *did* bring a lot of walls. In mid-2007, an average U.S. Army engineer unit in Baghdad emplaced two thousand barriers a day.[31] Local contractors put in thousands more. But blast walls—whether Alaska, Texas, or Jersey—didn't address the root causes of violence. No amount of concrete was going to force the Shia-dominated government to develop an acceptable power-sharing arrangement with minority Sunnis and Kurds. Nor could millions of barriers produce an equitable division of Iraq's vast oil reserves. At one point in April, Iraqi prime minister Nouri al-Maliki even ordered a halt to the walling of Baghdad's neighborhoods, fearing the barriers would "aggravate sectarian tensions by segregating them" further.[32] American wishes eventually prevailed. We had the money and the troops, and therefore the power. Iraq's prime minister was not going to stand in the way of "progress." At least not back then.

### HUMAN INTERLUDE 4: ALEX FULLER
### AND THE ASHURA HOLY DAY

Cultural ignorance got a lot of people killed. Several accounts indicate that President Bush himself was unaware of the divide between Iraq's Sunni and Shia communities. "I thought they were all

Muslims,"[33] he'd supposedly said during a cabinet meeting. Sometimes, though, our obliviousness was altogether more innocent, and occasionally darkly comical. It all started with a new, temporary mission. FOB Rustamiyah was getting hammered with mortars—more than usual, even—and several soldiers were wounded. Our platoons were tasked with stopping the attacks. Easier said than done. Even if we could pinpoint the origin of enemy fire once the rounds started landing, we couldn't *stop* it from happening in the first place. That was nearly impossible. A mortar tube is small, easily concealable, and takes only a minute to fire off a few rounds, before quickly withdrawing. But something had to be done, so 2nd platoon was sent on twelve-hour "terrain denial" missions.

Essentially, we'd drive to the areas insurgents regularly used for mortar attacks and just *stay there*. We literally denied them use of the terrain. That's it. Sometimes it worked and sometimes they just shifted locations. We'd switch up our own positions, employ multiple platoons simultaneously, and more often than not the mortar threat decreased. Nevertheless, the mission was ultimately ridiculous. Sure, we protected the FOB from mortar fire—and that was a good thing—but it certainly didn't get us any closer to victory. In fact, the mission ate up combat power and distracted platoons from other business. Rather than expand the sphere of U.S. and Iraqi government control, we just maintained a tenuous hold on our existing presence. Back in January 2007, though, we didn't care all that much—countermortar missions were boring, easy, and generally *safe*. Ironically, of course, a platoon on just such a predictable countermortar mission was later ambushed and lost several soldiers killed and wounded. We probably should have seen the danger, but at the time the mission seemed pretty cake.

The 2nd platoon's area of responsibility was the southeastern Baghdad neighborhood of Al-Amin, a densely packed, lower class Shia stronghold.[34] We'd drive along a raised dirt berm road on the edge of the Diyala River and survey the Al-Amin district. Mostly, though, we just parked our HMMWVs in dirt fields and watched the kids play soccer. Occasionally I'd send small dismounted patrols down alleyways to keep potential enemies on their toes and gather intelligence about the insurgent mortar teams. A month earlier, Sergeant Fuller had finally left the gun turret. He loved our crew and would miss being the LT's gunner, he'd said, but just *needed* to be on the ground where the action was. DJ had been our dismounted team leader—in charge of organizing and employing the scouts who accompanied SSG South and me on foot patrols and raids—and now the job was vacant. Fuller begged and begged to take over after DJ got shot. He was definitely the best qualified—a young, fit, popular, and motivated sergeant—but selfishly I wanted to keep him on my crew. By Christmas I relented. I've regretted it ever since.

Anyway, one evening as the sun set, we could hear some commotion a few streets over. Certain it was just a rally or something, I stayed put and sent Fuller with a handful of dismounts to take a look. Minutes later Fuller's panicked voice blasted over the radio: "Ghost 1, this is 1-Delta, mount up—we're coming in! We got a crazy crowd on our ass!" Within seconds Fuller and his team were visible, sprinting down an adjacent alley toward our trucks. I had no idea what was going on. I hopped out of the truck and stopped him. Smith yelled out: "Fuller, what the fuck?" Fuller struggled to catch his breath and answered us both, panting: "Oh shit, son, we need to get up outta here—there's some crazy shit going on down in there. Hajis be banging gongs and shit,[35] marching our way, yo. It's like Indiana Jones and the motherfucking *temple of doom*, bro."

It only took a second until Fuller's gong-toting assailants became visible. They weren't insurgents at all—just a religious parade, replete with men, women, and young children. There were several hundred of them carrying banners and definitely banging on a drum of sorts. It was Ashura, and this was a march to mourn the martyrdom of Imam Husain. An extremely important holiday among the Shia people, Ashura manifested itself in some extreme ways. Some in the crowd took part in *tatbir*—rituals of self-flagellation in which men cut themselves using chains affixed with blades (*zanjeer zani*) in order to shed blood in commemoration of Husain's sacrifice.[36] If you've ever seen Ingmar Bergman's classic film *The Seventh Seal*, you will remember the famous scene of flagellants parading in medieval Europe—whipping and punishing their bodies to ward off the plague. The Ashura crowd looked a bit like that. As the peaceful march wound past us, I couldn't help but chuckle. Fuller, only slightly embarrassed, admitted his error, but "still, though, ya gotta admit—that's some freaky shit!" It was. But that's not why I'd laughed. It had something to do with the absurd gulf between Alex Fuller of New Bedford, Massachusetts, and the Shia pilgrims of east Baghdad, and perhaps—just maybe—the tragic gap between American goals and comprehension.

# Ushering in the "Surge"
## Farewell Mada'in, Hello Baghdad

JANUARY 2007

By New Year's Day 2007, Baghdad was an absolute disaster. Civilian deaths were staggering (over three thousand dead in January alone), attacks on and fatalities among American soldiers were rising. The prior November, Democrats—running in what seemed a referendum on the war—won control of both houses of the U.S. Congress. Both senior U.S. commanders in Iraq, generals George Casey in the Green Zone and John Abizaid at CENTCOM,[1] were advocating gradual troop drawdowns in the near future. Love him or hate him, you've got to admit that only President George W. Bush was capable of what came next. Ignoring the new congressional mandate and overwhelming opinion polls, against the advice of the bipartisan "Iraq Study Group," and despite the spiraling war effort in theater— Bush doubled down. On 10 January, in a televised speech, Bush told the nation: "America will change our strategy to help the Iraqis carry out their campaign to put down sectarian violence and bring security to the people of Baghdad. This will require increasing American force levels. So I've committed more than 20,000 additional American troops to Iraq. The vast majority of them—five brigades—will be deployed to Baghdad."[2] The Surge decision had many fathers. Influential retired generals, conservative political aides, and a small cohort of counterinsurgency enthusiasts in the active duty military all guided Bush toward the policy shift.

The Surge speech threw our world into disarray. Though long cynical about the war's purpose or prospects, I selfishly hoped that the troop increase would take some pressure off our squadron. Of course, that was pure conjecture—we didn't really know what the new deployments would mean. In practice, however, the decision had immediate effects. Within days, the squadron received orders to shift two troops (Apache and my own Black Knight) from Mada'in to Baghdad city. Coldblood Troop would remain in Mada'in and hold the line as best as they could until the Surge brigades arrived. Our troops would temporarily occupy (read: babysit) the districts of New Baghdad, Amin, Mashtal, and Beladiyat for about a month until we'd *again* swap out and move into east-central Baghdad. The cavalry still plugged holes and rode to the sound of the guns—it seems not much had changed since the Indian Wars of the old Western frontier.

It was going to be tough. Both A and B Troop patrolled a sector that was eventually taken over by a *battalion*—four or five times our size. C Troop (with about eighty-five guys) held down the entire Mada'in Qada—more than 500 square miles—until relieved by a full *brigade* of more than thirty-five hundred soldiers. And we thought we were stretched thin before! As always, though, we made do. Our troop primarily handled the neighborhoods of Amin and Mashtal. The area was vastly different from Salman Pak. Amin was densely populated, exclusively Shia, and the threat of firefights drastically dropped. Mada'in presented an array of dangers: gun battles, IEDs, sectarian murders, car bombs, and so forth. In al-Amin, the threats were far fewer but severe and extremely concentrated: snipers and sophisticated IEDs were the main problem. The learning curve was steep, and we'd only be there for about a month. As we left Salman Pak for the last time, I was strangely sad to say good-bye—it felt like we had unfinished business in the ancient city. But with little time for sentimentality, we headed north to learn all about a new sector, just in time to turn it over and move again. A few months later our morale received a heavier blow. The U.S. Army was severely overextended fighting two wars—in Iraq and Afghanistan—and simply didn't have the requisite troops to fulfill the president's strategy. Something would have to give. Truthfully, we'd heard rumors and seen it coming for a while, but Bush's decision took the life right out of us. On 11 April he announced that all current troops would be extended in Iraq for ninety additional days—a fifteen-month tour. They were unsettled times.

In east Baghdad the insurgents were less willing to stand and fight the U.S. troops—that much was immediately apparent. Shia militiamen of the Mahdi Army were more interested in murdering Sunni civilians and extorting money at local gas stations than shooting it out with American patrols. That said, the militias were no less deadly— just different. IEDs were a huge problem in Baghdad, especially along the main thoroughfares. These key routes served as logistics arteries for U.S. Army, Iraqi police, and contracted supply convoys. Unsurprisingly, insurgents littered them with bombs. Route Pluto was the main freeway in east Baghdad. Running generally south to north, it cut the east side in half and was the fastest way to get anywhere, but also one of the most dangerous. IEDs became such a problem that some combat platoons avoided Pluto completely, preferring instead to snake slowly through the winding alleys of Baghdad's neighborhoods. That could take a while, and besides, the larger logistics trucks often didn't have that option, because of a combination of tight turns and low-hanging electrical wires. Route Pluto needed to stay open. Once again, 3-61 CAV received a terrain denial mission. Here we go again—I thought—babysitting a roadway, this time to deter IED (instead of mortar) emplacers. Only Route Pluto was more dangerous.

On 20 January our platoon drew a daylight IED denial mission on Route Pluto. We knew the threat of attack was fairly high, so I'd instructed the guys to stay in the vehicles for most of the day. Just before noon, Faulkner jumped out of his truck to take a piss on the side of the road. He had been out for less than a minute when he opened his door to re-enter the back seat. Lifting his arm above his head to steady himself before jumping in the truck, he felt the sting of the bullet before even hearing the sound. Raising that arm and ducking his head likely saved his life. A sniper had been sitting patiently in one of the adjacent apartment buildings, waiting for one of us to get out of the vehicle. Ed Faulkner just happened to be the guy with the smallest bladder that day. He shrieked in pain, then screamed out to SGT Pushard—his truck commander—that he'd been hit. It was 11:58 a.m. The start of a bad day. Our gunners scanned for a target but couldn't find anything. With dozens of tall apartment buildings and hundreds of low-rise row houses within range, it was a sniper's paradise. There was no *way* we'd identify the shooter.

Ford went to work bandaging Faulkner's bloody forearm and we quickly made our way back to the FOB. Lucky for Faulkner, we were close by and got him to the aid station within twelve minutes. The FOB's physician assistant put on a fresh bandage and a quick X-ray determined that the bullet had shattered Faulkner's forearm. He'd have to be evacuated for surgery, but his condition was quite stable. I really liked Ed. He was one my favorite soldiers—dry, sarcastic, and smart. We'd smoked more than a few cigarettes together the last several months, and I hated to lose him. Standing by his side as the medics worked, it was tough to see him in such pain. All in all, he handled it pretty stoically. Just before they carried him out to the MEDEVAC helicopter, Ed Faulkner called my name: "LT, LT, can you come here for a sec?" Sure, I thought, anything—he must want to tell me something heartfelt and meaningful. I braced myself for a dramatic moment and leaned in. "Sir, sir, what happened to my cigarettes? I'm gonna need some smokes!" I should have known. Smiling through my foolish tears, I pulled my own pack from a shoulder pocket and put them in his good hand. As the bird took off, I had to laugh. I didn't see him again for six months. That's how I'll forever choose to remember him.

January 20 turned out to be a bad day all around in Baghdad. Actually, it was awful across Iraq. At 2:58 p.m. a Blackhawk utility helicopter carrying twelve passengers and crew was shot down northeast of the city limits. The bird was carrying a group of senior leaders from a National Guard unit, including three colonels, two sergeants major, one major, and a captain. Helicopters didn't crash often, but when they did it was a big deal. The code word for a downed bird was "Fallen Angel," and as soon as the term blasted across the radio, the nearest unit had to zip over and secure the crash site ASAP. The reasons were obvious—protect any surviving crew from enemy attack or capture, safeguard any dead bodies, and eventually recover or destroy the wreckage itself. Being the most mobile and proximate squadron, 3-61 CAV got the mission. Our platoon was off the hook, having already been on patrol and in contact earlier that day, but several other units eventually converged on the crash site. Without a direct east-west road, our patrols had to swing far south and east of the city before turning north. That, combined with the remote, unfamiliar desert terrain meant that no one arrived until 3:48 p.m. Luckily the site hadn't been exploited by the insurgents. The first platoon on site surveyed the wreckage—there were no survivors. The leaders at the crash—mostly from Apache Troop—kept the soldiers away from the carnage and handled the bodies themselves. It took until after 2:00 a.m. to fly out the bodily remains.

Unfortunately, most of A Troop had to stay on site until the next morning, when a large truck would arrive to recover the wrecked fuselage. It was a long, gruesome night. In an effort to swap out one of the elements that had been on site longest, headquarters sent the squadron mortar platoon up as a relief force. At 6:30 p.m., Lieutenant Luke Pereira's mortar platoon was just 1 kilometer out from the crash site when the second vehicle of the convoy hit a buried IED. The right rear of the truck was blown out, resulting in four casualties. One—Private Allen Jaynes—was in critical condition. They needed a MEDEVAC, and fast. The remote location, combined with a long flight and some sporadic alleged enemy ground fire, caused a delay. The birds didn't go "wheels up"—leave the blast site—until 7:44 p.m. Jaynes didn't make it.

The whole thing wasn't anyone's fault, really, just one big mess from start to finish. The helo crash set off a chain of awful events no one could've foreseen or controlled. Had the bird not gone down, the mortar platoon wouldn't have even been there. Were the crash not so far from a U.S. base, and in an unfamiliar area, the chance of an IED attack would have been significantly lower. That's the crux of it—chance and contingency—it's what war is all about. Who could have predicted it? Was anyone responsible? Not really. Back then, though, living through it all, we struggled with anger and the assignment of blame. Luke lost a soldier—one of his boys—and he was fucking pissed. Pissed he'd been sent up to a site that was already secure, and furious with the pilots who refused to land because they claimed to be under fire—shots that the guys on the ground didn't even hear. Who could blame him? It was a shitty little war. Anger, at least, gave all the death and despair some semblance of meaning. You did what you could.

All told, twenty-five U.S. soldiers died on January 20—the Iraq War's second deadliest day. Twelve national guardsmen died in the Blackhawk crash, five more soldiers in an attack on a Karbala security station, four in an Anbar province bombing, another soldier in an IED attack north of Baghdad, an engineer in northern Iraq, a marine corporal shot in Anbar, and of course Private Allen "Fuzzy" Jaynes from Luke Pereira's mortar platoon.[3] It was a bad day for Baghdad more generally—albeit typical—with twenty-nine civilian bodies recovered throughout the city, most with gunshots to the head.[4] So it went. The anti-American insurgency and the related sectarian war pressed on.

▬▬▬ Snipers were a growing problem now that we'd moved into Baghdad proper. The threat was heightened by the urban sprawl and its countless hiding spots. The snipers were confident enough to *film* their work. The Iraqi Islamic Army (IIA), one of the Sunni-affiliated insurgent groups, released several "Baghdad Sniper" videos on the Internet. The YouTube clips contained real footage of American soldiers struck down by single shots. It was highly disturbing to watch. The videoed attacks—all allegedly conducted by a single, expert sniper—were designed to taunt and demoralize us. Rumors spread throughout the city about the sniper—she was a *female*, he was *Chechen*, he was trained by Bin Laden in Afghanistan, and so on. Terror fed the rather creative imaginations of our soldiers, and after Sergeant Snell was struck down with a single shot to the head, the fear only spread.

The sniper was *probably* just a composite of many insurgent shooters, but the threat was nonetheless distressing. We felt helpless against snipers. Unable to identify the shooters, we devised pathetic tactics to protect ourselves. We'd limit our time outside the vehicles, stick to confined alleyways, and patrol at night. If we had to be outside during daylight, we'd dance the "Baghdad shuffle"—zigzagging, doubling back, and constantly swaying from side to side—anything to throw off an insurgent's aim. Legends of the "Baghdad Sniper" aside, the *real* threat—we all knew—was from IEDs, more specifically the new lethal EFPs.

EFPs were the bane of our existence. We first heard about them from one of Steve's West Point track buddies, a guy stationed on our FOB. He was an officer in 1st Battalion 26th Infantry, of the 1st Infantry Division. His unit worked up in northeast Baghdad and had a long, rough commute into their sector of Adhamiyah, one of the most notorious neighborhoods in the city. The 1-26 Infantry, the "Blue Spaders," had the ignoble distinction of being the hardest hit battalion of the whole war. They took more casualties during this tour than any other unit in Iraq or Afghanistan.[5] The 1-26 IN had thirty-one soldiers killed and several times that number wounded in a single battalion of about six hundred soldiers. Sitting at the FOB Rustamiyah dining facility listening to tales of these "super IEDs"—without a single patrol yet under our belts—was terrifying. The tone of the conversation, in fact, led me to believe this guy was *trying* to scare us. Mission accomplished.

EFPs were essentially homemade but sophisticated shaped charges. Much of the required expertise, however, came from Iranian Republican Guards allied with the Iraqi militias. The EFP slug penetrated even the thickest modern armor like a hot knife through butter. This was a no shit game changer. HMMWVs were shredded like Swiss cheese, and even the army's main battle tank, the M1A2 Abrams, was sometimes pierced by this lethal device. Consider this: the new, often homemade bomb was more effective against American armor than all the Soviet-supplied tank rounds of the entire Persian Gulf War. The nightmare had only *begun* once the EFP pierced a vehicle's armor. In a process known as spalling, or back spalling, the penetration of the slug turned the external metal armor of the HMMWV or tank against its occupants. The armor fragmented into a storm of jagged shrapnel that burst inside the vehicle like the spray of a shotgun blast in a tiny crew compartment. The result was devastating.

Relatively simple to manufacture and built in a basic machine shop, this type of EFP was first used against Israeli troops in southern Lebanon by Hezbollah militiamen in the 1980s.[6] Nevertheless, when they first hit American patrols in Iraq during 2006, EFPs caught the army flat-footed. We have a notoriously short institutional memory and a weak grasp of recent history. Maybe it's an American thing. Read the headlines from the summer of 2003 and you'd think those first IED attacks were some sort of revolution in warfare. The army had essentially zero effective tactical doctrine for such attacks, and many of our vehicles were woefully lacking armor. Never mind that the Irish Republican Army had used almost identical devices against British patrols in Northern Ireland. Or that British officers had coined the very term "improvised explosive device" (IED) and written about such bombs in our own military's professional journals in the mid-1970s.[7] Perhaps it should come as no surprise that EFPs shocked our system.

Those of us patrolling Baghdad's streets in 2006 and 2007 couldn't concern ourselves with such institutional failures to forecast the EFPs. We had to find a way to stay alive. Nothing in our existing arsenal could definitively defeat this weapon. American soldiers were at a *disadvantage*. That is not a comfortable condition or one that most Americans would consider possible. Lucky for them, the war, even at its height, received less media attention than did standard celebrity gossip. We, the volunteers, adapted as best we could. Patrols all across east Baghdad crafted a succession of desperate, sometimes feeble attempts to protect themselves.[8] Our internal countermeasures blocked certain detonation mechanisms, but insurgents quickly adapted other means of ignition.

When EFPs hit a vehicle, the devastation was unreal. The carnage inside these HMMWVs was too gruesome to comprehend. Sometimes, multiarray EFP attacks (those with multiple charges), pierced the vehicle's external frame with a few dozen holes. Oddly enough, some soldiers noticed, the reinforced glass windows *did not* seem penetrated. Theories arose that for some reason EFP slugs couldn't puncture glass. I'm not sure an actual study ever came out and it seemed like a myth, but we wanted so badly to believe the devices were fallible. Overnight, some platoons began welding extra glass windows all over the outside of their HMMWVs. The result looked ridiculous, like something out of the *Beverly Hillbillies*, and inevitably the extra gear weighed down the trucks. Nor could the glass cover every square inch of armor. But no shit, for a brief moment east Baghdad faced a veritable glass shortage. There wasn't a window to be had on the FOB.

We also changed our driving habits. And here, characteristically, there is a backstory. In Iraq, American patrols constantly shifted the way they drove. This process began in 2003 and underwent a variety of mutations during the next eight years. This mattered because for many Iraqis, vehicular patrols were the public face of the U.S. Army. Add to that the complexity of Baghdad's traffic patterns. Several million people lived in Baghdad, a major urban city with municipal topography not dissimilar to Brooklyn, New York. Yet, I never saw a functioning traffic light or very many road signs. Millions of cars jammed the few highways and narrow streets in a chaotic maelstrom of daily gridlock. It made Los Angeles look like Kansas by comparison. Then we'd inject hundreds of military patrols full of nervous soldiers rushing across the city like they owned the place. It got messy.

To understand the shifting dynamics of U.S. mounted patrol techniques, one must understand something of the nature of IEDs and American tactics. An IED attack has essentially three key components—a holy trinity if you will. First, is the explosive itself. This could range from unexploded artillery shells to homemade devices, or from mortar rounds to sophisticated EFPs. Next, is the detonation method and the "trigger man" himself. These two components are related. The least sophisticated was command wire (CWIED) detonation, whereby someone ran electrical wire from the explosive to a hiding place and then set it off while watching the American patrol roll by. This method was generally reliable but also dangerous for the insurgent. Depending on the speed of the convoy and the skill of the operator, timing could also be a problem. Remote controlled detonation (RCIED) was another method. This was popular for quite some time in 2004 and 2005. The trigger man could be farther away and less conspicuous while setting off the bomb. Insurgents initially liked this method because they could stay away from the blast site and weren't fixed to an incriminating command wire. However, depending on the sophistication, the remote could still require line of sight to the explosive; and the army quickly developed countermeasures to thwart the devices.

In 2006 my unit began to see more victim operated devices (VOIED). These included trip wires and other booby traps, but the most common form was what we dubbed crush wire IEDs. Essentially, the insurgent ran a series of wires, sometimes in a small tube, across the road. Then he would camouflage them with some dirt or trash. Because wires were harder to conceal on blacktop roads, this technique was more prevalent south of Salman Pak than in downtown Baghdad. When a vehicle rolled over the wires, it would crush them together, completing the circuit and detonating the explosive. Insurgents loved this method because they didn't even have to *be* there. There were, however, some issues. The crush wire couldn't discriminate between our vehicles and civilian cars or trucks. Also, if you drove slowly and knew what to look for you could often find the wires before you hit them. The Ghost Riders became very proficient IED-finders. Our lead section sergeant, Staff Sergeant Damian South, found more than a dozen VOIEDs in just a few months. We were rather proud of that at the time. For these reasons, the crush-wire IED saw more use in remote rural areas with light vehicular traffic. The insurgents would warn locals or mark the IEDs—often with a rag tied to a tree nearby—so the civilians knew to avoid certain roads. The final detonation method was the passive infrared (PIR) IED. This was the most sophisticated and difficult method to counter, try as we might.

The way we drove was a big part of our survival strategy. U.S. soldiers had one foremost goal on the roads of Iraq. Stay alive. Second to that was avoiding bystanders or other vehicles. Last on the list of priorities was courtesy. Insurgents had their own hierarchy of goals when emplacing an IED. Number one—do not get killed or caught. Number two—try to kill an American. And a distant third—avoid hurting civilians so as not to alienate the populace. The conflicting goals of U.S. troops and bomb-wielding insurgents began a cat and mouse game of threat and countermeasure that played out on the streets of Baghdad for several years. Often, those who suffered most were average Iraqi citizens watching this contest each and every day. It must have been hard to keep up.

Early in the war, as the maelstrom kicked off in summer 2003, insurgents unleashed a variety of IED attacks. At first they were mostly small and unsophisticated, usually surplus mortar/artillery rounds or homemade devices left unconcealed on the roadside. The majority were command detonated by a trigger man. It wasn't easy for the insurgents. They had to time the detonation *just so* in order to score a hit. Besides, U.S. patrols quickly adapted, driving fast as hell down the center of the road—civilian traffic be damned—to avoid the roadside bombs and throw off the trigger man's timing. Once an IED blew, the HMMWVs often engaged in a "spray and pray" technique—shooting turret-mounted machine guns in the probable direction of a trigger man. Sometimes civilians were hit. But it scared the hell out of the insurgents and they soon changed tactics.

In response, the insurgents began burying IEDs in the ground, often under the center of the road. In some cases, they even broke through the asphalt, emplaced a bomb and then quickly patched the roadway. To protect the trigger man, they used a combination of remote controlled and crush-wire detonation. They also increased the amount of explosive charge, sometimes stacking several antitank mines and or artillery rounds in the same hole. If they scored a direct hit, some IEDs were absolutely catastrophic. In several instances, three, four, or even five soldiers perished in a single blast. The American countermove was twofold. First, we began driving on the opposite side of the road, *against* traffic. This caused some serious gridlock, but it forced the insurgents to guess correctly when choosing on which side of the road to bury the IED. We also drove more slowly, realizing that you can't physically outrun the blast itself, only disrupt the timing. Crush wires removed even that method. Now we had to drive slowly and keep our eyes peeled for wires across the road, disturbed earth, or a civilian marking device. We learned to look for anything out of the ordinary. Paranoia set in—patrols called explosive ordnance teams (EOD) to check out thousands of innocent rocks and piles of dirt. It was all in the game.

Counterinsurgency theory holds that the occupying army must do everything in its power to isolate the insurgents from the mass of civilians. The insurgents, conversely, wish to drive a permanent wedge between the people and the army. Certain enemy tactics did just that. Suicide car bombs, or, in army jargon—vehicle borne improvised explosive devices—rendered vehicular courtesy almost out of the question. In dozens of high-profile attacks, Sunni extremists drove explosive-packed cars directly into American convoys. Scores of our soldiers died. Also significant, fear of VBIEDs spread like wildfire in the ranks. Suicide attacks changed everything. Given that an approaching car gave a HMMWV gunner only seconds to decide whether it posed a threat, the army was forced to keep civilian vehicles at a safe distance—both for our security, and theoretically, theirs. If a civilian car came too close to an American vehicle, the gunner would wave the local driver away then shoot a flare at him. If that didn't work he might fire a warning shot. Never mind that our convoys still drove against traffic, crossed over medians, and moved at erratic speeds. We expected Iraqi cars to move aside—and fast. We were scared; how could we not be? But these were *their* roads. The whole situation made for deteriorating relationships on both sides. Eventually we affixed Arabic language warning signs in bold red and black letters on the backs of all vehicles. The signs read "Keep Back" and warned that violators could be shot. Some were. The stats bore that out. Seven civilians killed per week in 2005—mistaken for suicide bombers—more than 350 in one year.[9] The year 2007 heralded thirty-six casualties per week.[10] Most were innocent.

Luckily, car bombs are expensive, and even back in the bad old days (2005 to 2007), suicide bombers were in relatively short supply. Most Iraqis, and even most foreign jihadists, didn't have the stomach for suicide. Plus, our patrols gradually improved the escalation of force procedures to reduce civilian casualties while simultaneously deterring suicide attacks. What the insurgents really wanted was something as deadly as the VBIED and easy to emplace as a standard IED. They found their answer in the EFP, which sent our patrols into absolute freak-out mode and left us scrambling for solutions. The sad reality is that for most of 2006 and 2007, few of our countermeasures worked. American patrols left the base and faced a tactical mismatch on the streets. Thank God the militias never had enough of the devices to really change the momentum, but they did have a sufficient supply to sow terror. If an EFP hit a patrol, we felt utterly powerless. We didn't get the basic psychological comfort of *seeing* who was attacking us. Nor could we outrun these devices or count on changing lanes to limit exposure.

We did what we could. Most patrols drove excruciatingly slow—like 5 miles per hour—and scanned the road. We stopped for almost any suspicious item and endlessly scrutinized the boulevards. It helped, but it now took up to three hours to travel a few miles. The stress was overwhelming. Even the slow roll wasn't a foolproof solution. Finding an EFP was like looking for a needle in a haystack, or more accurately, finding a piece of trash in a pile of garbage.

Most were arrayed inside coffee cans or similarly shaped rubbish. Without regular sanitation, the roadways of Baghdad were literally coated with refuse. Finally, we totally altered our driving technique. Off came the "Keep Back" signs and gone were the warning shots. Our patrols began weaving *into* Baghdad's normal traffic patterns. Our gunners—instead of shooting at nearby cars—began waving civilian cars *into* the military convoys. The idea was as simple as it was brilliant, the idea being that mixing with traffic would induce insurgents to shut off the IED sensor for fear of killing civilians. In a sense, we used the Iraqis as (unwitting) hostages. The irony is that Americans are quick to criticize Hamas and similar Mideast paramilitaries for using civilians as "human shields." No doubt our techniques differed and, to be fair, so did the scale. That said, one has to wonder what's so different about the *moral* calculus. In the moment, however, these tactics felt necessary. Besides, it usually worked, and civilian casualties were actually minimal. Nevertheless, you can imagine the locals' hesitancy. Our schizophrenic behavior on the road caused confusion and fear. Imagine a foreign army driving through an American city in that manner! How would we perceive them? My guess is half the population would be ready to go all *Red Dawn* on the occupiers. Nonetheless, in Baghdad choices were limited when trying to stay alive as a smart, adaptive enemy desperately tried to kill you.

The cat and mouse IED game absorbed enormous resources and brainpower—on both sides. No technological innovation or tactical solution had any definitive permanence. The facts remained; in 2006 and 2007, Baghdad's roadways were permanently treacherous. EFPs remained exceptionally deadly. Military responses were never adequate. In the end, everyone coped with the uncertainty in his or her own way. It got pretty morbid—the jokes and the strategies. Some guys rode in their vehicles with arms and legs exaggeratedly spread apart, the idea being if an EFP struck at least you'd keep a few limbs. I never had the discipline for that. So I kidded about my inevitable death and saddled up anyway. I fashioned a cigarette holder on the dash of my HMMWV, ripped the top off my pack, and slid the box inside. As we drove a couple miles per hour down serpentine streets, I'd chain smoke Gauloise "Blonde" cigarettes—like a fuckin' foreign legionnaire, as I liked to say. Lighting one cig off the other, Smith, Singleton, Fuller, and I would hold our breath as the truck rolled past some suspicious trash. Then we'd exhale and try to act brave. Each did what he must to get by.

# 10
# Troop Shortage, Troop Surge
## Good People, Bad Advice

It's 2 February 2014. I'm bored of waiting for the Super Bowl to begin, so I throw on C-SPAN (I'm a super dork) to kill some time. I watched a book talk by former secretary of defense Robert Gates. His book, *Duty: Memoirs of a Secretary at War,* was receiving a bit more than the usual attention because of some alleged criticism the former SecDef leveled at President Obama. I wasn't particularly interested in the latest manufactured controversy of the Obama administration and its detractors. Then something Bob Gates said caught my attention. It was a vignette about the Surge in Iraq and his decision to extend army brigade tours from twelve to fifteen months. I paused the program and began one of my ubiquitous rants. As always, my wife served as the primary audience.

Let me begin with a disclaimer. I happen to think, for what it's worth, (nothing) that Gates was a solid secretary of defense and is a genuinely good man. He served two presidents, from two parties, with two radically opposed styles and (at least initially) foreign policies. He managed two wars and two troop surges. He also downsized the defense budget and fired a record number of flag officers, all the while maintaining the general respect of civilians and soldiers alike. This is no small feat. After the Rumsfeld years, Gates's tenure and tone seemed like a breath of fresh air. I was happy when he agreed to stay on with the Obama administration.

But I hated his story. Mostly because it demonstrated how even this intelligent, well-meaning, competent man of character could be so misinformed and out of touch—often through no fault of his own. On this particular C-SPAN BookTV program, Gates was answering presubmitted audience questions fielded by a reporter from the

*Philadelphia Inquirer.* I don't even remember the question, but it had something to do with receiving military advice from senior generals and the place of the chiefs of staff in the chain of command. Suffice it to say that Gates answered that question and then expanded with a tangential vignette about the advice he received from his own military advisers. He spoke of difficult decisions in the wake of President Bush's decision to "surge" thirty thousand additional troops into Iraq in early 2007. Gates, it seems—to his credit—particularly anguished over the decision to extend army tours from twelve to fifteen months. Then, he said, his senior military advisor (one assumes a general or admiral) cornered him and said something like, "Sir, pardon my candor, but the troops *know* you *have* to make this decision, and they think you're an asshole for not making it yet, so just go ahead and do it." Wow. Really? Who exactly had this general polled about how *we* felt? Did he call up individual soldiers in Baghdad? If so, did he find such consensus? Or maybe this "senior advisor" was the asshole.

The whole thing was more complex. At least to those of us in Iraq at the time. I can only speak for me, my soldiers, and my peers in one unit, in one city, in one part of the country. But no one I knew seemed to understand that Gates *had* to extend tours, nor did they hope he'd "just get on with it!" I'm not sure who this guy asked, but I don't remember it like he did at all. Most of my peers and soldiers were stunned by the decision. When official word came down, I felt like I'd been hit by a train. I couldn't even speak. I hesitated to perform my duty and talk to the platoon. Instead, I sat against the brick wall of our barracks and chain smoked about a dozen cigarettes with close friends.

We tried to process the whole thing. We were sad, scared, and angry. I hated President Bush in that moment, and the war, and the American people, who didn't seem fazed by it. And I wasn't the only one. Soldiers, at least as a cross-section of Americans, are probably more conservative and supportive of presidential policy than most citizens. But as I broke the news to my guys, fielded questions, and listened in on barracks banter the next few days, I heard nothing resembling Gates's advisor's take on how soldiers *felt*. My guys were angry and frustrated. And scared. They didn't see the Gates decision as inevitable or welcome. They wondered why soldiers had to serve fifteen months when marines, sailors, and airmen did no more than seven. They couldn't understand why the army didn't expand—if necessary through a draft—in order to meet the needs of a new national policy. "Sir, if this mission is so important, why aren't we asking more people to join up so the army isn't so fucking stretched?" A fair question.

That being said, look, I actually did understand intellectually that the SecDef probably had little choice but to extend tours in order to fulfill the president's (not Gates's) order. The army was just stretched too thin and had no brigades on hand with which to "surge" into Iraq. The only other alternative, it seems, was to send units back that had been home less than a year. So I get it. It was the policy *itself* that many of us took issue with. Nevertheless, the pretentiousness of this senior advisor—back in Washington, DC!—to speak for those of us who were there, in Baghdad, and had to deal with the complicated emotions of being extended in a war (that was not going well) for three additional months—is staggering.

Generalizations tend to miss the human element. The war was going poorly. Some 115 American troops died in December 2006, scores in Baghdad alone; 86 in January 2007; 85 in February; 82 in March; and 117 in April.[1] That was just the dead. There were 706 wounded in December; 647 in January; 520 in February; 620 in March; and 651 that April.[2] The totals were almost double the previous year's casualties. Increasing attacks by EFPs were devastating convoys and shredding our HMMWVs. Protective armor was often insufficient, and our detection mechanisms had not yet caught up to this new (Iranian-supplied) threat. Spirits were often low.

The extension affected soldiers in a myriad of ways. Some guys had to change major life events, reschedule weddings, or miss the births of their kids. Dozens died during those extra three months. Time they shouldn't have even spent in Iraq. We young officers had to explain the new policy to our overworked, stretched, and stressed soldiers. We had to process our own emotions and listen to our soldiers' concerns. All of us lost another three months of our lives. Time you don't get back. That decision, its effect, and our opinions, were countless, complex, and nuanced. Whoever that general was—he's a jackass, and a sycophant. He told his boss (Secretary Gates) what he wanted to hear, to help assuage the anguish of Gates's decision, and he probably hoped to look like a can-do professional in the process. It's nearly seven years later, and I find I'm still angry about it. Gates's advisor sure didn't speak for me.

### "THANKS FOR YOUR SERVICE"

"Support the Troops" is the worst kind of platitude—hollow and insincere. What started out as bumper sticker encouragement gradually entered the digital age as some citizens took a moment to forward a mass email or post a yellow ribbon on their Facebook wall for Veteran's or Memorial Day. Support the troops—*how*, exactly? It was 2007—Iraq was on fire—and the country had too few active soldiers to complete the president's new directive. So, did the military's countless champions line up outside the recruiting stations? Nope. Instead the army began accepting felons and more recruits without high school diplomas, just to stay afloat. In April 2007, all U.S. Army tours in Iraq were extended from twelve to fifteen months. "That's a shame," some people privately muttered, but few citizens broke stride for a moment, and only a minuscule number took the tangible action of enlistment to *actually* lessen the soldiers' burden.

Early 2007, the Surge, was a key moment. Here was our nation's venerated professional army: extended to its breaking point, losing a hundred soldiers a month, sending the same kids back for their second, third, fourth tours, and now forced to keep them in the war zone for three additional months. And the country barely blinked. Or noticed. No major debate ensued on the nature of military service or citizens' obligation to the state. Those few voices that did speak out in favor of a draft, such as New York congressman Charlie Rangel, were derided as unrealistic cranks.

How, precisely, did the country and its elected leaders propose to support it's "heroes" deployed overseas? Certainly not by joining up and shipping out. Did they pay more taxes to substantially increase military salaries or revamp HMMWV armor? Not by a long shot. Did they improve education benefits for the troops? Well, yes, actually. Sort of. The new post-9/11 GI Bill was a huge improvement on the older system and continues to provide significant opportunities for a generation of veterans. But not everyone liked the idea. The bill's primary sponsor, Senator Jim Webb (D-VA), introduced the legislation in January 2007. Webb was a decorated Marine Corps veteran of the Vietnam War. Among his primary cosponsors, Senator—and later Secretary of Defense—Chuck Hagel (R-NE), was a U.S. Army foot soldier in the same war.

One would think the bill would breeze through the Congress with near unanimous support. After all, this was about veterans' education, and this was the low point of a long war that saw soldiers return for multiple combat tours. Instead, it took eighteen months to pass and faced significant opposition early on. From whom you ask? It was opposed by President Bush and many Republicans. Bush initially threatened to veto the bill and considered its $5.1 billion annual price tag "exorbitant."[3] Of course, the cost equaled less than a month of spending for the Iraq War at the time. Even Senator John McCain (R-AZ) withheld early support out of fear that such generous education benefits would hurt retention.[4] Better that the soldiers all return for a fourth or fifth tour, I suppose. He and Senator Lindsey Graham (R-SC) introduced a far more modest increase in benefits meant to encourage re-enlistment. A soldier would need to spend *twelve years* in uniform to receive the maximum tuition assistance.[5]

None of this should have been a surprise. With the exception of McCain, few of the Iraq War's early proponents were themselves veterans. The bill failed to pass in 2007 because of the president's outspoken opposition and a lack of votes. With only fifty-eight supporters in the Senate, Webb's initial bill was just short of a veto-proof majority. One major sticking point involved funding. The original House version of the law proposed to pay for the veterans' education benefits with a tax increase of 0.47 percent on couples earning over $1 million annually. This modest proposal met a firestorm of Republican opposition. The bill eventually passed, mainly because a compromise resolution dropped the original funding plan and attached the new GI Bill to the main Iraq War appropriations bill in 2008. With the Pentagon warning that a lack of additional funding would result in a shutdown in operations by mid-2008, President Bush couldn't veto the bill.[6] It passed and the president quickly took credit for the popular new law, but at the outset, fiscally conservative ideology trumped "Support the Troops." Such is life.

So, how else did Americans tangibly "support our troops"? Perhaps the people decided en masse to pull the troops out and redirect U.S. foreign policy? Maybe they took to the streets in massive public protests against the war, a la Vietnam? Hardly. Why should they? No one feared a draft—they simply had no skin in the game. The middle class didn't *feel* this war. In 1968, a mother might open her daily newspaper or listen to Walter Cronkite on the nightly news and face the horror of the Tet Offensive in Vietnam. She would know that her teenage sons were subject to conscription as soon as they left high school or college. She might not otherwise be political, but the war would become real to her and she needed to decide how she felt about it. Was it worth it? Did the ends justify her son's potential death? A mother in the age of national service lived with those questions. So did a father. So did a young man.

In the age of Iraq, one mother did take to the streets and the airwaves to protest the war. Cindy Sheehan lost her son to the war. *She* had skin in the game. And look at how she was treated by the media: regarded as a kook, an oddball, an American-hating communist lunatic. No one in the corporate media gave her a fair appraisal. People said times had changed. Her son was a *volunteer*, after all. She had no right to "dishonor his memory" by protesting the war. Consensus emerged around these beliefs that bordered on character assassination. Fred Barnes of Fox News called her a "crackpot," and right-wing blogs lit up with "tales of her divorce and her angry Republican in-laws."[7] The ironic thing is that many of us have someone in our family widely considered a "flake." You know the type—the flighty vegan aunt who brings petitions to Thanksgiving, marches for animal rights, lives for her new juicer, and might even protest the war. Mine is named Patti, and she is genuinely passionate. We laugh at her—you probably laugh at yours, too—but at least she cares and at any rate she *does* something. I'll never agree with everything Patti says; I didn't subscribe to all of Ms. Sheehan's stances. But life has taught me not to dismiss these people. Cindy Sheehan was a heartbroken mother with a reasonable argument. Few noticed, fewer cared. Such is the fallout from our current American system to provide for the "common defense."

Some things you just can't make up. On 2 July 2007, a platoon from our Apache Troop hit an IED at a busy intersection. One section raced off to the nearest FOB with a wounded but stable trooper. A nearby military police platoon—in a display of solidarity—drove straight to the blast site and helped secure the remaining scout section until further reinforcements could arrive. A few minutes later, our B Troop platoons showed up and cordoned off the area. The MPs—including one young sergeant—fanned out to keep gathering bands of pedestrians away from the blast site. As the MP sergeant walked away from the cordon, he was hit across the head with a powerful blow from behind that he said felt like a "clothesline tackle."[8] The MP stayed on his feet, turned, and wrestled his assailant down to the ground. His squad mates pulled them apart and detained the assailant. "I remember being pretty pissed off," the sergeant recalled.[9] His medic, meanwhile, tugged at the wounded man's arm and told him to "sit, calm down, and leave the knife in."[10] Knife? The guy had no idea he'd been stabbed, nor that 4 *inches* of a 9-inch blade—a kitchen knife—were embedded in his skull. He was wearing the proper protective gear, but the blade entered just below his helmet. Medics did what they could on scene but were afraid to remove the blade. They carefully bandaged the sergeant's head and placed a Styrofoam coffee cup over the knife. Within minutes, they got him to FOB Shield and into a helicopter bound for the U.S. Air Base at Balad.

His troubles were far from over. Once he was in Balad, the surgeons were initially at a loss. They were used to seeing blunt, traumatic head injuries from IEDs and sniper bullets, but this was something wholly new. X-rays revealed that the blade had just missed the sergeant's brain and come to rest in his cavernous sinus. The real problem was that the knife had also nicked his carotid artery and was literally acting like a cork holding in the blood. Surgeons at Balad decided to risk removal, breathed deep, and yanked out the blade. Blood gushed out of the wound and the air force surgeon thought his patient might die right then and there. Amazingly, they managed to clamp the carotid artery, saving his life, but not before the sergeant lost two-fifths of his body's blood supply. With no precedent for this type of injury in

Iraq, the surgeons needed guidance on what to do next. They contacted the army's top neurosurgeon at Walter Reed Army Hospital, who pulled over in Washington, DC, traffic to take the call. Taking a look at emailed X-rays and photos, the doc advised that the wounds be closed up and the sergeant be sent back to the States ASAP.[11] The MP came out of an induced coma four days later, and despite doctors' fears, he maintained his eyesight, body functions, and memory. Within thirty days he was home in North Carolina.

Stabbing injuries were extremely rare. In Iraq, injuries from hostile knife attacks were outnumbered by drowning and electrocutions. According to the Defense Department, this was just the second stabbing victim of Operation Iraqi Freedom.[12] The scarcity of stabbings has to do with technology, of course, as other weapons are far more effective against gun-toting soldiers wearing Kevlar vests. Besides, running up and stabbing an American soldier was basically suicide—and not of a tactically or psychologically effective form, such as suicide bombing. You'd have to be literally crazy to attempt it. Some of the guys in our 1st platoon were ready to shoot the teenage "insurgent" who had attacked the sergeant—which was understandable. To their credit, and especially to the credit of the disciplined leaders on the ground, the "insurgent" was safeguarded and detained according to regulations. It could easily have gone the other way.

It turned out that the teenager was all but off his rocker, unstable and possibly a bit slow. Some locals tried to explain that the boy wasn't an insurgent but just a crazy kid, the neighborhood's village idiot. That could very well have been true. Jihadist stabbings were just rare enough (as in they basically never happened) that one can assume this guy wasn't all there. Nevertheless, he was sent off to jail. Sometime later, the victim testified via teleconference at his attacker's trial, which was prosecuted by Iraqi authorities. The sergeant wasn't aware of the man's fate at the time of trial, but told reporters that the Iraqis planned "to lengthen his neck a little bit."[13] Maybe they did hang the guy, or maybe he was released along with thousands of prisoners in Iraqi jails after the worst violence died down. I'm not sure it matters in any real sense. Just one more irrational act lost in the absurdity of the war. But it's a story I'll probably never stop telling.

# 11

## A Night to Remember

### 25 JANUARY 2007

Some guilt you never lose, and some dates you never forget. For most people, birthdays, anniversaries, maybe the birth of a child top the list. Sure I remember those too, but I remain fixated on another. The date is engraved on a bracelet and in my thoughts.

After DJ was hit, Fuller took over the dismount team. He now rode in the lead vehicle, ready to hop out and lead raids at a moment's notice. SFC Gass went on leave in mid-January. SSG South stepped in temporarily as platoon sergeant and SSG Rittel started leading patrols as our senior scout. Our platoon now patrolled the al-Amin district of southeast Baghdad. These were the facts as they existed on 25 January 2007.

With DJ and Faulkner both wounded and shipped home, the platoon was short a couple of guys. Recently we'd received a new soldier—PFC Michael Balsley from Hayward, California. Balsley had transferred over from 3rd platoon and fit right in. He was a quiet, unassuming, genuinely nice guy and meshed well with his truck commander—SSG Rittel—who had a similar disposition. Balsley was my age, a few years older than most of the other Joes. He'd been a poor student and gotten in some trouble during high school. After graduation he'd worked with his father, Jim, a Vietnam veteran, at a local auto parts warehouse. After the 9/11 attacks, Michael—still in high school—decided to enlist. He completed basic training as a Cav scout in Fort Knox, Kentucky, then did a tour in South Korea—just as Alex Fuller had done. At Fort Carson, Michael met and fell for Samantha Wall. They married in 2006.[1] Before we deployed, Michael was in the process of adopting her one-year-old son, Logan. PFC Balsley was well liked and a natural fit on SSG Rittel's crew. He was driving that night.

Our missions in late January were sort of thrown together. In Salman Pak, we had had a set campaign plan and a sense of what we intended to accomplish—however fanciful those goals might have been. Protect the city from Sunni insurgent invasion, limit the sectarian violence, and gather intelligence on AQI's next move. Up in al-Amin, we were still learning the ropes: how to get around, who the key powerbrokers were, what role, exactly, the Mahdi Army played in the area. The first and last thirty days of any deployment are the most dangerous. The last thirty because everyone is getting complacent and lets their concentration slip away to home. The first days because you don't yet know *what* to look for, don't yet have a sense for what's out of place in your sector. Unfortunately, by moving districts three times, we faced the "first thirty" over and over again.

On 25 January, we were supposed to drive up to the NP station in northern al-Amin and link up with the police for an overnight observation post (OP). I hated the whole concept and here's why: EFPs detonated by a sensor were our number one threat. Fortunately, these devices were potentially dangerous to civilians and thus in only limited daytime use. *However,* after nightfall and the government-enforced curfew took effect,[2] the *only* vehicles on the road were American or Iraqi police. We couldn't mix in with traffic, and our ability to scan the roadsides was diminished in the dark. There was *no reason* to be out on those roads after dark. The only exception would have been an emergency or extremely valuable intelligence gathering opportunity. Our mission that night was neither. I fought my troop commander at some length over the patrol schedule, asking either to leave early or wait until morning, but it didn't fly.

You see, by 2007 we weren't supposed to use the term "presence patrol" to describe routine missions any more. The phrase was long out of vogue, replaced with the profound concept that all missions must have a clear task and purpose. Unfortunately, the distinction was more semantic than tangible. Counterinsurgency theory called for the occupation forces to provide sustained security, and that meant *presence.* In practice, this was manifested in a directive from our headquarters to maintain at least one platoon in sector at all times. It looked a lot like presence patrolling. The captain wrote the patrol schedule, which directed our platoon to leave the FOB at 10:00 p.m.—after curfew—and he didn't appreciate my complaints about the timetable. After two days of choice words exchanged, I was decisively overruled. We'd be taking off as scheduled.

We had bungled a mission in the area the night before, and I wasn't particularly keen on rolling through the sector anyway. Technology is great, but it has its limitations. On 24 January a drone had spied some "military-age males" carrying a large box into a local mosque. Whoever was watching the monitor at headquarters suspected local militia members were storing weapons. Given our past experience with the Salman Pak mosque raid, it wasn't a bad hunch. There's just one problem: eyes in the sky at several thousand feet—no matter how high-tech the cameras—see things *way* differently than men on the ground. Mistakes are made. Our platoon was in the vicinity, and squadron headquarters tasked us to check things out. Of course we couldn't enter the mosque, but lucky for us the drone now observed the men carrying a large object back *out* of the mosque to a truck bed parked in front. We zipped over, surrounded the truck, and temporarily detained everyone on site. We had the men sit on the curb, guarded by a few soldiers. The eldest Iraqi was vehemently shouting something at the interpreter as our guys checked the truck. They did, in fact, find one long, wooden box covered in a sheet. Opening the lid and lifting another sheet, they found . . . a corpse. Shit. The old man had been trying to tell us they'd been ritually cleansing and dressing the body of his deceased son—*not* transporting weapons. All that was left to do was apologize, profusely, and let them all go. They weren't amused.

About 9:45 p.m. the next night I grabbed my gear and started to make my way down the hall to the door. I was headed out to the trucks to give a standard patrol brief—a verbal reminder of our mission, route, and plan in the case of an attack—and was running a few minutes behind. From over my shoulder, I heard Fuller's voice.

*"Yo, Sir, Sir. You gotta check out these pics of Stacey."* [She was several months pregnant.]

Exasperated from my earlier argument with the troop commander, I wasn't really in the mood, but this was Fuller—my guy—so I stopped and laid my vest against the wall. He handed me some snapshots and peered over my shoulder. Stacey, a petite girl of no more than a hundred pounds, was beginning to show.

*"Sir, look at her BELLY! She's so beautiful. It's gonna be a girl, you know, right? Yeah—I told Stacey we gotta name her Aliciah. You know—like Al—Aliciah."*

Fuller and his wife were in love. I didn't know Stacey that well but could tell. Back in Colorado, the platoon had spent weeks at a time in field training. In between, we broke up into groups and partied in some of the same downtown Colorado Springs bars. Both at work and off duty, Fuller and I began to spend a lot of time together. He talked about Massachusetts and his friends. About Florida, his family, and his past dealing drugs. But much of the time he talked about Stacey, of how young they were when they got together: thirteen and fifteen. How he knew she was the one from the start. Sure, everyone in the platoon knew they had problems. Tales of their fights were epic. Among the troops, Alex and Stacey became synonymous with "Sid and Nancy." Fuller would try to avoid the fighting. Sometimes he'd lie about where he was. He stayed long hours at work after everyone else went home. Much of the time, it was just him and me. Occasionally he'd tell Stacey he was at work when he was elsewhere. At least once she called my personal cell to ask if Al was with me. I'd try and cover for him.

This was a highly unusual conversation between a lieutenant and one of his soldiers' wives. In retrospect I walked into it. I was probably too close to Fuller. He quickly became my protégé. He was known as "LT's guy" within the platoon. Sometimes after work I'd drive him to grab Burger King (he was often short on cash), sit in my car, and just talk endlessly. I loved those times—probably because I liked to think I could relate to Fuller, that I had more in common with him and soldiers like him than I did with my own peers.

I guess I'd felt that way since West Point, where I met thousands of cadets from affluent families. I struggled to maintain my individual identity and part of that came from crafting a narrative whereby I was a product of tougher, working-class circumstances. Thus, I was different from the more sheltered officers I served with. Some of this was unfair to my peers and to my own family, but much of it was true. I know now that none of it mattered. One night Fuller started talking about Stacey. He said he knew what people said about their relationship. He admitted they fought a lot and that things could get crazy. He also confessed he wasn't a perfect husband. But then he gave me a serious look and said he loved her, always would, and just couldn't help it—she was his girl. I believed him.

On this night, Fuller was legitimately giddy. I flipped through all the shots and he pointed at each one adding some sort of comment. Fuller was always energetic, but something was different that night. He was buoyant with excitement and didn't seem to want our conversation to end. Eventually, I handed him back the photos, slapped his back, and told him we needed to head out. We walked down the hall together.

I finished the routine patrol brief and walked over to SSG Rittel's truck. He'd be leading that night, and I wanted to go over the route with him one last time. Rittel back-briefed the plan and then asked me to stick around for a second. It seems he wanted his crew to show me something. "Ok, fellas, do the song for the LT." Ducks was up in the turret, Fuller and Balsley down in front of the truck. Fuller counted down from three and they broke into song. You could tell Balsley—shy as ever—wasn't too excited about it, but under Fuller's prodding sang along anyway. They'd changed the lyrics to the famous ditty from *The Lion King*—"Hakuna Matata," substituting "Moktada al-Sadr." Performed with energy, it sounded pretty damn good:

"Mok-ta-da al-Sadr, what a wonderful name.
Mok-ta-da al-Sadr, ain't no passing craze.
He-gives-us worries, every single day.
He's got I-E-Ds, and E-F-Ps, Moktada al-Sadr."

Rittel and I gave a resounding applause and Fuller slapped Balsley on the back. We all smiled. It was a fine moment. After the song and dance, Ducks turned to Balsley and said he had a bad feeling about the night's mission. He'd only done this once before—on 14 December—a couple hours before DJ was shot. A few minutes later, we took off.

After about ten minutes, we were just over halfway to the NP station. Then Rittel turned right on an unnamed road we called 8th

Street. What happened next seared into my memory the cluttered disarray of sight, sound, and smell. The loudest explosion I'd ever heard shattered the night, rocked our eardrums, and forced my head against the window. It was 10:24 p.m. Dust blanketed everything, and I was afraid we'd smash into the lead truck. I screamed at Smith first to speed up—to get us out of the "kill zone"—then to slow down to avoid rear-ending SSG Rittel. I'm not sure he could even hear me. Within seconds—or maybe it was minutes—the smoke cleared enough and I saw Rittel's truck veer slowly to the right and crash against a telephone pole. As we pulled up alongside, we heard a piercing shriek—unmistakably Ducks—bursting out the turret. Something was terribly wrong.

The bomb blew on the north end of 8th Street out of a pile of garbage along the roadway. The blast concentrated against the driver's side of SSG Rittel's vehicle. Smith and I were the first ones out of the truck. SGT Pushard, Doc, and Ford were close behind. The smell—which will never leave me—was the first thing I remember. I now know that it was a mix of burned metal and flesh. The entire driver's side was ripped to shreds, leaving the HMMWV resembling a slice of Swiss cheese. Someone opened the driver's door and Balsley's lifeless body fell to the pavement. A copper slug had pierced his skull and killed him instantly. I froze and stared at him for a few seconds. I couldn't shake the image of that last expression forever frozen on his face. Yet somehow it didn't seem real. Ducks was screaming bloody murder and the guys were slowly pulling him out of the turret. His legs and torso were littered with shrapnel and his left arm was nearly torn off. The bleeding was profuse. Doc Schrader worked furiously to stabilize Ducks and staunch the blood flow from dozens of shrapnel wounds. In the confusion, Doc accidentally stuck his *own* thumb with a morphine injection intended for the wounded. Ducks was in serious condition. His arm was hanging on by a thread, and—unbeknownst to him—a flare inside the truck had kicked off and hit him square in the back. As Doc and Ford worked on him, Ducks's only thoughts were of his crewmates.

As I circled around to the passenger side to check on Ducks, SSG Rittel opened his door. He looked stunned and stumbled a bit as he stepped forward. Realizing his elbow was bloody, I steadied him and pulled out a bandage. As I dressed the wound, Rittel kept asking about Balsley. I don't think I answered. After I tied the dressing on Rittel's arm, I started to jog back toward SSG South's vehicle. My plan was to update him on the casualties so he could relay the MEDEVAC report. Before I got around the back of the vehicle, I almost ran into SGT Pushard. I stopped and instructed him to keep an eye on Ducks while I ran back to SSG South. For some reason, I verbalized the report I was about to give: "Ok, so we've got one KIA [killed in action], and two WIA [wounded in action]. Oh yeah, and grab Fuller, too," I heard myself saying.

Pushard stared at me confusedly. "Sir. Sir, Fuller's dead. He's gone."

"WHAT?!?" I said. "Wait, did you check him out, did you work on him? Are you sure?"

Pushard grabbed me by the shoulders. "He's gone. Look, Sir, there's nothing left of him. Sir, don't even look back there, please."

The whole moment remains extremely fuzzy, like my memory is shrouded in a thick fog. It was—and is—so surreal. Looking back, I wish I'd taken SGT Pushard's advice. I turned to leave, looked once into the backseat, and glimpsed the horror within. I have neither the words nor the desire to describe what I saw. I just spun around and continued to walk.

I'm still not sure where the energy came from, but somehow I continued to function. I relayed the report to SSG South, using his first name. "Damian, we've got one urgent surgical casualty, Ducks. He's bad. Rittel is walking wounded—shrapnel to the arm. Balsley and . . . Fuller—his name stung as it leapt off my tongue—they're dead. KIA. Both. Make sure you get the battle rosters up. We've got to get Ducks out of here."

Damian looked stunned, but he was on his game as always. He'd already sent up an initial report and coordinated to have a platoon from Apache Troop take over the site and gather up the bodies while the rest of us took the wounded to FOB Loyalty, the closest American base. Our squadron commander had *personally* gotten on the radio with Damian and tried to send a helicopter our way. Damian bucked: "Sir, there's no *way* you're gonna get a bird in these narrow ass streets," he yelled into the mic—*not* the customary way a sergeant talks to his colonel. The SCO knew South by reputation and must have heard the urgency in his voice, because he approved Damian's plan and simply told him: "Do what you've got to, sergeant." When I got over to his truck, our whole conversation sounded fake, like we were on a training exercise or performing in a stage play. We agreed on the plan—get Ducks to the FOB ASAP—and I ran back to the shattered truck to gather everyone up.

After I left, Brian Longton called down to Damian from the gun turret. "Sergeant South, look at Balsley lying on the ground. We've *got* to go pick him up." Damian wanted to gather Balsley's body just as much as anyone, but he knew we'd have to leave that for the relief platoon. Right now, all that mattered was getting Ducks to the hospital. He knew there wasn't a second to waste. Damian told Longton so, and it killed them both inside. When I made it back to Rittel's truck, Pushard was seething with anger and pointed up at an open window right above us. "Sir, I'm gonna put a few rounds in that fucking window." It made no sense. The EFP that hit us—a multiarray sophisticated device as it turned out—was almost certainly set off by a sensor. Any insurgents had long since left the area, and no one was using that window for anything nefarious. He let off a few meaningless shots from his M4 into the blackness. Thing is, our boys were dead. A whole crew effectively wiped out. And there was *no one* to blame, no one to take it out on. It wasn't even like war; it felt more like murder. The spot looked and smelled like a crime scene, and I couldn't shake the feeling that *I* was the perpetrator.

We took off at full speed through the dark, narrow streets. Ducks was laid across the backseat of South's vehicle, and Frunk—driving the truck—kept yelling out profuse apologies as he slammed into the inevitable Baghdad potholes. Within a few minutes, we screeched to a halt in front of the FOB Loyalty aid station. The boys carried Ducks in before I even had a chance to catch up to them. He'd lost an immense amount of blood. I walked into the station alongside SSG Rittel. The physician's assistant and medics went to work on Ducks. They kept us at a distance and stabilized him. Time flew by and the next thing I knew, he was being carried to the helipad. Both Ducks and Rittel took off for the CSH in the Green Zone.

A chaplain walked me out to the trucks and I sat down on a curb. He asked me how I was and made me tell him about Fuller and Balsley.

I tried. The chaplain was a stranger to me, though, and sometimes—looking back—I wonder if he even existed or was some sort of figment of my imagination. Back at the trucks, all the boys were carrying on hushed conversations in small groups. Next thing I remember, I was standing with Damian and we smoked a few dozen cigarettes. Everyone was terrified to drive back to our own FOB. They begged me to wait until morning. I jumped on the radio, asked to stay put, but was instructed to head straight back. I was afraid I'd have a mutiny on my hands. I called Singleton and Smith together and gave it to them straight. "Look, fellas, no one is going to leave here unless I lead them out. I'm the LT, and I've got to do it. Can you guys handle that? Are you ready?" Smith fired back: "Hell, yeah." Singleton said he was in, too. I know it sounds trite, and might seem insignificant compared with hitting the beaches at Normandy—but that was about the gutsiest thing I'd ever witnessed.

It was 1:41 a.m. when we finally left FOB Loyalty. We drove so slowly that it took thirty-seven minutes to make a ten-minute trip. For all his courage, and verbal bravado, Smith's hands and legs shook the whole way. I tried not to stare. Besides, I was shaking worse. When we got back, everyone in the barracks looked at us with blank stares of pity. Steve hugged me and said, in sincere tones, how truly sorry he was. I don't remember much of it. The platoon—what was left of us—gathered up in one of the rooms on the second floor. We sat around in a circle for a few hours, smoking cigarettes and trying to make sense of the whole thing. A year earlier, I'd craved these intimate moments. I remembered back to the first time I sat around with these boys as Fuller danced across the room re-creating the scene of Artis's arrest. If only I'd known. Some of the guys were already saying they didn't want to go back out on patrol—ever. "What the fuck *FOR*?" "How in the world do we fucking *stop* those things [EFPs]?" "We don't even have a *chance!*" "Fuck the Iraqis—it's *their* country." As I walked down the stairs to my room, I knew I'd have to figure something out. I turned right instead of left, walked into the night, lit a smoke, and pictured Fuller's face. Tears flowed effortlessly, and I finally let myself cry. I was alone.

Fuller and Balsley. Two young men, one my close friend—gone. Just like that. Life, extinguished. Unless you've seen it, it's hard to explain the effect. They were there, and then in a moment—they weren't. The randomness of death, the suddenness and finality still mess with my head. Some days, I worry about living life to its fullest and on others I'm struck by the essential absurdity of it all. Nothing was ever the same.

At best, most Americans catch a name in the paper, read aloud on *This Week with George Stephanopoulos*, or see a couple of faces flash across the TV screen. But every one of those faces was a unique individual, loved by some and mourned by many. They were real to me—my soldiers and my friends. Jim Balsley said he wants his son to be remembered as a patriot. "Michael was a real person," he said. "Michael was not just another name in the newspaper about another fallen hero defending the United States. Michael was a real individual."[3] Most people just see numbers, the statistics. Like this one: Alex Fuller and Michael Balsley were the 3,068th and 3,069th soldiers killed in Iraq.[4] This too, though: their stories matter.

### HUMAN INTERLUDE 6: ANGER AND FUTILITY
JANUARY 2007

My brother had a book he would hold with pride
A little red cover with a broken spine
on the back he hand wrote a quote inside
"When the rich wage war, it's the poor who die"
— "Hands Held High," Linkin Park

Once, not that long ago, artists, poets, and musicians wrote extensively about war. As recently as the Vietnam era, pop stars addressed the subject in a variety of ways. When one thinks of antiwar protest songs, Woodstock and the 1960s immediately spring to mind. But the songs of that era actually ranged from Sergeant Barry Sadler's pop hit "The Ballad of the Green Berets"—a patriotic yarn written by Sadler, an actual Special Forces veteran—to Neil Young's "Ohio," an indictment of Nixon, Vietnam, and the Kent State massacre.

Compare that with contemporary wars, the longest in our history, and the utter lack of associated music. Off the top of your head, how many songs with an explicit or even *implicit* reference to Iraq can you think of? My guess is somewhere between zero and one. Bruce

Springsteen bucked the trend. His 2006 album *Magic* was essentially an extended condemnation of the Bush era war policies. The best track, "Long Walk Home," addressed the struggles of a returning veteran. *Magic* is a phenomenal album and reflects its moment better than anything else done at the time. Nevertheless, most of its songs never made it to the radio, and how many people—besides Bruce fanatics, among whom I must count myself—knew anything about it? Watch *Fox News* and if Springsteen does get press, it's heavily negative, along the lines of "socialist, liberal celeb is once again telling us how to think." Springsteen has the name, reputation, and established fan base to take creative risks, but an up-and-coming band doesn't have the luxury. In a corporate music market where politics don't sell, and the consumer public doesn't *care* about the war, topical songs don't stand a chance.

That's just it—no one is invested in these wars. I mean, no one *besides* the tiny minority of actual soldiers. That said, many of us *were* angry and sought artistic outlets for that rage. We had to look into the deep tracks to find it. In 2007, Linkin Park's "Hands Held High" from the *Minutes to Midnight* album became our anthem. Several of my fellow LTs loved the song. I didn't even like Linkin Park or their style of music—not really, anyway. I still don't. Nonetheless, "Hands Held High" is an all but unknown classic, and I'm forever grateful they took the time to write something meaningful about the war. The lyrics were perfect, a snapshot of the times, and our response to those days. We were *angry*. Some of us, at least. Because we all "volunteered for this," no one ever talks about our anger, but we *were* fucking pissed. Someone has to describe this moment in time—how we felt, what we clung to, how many of us viewed the world. Some of us saw through a very dark lens, indeed.

> It's ironic, at times like this you pray
> but a bomb blew the mosque up yesterday.

The days after Fuller's and Balsley's death remain a blur. The platoon got a few days' reprieve from patrolling—after all, we didn't even have enough guys left to man four trucks—and some of the soldiers spoke with the chaplain. Sometime in the days following the attack, Damian and I flew into the Green Zone to visit Ducks and SSG Rittel.

Ducks was in rough shape, and would lose most use of the arm, but was in pretty good spirits. The night before, heavily drugged up and high as a kite, he'd called his mother. The day of the visit I also called with a more accurate status on her son. Ducks was heading home for good. Rittel's physical injuries were minor, and we took him back to the FOB with us. Inside, though, Rittel was shot. He'd survived a blast that tore his entire crew apart, and he was racked with survivor's guilt. I didn't know what to say to the guy. We smoked some cigarettes, reminisced about the boys, and waited for the next bird back to FOB Rusty.

A couple days later the squadron held a traditional memorial ceremony for Fuller and Balsley. Set on a small stage inside the squadron headquarters were two pairs of combat boots, each with an upside-down rifle stuck in the ground by a fixed bayonet. On top of the rifles sat two helmets with two sets of hanging dog tags—their dog tags. The ceremony is intense. Friends make speeches honoring the deceased, then the troop and squadron commander each speak. The squadron commander—doing what I'm sure he felt was his duty—exhorted us to use Fuller's and Balsley's deaths to "*rededicate* ourselves in our mission to secure the Iraqi people." What a load of bullshit, I'd thought. What happens next is the most haunting part of every memorial. I've been to dozens now, and the effect never diminishes. The troop first sergeant—the senior enlisted soldier in the unit—starts calling out names of the guys in the platoon.

"Private Smith?" he yelled, taking roll.

"Here, First Sergeant!" Smith bellowed back.

"Private Frunk?"

"Here, First Sergeant!"

"Specialist Longton?"

"Here, First Sergeant!"

"Sergeant Fuller?" [Eerie silence.]

"Sergeant Alexander Fuller?" [Nothing.]

"Sergeant Alexander *Henry* Fuller?" [No answer.]

The process was repeated for Balsley. As soon as the last unanswered question of this final roll call left the first sergeant's tongue, an honor guard fired three rifle volleys into the air.

"Ready, aim, fire!" [Called out the NCO in charge.] *CRACK!*

"Ready, aim, fire! "—*CRACK!*

"Ready, aim, fire! "—*CRACK!*

With the last discharge of rifles, the witching melody of Taps played on a trumpet. Almost no one can resist the tears. The ceremony is an emotional rollercoaster and does a number on most spectators.

Just like that—it's over. Each individual in the crowd slowly walks up to the stage, salutes, turns right, and walks out. Along the way they pass through a receiving line of mourners that includes the troop commander, first sergeant, platoon leader, and platoon sergeant. Everyone expresses apologies and some hugs are exchanged. I can't remember any. Except one. SFC Chris Lyons—3rd platoon sergeant, and one the finest NCOs I've ever seen—pulled me close and whispered, "You're a good platoon leader, Sir." More than anything in the world, I needed to hear *those words* right then. Maybe he sensed it, or maybe it was a coincidence, but I've never forgotten that moment. Stricken down with guilt, heartbroken, and a little afraid, I suppose I was desperate for some validation. It meant all the more coming from a guy like Chris Lyons.

The anger doesn't just go away. After the memorial, I spent a couple hours around a bonfire with my guys. There was a lot of crying, plenty of reminiscing, and even some laughing. Afterward, I sat around with my peers—LTs Scott Maclaren, Steve Migliore, and Keith Marfione, among others—and talked endlessly. We discussed Fuller, EFPs, the Iraqi police, and the futility of the entire war. Then Keith and I got to carping about the squadron commander's speech, not just at this memorial, but at all of them so far. We were angry and, perhaps foolishly, took it out on him. What we couldn't stand was his whole "rededicate yourselves to the mission" shtick. Then and there—late at night, hopped-up on Red Bulls and emotion—we made a pact. Should one of us die—and with the EFP threat increasing, that seemed a real possibility—we promised not to let the SCO, or *anyone*, hijack our memorial. No, we decided, if Keith died and the commander started that shit, I'd jump out of my seat and interrupt him like a jilted lover at a wedding service. "Fuck that," I imagined myself saying. "Keith didn't believe in this war for one second. He wouldn't want you all to rededicate yourselves to much of *anything*, let alone this shithole mission and dying for the sake of advancing some asshole's career!" Or something like that. And vice versa. We swore on it. Fact is we'd have probably been fired for such a stunt, but I'm pretty sure Keith would've done it. I know I would've.

# 12

# Shouting at Lindsey Graham

> I confess, without shame, that I am sick and tired of fighting—its glory is
> all moonshine; even success the most brilliant is over dead and mangled
> bodies, with the anguish and lamentations of distant families. . . . It is only
> those who have never heard a shot, never heard the shriek and groans
> of the wounded and lacerated . . . that cry aloud for more blood, more
> vengeance, more desolation.
>
> — GENERAL WILLIAM TECUMSEH SHERMAN, May 1865

I have a confession. I watch *The Daily Show with Jon Stewart*—
religiously. I know there is nothing more stereotypical for a young,
self-designated progressive to do these days, but I don't care. The network and cable news are hardly less partisan; besides, I happen to
like the show. One of my favorite recurring skits is Stewart's Scar-
lett O'Hara–style impression of Senator Lindsey Graham (R-SC). Two
things: Graham's accent is ridiculous, and second—what kind of
name is Lindsey? I tend to disagree with nearly everything Graham
says and get a good laugh out of Stewart's endless attempts to dem-
onstrate the senator's hypocrisy. Nevertheless, I never gave the man
much thought. That is, until the latest round of spectacular violence
hit the major media outlets, but slightly before ISIS overran nearly
all of western and northern Iraq. It was mid-January 2014, and I was
watching a Senate debate on C-Span. I don't remember the official
subject, but it had to do with the budget or something—definitely *not*
foreign policy. Yet up stepped Senator Graham to the podium. What
took place was a long rant against the alleged failures of the Obama
administration in the Middle East. I began paying attention.

Graham was relentless. It was the typical militaristic yarn. "Obama
pulled the troops out of Iraq too soon." "He cut and ran on American
security." "Obama wasted all the hard-won American *gains* in the Iraq

War." "He squandered the effects of the Surge." I listened for a minute and then lost it. I was sitting alone but found myself screaming at the television. It was hard to believe such ignorance passed as not only acceptable, but *mainstream* thought about the war. I used to think that most Americans didn't know their history. I've come to believe they don't even know their present.

Graham claimed that Obama pulled the troops out too soon. Never mind that the last American soldiers didn't leave Iraq until mid-December 2011. That's eight years and eight months. In other words, 2.4 times longer than in World War II, or about as long as combined U.S. involvement in both world wars and the Civil War. Quite a commitment. Graham belongs to the school of Surge-worshippers, congressional hawks that never cease to espouse the heroic accomplishments of the Petraeus miracle. For starters, the very foundation of this explanation is questionable. Violence decreased in 2008 and 2009. That is undeniable. Attacks on U.S. troops, sectarian killings, bombings, and shootings all declined. But why? Was it a new general armed with enlightened counterinsurgency methods? Or the additional thirty thousand–odd troops added to the streets of Iraq? Many senators, defense analysts, and authors initially answered with an emphatic yes on both counts.[1] Particularly at the time. Recently, with the hindsight of a seemingly less than triumphant application of Surge principles to Afghanistan and some closer scrutiny, a number of scholars have begun to question this prevailing narrative.[2] This came as no surprise to me. Many of us leveled these criticisms at the "Surge narrative" before it even got off the ground.

Petraeus didn't take over until January 2007. By September, during his first congressional testimony on the new strategy, the general claimed a great deal of progress. Democrats doubted the statistics; Republicans lauded the new policy, grit, and determination of President Bush and his new hero—Dave Petraeus. Both sides used the war as politics. Plain and simple. Many of my fellow officers in Baghdad saw a different story unfold.

First, by late 2007, an Iraqi sectarian civil war (although few military officers or supporters of the administration dare use the term) had raged on for almost two years. Millions of people were forced from their homes or left the country in fear. Tens of thousands were killed. One result was an ever-greater segregation of the opposing ethnic and religious communities. A once heterogeneous Baghdad became largely Shia dominated, and other Iraqi cities became similarly Balkanized. Few truly mixed neighborhoods or towns remained. Before 2006, estimates had placed the city's district breakdown as 40 percent Shia, 20 percent Sunni, and 40 percent mixed. By mid-2007 half the Sunnis had left and 60 percent of neighborhoods were solidly Shia.[3] Thus, by the time of the Surge, much of the work of death and displacement was complete. Violence began to decrease as the opposing groups settled into geographically separated, armed camps. We watched this firsthand. In November 2006, it was still possible to find streets in Salman Pak and southeast Baghdad with alternating Sunni and Shia households. By the time we began formal census taking in late summer 2007, that was a thing of the past.

Second, in 2006, months before the Surge, one American army armored brigade astutely exploited growing tensions between Sunni tribal leaders and Al Qaeda extremists in far western Anbar province.[4] This unit laid the necessary foundations for an eventually expanded policy of placing former Sunni insurgents on the American payroll to battle AQI fighters. Many of our new allies were themselves former insurgents and had undoubtedly killed American soldiers in the recent past. Occupation is an ugly business. In the bad old days of 2006, whether such a policy had long-term benefits or would portend future national unity was beside the point. What mattered was lowering violence. This breakthrough long preceded the Surge and was not dependent on the thirty thousand extra troops. The tribes didn't turn because of *more troops*—2006 was pre-Surge—and besides, most of these Sunni leaders *hated* and had once attacked Americans.

The tribes in Anbar turned because they saw AQI as the more existential threat. AQI carried all the arrogance and fanatical brutality of extreme fundamentalist Islam into the Sunni heartland of Iraq. They beheaded those suspected of blasphemy, outlawed simple pleasures like smoking, and forced marriages between village women and AQI fighters. Most of the Anbar tribesmen didn't wish to live under a new "Islamic State of Iraq," as AQI dubbed the occupied region. This was not the sort of Iraqi society they were used to or the brand of social control most desired. Furthermore, the tribal shift against AQI and temporary alliance with U.S. forces were *not* indicators of Sunnis' acceptance of the new Iraqi government's legitimacy. Far from it. Rather, the Sunni "Awakening"—as it was called—represented an expedient; a short-term solution to the immediate threat posed by AQI. Widespread American misinterpretations of the Awakening and a misunderstanding of Sunni motives are now being played out, as violence once again significantly increases across Iraq. Here we go again: with many men once on our "Awakening payroll" joining ISIS—the latest manifestation of power vacuum extremism—and presumably threatening the United States. It's an inherently American, and tragic, story.

Third, the most violent and effective Shia militia, Moktada Al-Sadr's Mahdi Army, called a unilateral ceasefire in August of 2007. Internal strife, factionalism, and loss of central control had contributed to decreased effectiveness among the Mahdi Army for several months. It is hard to overestimate the importance of this self-imposed armistice. Sadr's units were responsible for the great majority of EFP attacks on American convoys. These were the deadliest and least avoidable weapons in the vast insurgent arsenal and struck absolute terror in the hearts of U.S. soldiers. The addition of Petraeus and his thirty thousand troops had only limited influence on the Mahdi Army ceasefire, which served as a reorganizational tool for Sadr rather than a sign of surrender. The pressure of additional "boots on the ground" undoubtedly played some role in convincing Sadr to lay low, but it was neither the primary reason nor a long-term solution.

At the time I didn't care what the reasons were. I knew that a Mahdi Army EFP had killed Fuller and Balsley, crippled Ducks, and wounded SGT Rittel, and might kill or maim the rest of us. I just hoped, even prayed, that the ceasefire would hold. For the most part it did. Petraeus took credit for the statistical drop in attacks, so did President Bush, congressional Republicans, and the anchors at Fox News. The Democrats were conflicted by these positive trends. Relieved that fewer of our troops were dying, sure, but also troubled by the potential political blowback and worried about the 2008 election. As for the soldiers—we just breathed a sigh of relief.

Finally, and this is pure speculation, I think many Iraqis—on both sides of the sectarian divide—simply got tired of the violence. Collectively, they inched up to the abyss throughout 2006, reached the edge in early 2007, peered over, and took a step back. This is hard to prove, being as it is unquestionably a form of psychoanalysis. But I walked the streets of Salman Pak and Baghdad that whole year. I spoke to thousands of Iraqis, on the road, in the market, and in their homes, often over countless cups of tea. Imperfect as my observations inevitably were, I felt—as did many of my fellow junior officers—that we got the pulse of the people. The war exhausted them. Many lost the stomach for a fight they might have believed in months earlier.

Civil wars, especially in densely packed settings, tend to degenerate into a cycle of revenge and retaliation. Things spiral out of control. The sheer horror of the violence sank to depths lower than anyone imagined. Most Iraqis were repulsed. In 2007, they paused. Little had been settled, but few had the stomach for war as it had been waged for the last year. Those whom it suited to do so (the aforementioned generals, politicians, and pundits, particularly on the right) chose to interpret this as success. Violence was down, after all, and some semblance of normalcy had reappeared. No one sought complex explanations. Why bother? Ask too many questions and you might find answers that don't support the approved narrative. But I knew it then. The Surge narrative was a sham. The tragedy was that no one realized this soon enough to prevent its application in Afghanistan just a few years later. Such is life.

This too must be said: from the moment the Bush administration decided to do it, from the very onset, it was *going to be* declared a success. Make no mistake, no matter what occurred, no matter why, and regardless of the actual reasons—interested parties in politics, the army leadership, and the media had already *decided* to declare "victory" and move on. Many stakeholders were invested in the Surge project. Republican lawmakers, conservative pundits, and dedicated military professionals all needed a win and couldn't tolerate defeat. In one sense, the Surge *was* a decisive triumph—a public relations coup of the first order. The historian in me can't help but conjure images of George W. Bush—"Mission Accomplished!"—or Richard Nixon—"Peace with Honor"—and wonder when, exactly, did the

United States last *win* a war? Sure, we've rebranded a few draws as wins and losses as draws, but I mean a *real*, decisive, meaningful victory.

All that being said, it wasn't Senator Graham's misunderstanding of the "Surge myth" that really upset me. Rather it was his unapologetic obtuseness—his total omission of the Iraqi people from his prevailing narrative. Graham decried Obama's retreat from responsible foreign engagement in Syria and Iraq. He feared that we would "lose everything we gained in Iraq." Utterly absent from his speech were the Iraqis themselves. The people I knew and loved. The families trying to survive and cohere in a world of death and terror. The children who never knew any other life. The women who once lived in a secular state and now covered their faces for fear of abuse, or worse in the case of ISIS: murder. No, they didn't count to Graham. What did *they* gain? What exactly did America *win* in Iraq?

I was angry as I watched the Senator slam the current president. I screamed at my television set. I wanted to say so much and wished *I* was a senator so I could debate this self-important man and call him on his bullshit. What would I say? How would I explain the reality of "what we gained" in Iraq?'

Then I thought back to early 2007, in the southeast Baghdad neighborhood of Al Amin. A predominantly Shia neighborhood, Amin had one large outdoor market where most of the people bought nearly all their necessities. Such was the model in many Baghdad districts. The majority of people lived just around the poverty line and rarely left their own neighborhoods. Once upon a time, a family might walk to the market together and buy food, drinks, and a few trinkets before strolling back home. Not so in 2006 and 2007. A series of deadly car bombs devastated the market and killed dozens of men, women, and children. On 12 December 2006—70 killed; 27 January 2007—15 killed, 55 wounded; 7 February—60 killed, 131 wounded.[5] This was just one market, in one neighborhood, in one three-month period.

The pattern repeated itself across the city. Shia-dominated public gathering places were attacked by Sunni insurgents, day in and day out. Thousands died, many more had their bodies maimed and broken. The violence and fear affected everyone. One family I met devised a solution to the problem. They set up a rotation and sent one of their young daughters to the market with a list of goods to purchase each week. The girl would run through the shops, grab all she could, and hurry home. The family had only one son. He was precious and never sent. Nor could the mother go. Her husband was dead and she was the only thing standing between the children and destitution. This woman made a choice, one that would be unthinkable for an American mother. Her daughters, while not expendable, were made available for the necessary and dangerous chore of providing sustenance for the family.

This is what our invasion wrought. We must never forget that. A mother—all that her children have in this world—who must choose which of her children to send out to the market. A place of recurring death and devastation. Right or wrong, intentionally or not, Americans brought more than democracy in 2003. We brought chaos. We unleashed forces beyond our control. By 2007, Iraq had been transformed into a Hobbesian universe in which cars exploded and mothers chose which child's life to risk. Senator Graham seems to have missed that. So do most Americans when they reflect on the invasion and occupation of Iraq. Perhaps if they met that woman or watched a young child hurry through a crowded market, they could begin to understand. Better yet, if they breathed in the sights, sounds, and scents in the aftermath of a car bomb—as many of us did— perhaps then they might take a moment to consider the Iraqis. After all, it was their country. It still is.

So, who won the Iraq War? That's simple—Iran. The increasingly authoritarian government of Nouri al-Maliki unapologetically allied itself with Iran and Syria. The new regime is flagrantly sectarian, its government, army, and intelligence services dominated by Shia Muslims. Even after Maliki finally stepped down, under pressure, in summer 2014, Iraq's government remained Shia-dominated. In fact, Iraq itself became little more than a geographic fantasy—alive on the map, all but dead in reality. Iran remains the strongman in the region, no longer balanced by countervailing Iraqi Arab power.

So let us reflect once more on "our hard won gains." The statistics are contradictory and imperfect. They are a battleground unto themselves. Human Rights Watch and the Defense Department will never agree on the casualty figures. They never do. Some love stats, others hate them, but to understand what the American invasion caused, and what it cost, you need to consider the numbers. Forget the money spent—estimates fall in the $1 to 2 trillion range (such is life)—but what was the human cost? It meant 4,486 American soldiers killed;[6] 32,223 American soldiers wounded in action; 797 amputees; hundreds suffered a major genital wound.[7] More than 10,000 veterans live with the varied results of penetrating head wounds and brain injuries. Modern medicine has kept thousands of those soldiers alive who would certainly have perished in past wars. Unfortunately, the science to cure cognitive deficiencies hasn't kept pace. Then there are the countless invisible wounds of war.[8] Some 235 troops killed themselves in Iraq.[9] Thousands more did so upon their return. And, as the U.S. Army enters Iraq once more (third time's the charm?), one must assume we'll only add to those casualty counts.

There is no agreement on the number of Iraqi civilian deaths. But here's a range and you can pick your poison. The Iraq Body Count Project—an independent U.S./U.K. joint group—estimates more than 120,000 dead.[10] The Costs of War Project estimates 134,000 civilian deaths.[11] The latest report by the Iraqi Ministry of Health supported by university researchers in the United States and UK counted 500,000 violent or avoidable deaths from war-related causes. Some were killed by errant American bombs, others by stray insurgent bullets, and most in sectarian murders. All were tragic. These were the war's real victims.

The number of Iraqi refugees is so staggering as to be difficult to enumerate. As early as mid-2007, a UN high commissioner report estimated that 2.2 million people had fled to neighboring countries. Another 2 million were internally displaced, living in a variety of conditions.[12] These were some of the people who inhabited my squatter zone in southeast Baghdad. So, upward of 4 million people were uprooted. Of the external refugees, the vast majority went to Jordan and Syria, where many remain to this day. More than 18,000 fled to Sweden. At the height of the civil war, in mid-2007, only around 700 were allowed into the United States.[13] In the initial run-up to invasion, Colin Powell supposedly warned President Bush about the consequences of war: "You break it, you own it," he cautioned. Maybe he was wrong. When Iraq was most broken, we took shamefully little responsibility for its refugees. Iraq's neighbors bore the brunt of it. The lucky ones got to Europe. At least Sweden had universal health care.

The war never really stopped. The Surge didn't create a democratic Mesopotamian paradise. The last U.S. troops left in December 2011. Some 4,584 civilians died a violent death in 2012. That number doubled in 2013,[14] and the trend continued in 2014. Listen to "Surge-as-savior" enthusiasts like Lindsey Graham long enough and you might believe we "won" in Iraq. That if we had just stayed longer the violence would have stopped. Unfortunately, the evidence just doesn't support that. Not the numbers. Not my memories. Prevailing perceptions about the Surge are dangerous for America's political and cultural health. Forgotten are the deceitful lies and omissions that led to an ill-advised foreign invasion. Sure, say the Surge enthusiasts, we made some mistakes and were unprepared for occupation and counterinsurgency—but we *fixed* all that. Enlightened generals and a sturdy president refused to quit, and American troops snatched victory from the jaws of defeat.

All this talk of "what-ifs" and lost Surge opportunities ignores one salient, if uncomfortable, fact: ISIS is an outgrowth of our *own invasion*. Operation Iraqi Freedom (OIF—as we gleefully named it) was more than just an awful euphemism; it spelled catastrophe—and chaos—for most Iraqis. American military force toppled Saddam's JV-squad of an army, to be sure, but destabilized an entire region and unleashed deadly pandemonium among the very people we sought to "save." OIF was akin to Doctor Frankenstein's monster. ISIS represents only the latest outgrowth of nihilism among disaffected Sunnis in a region plagued by civil war for more than a decade. The young men of ISIS, mostly Iraqis and Syrians mind you, grew up in this maelstrom. They fill the voids of unemployment, PTSD, political disaffection, and identity with extremist Islam. Power and status lay at the heart of the movement. Like drug kingpins in the United States or countless other insurgent groups in the region, ISIS demonstrates what happens when you continually cut the head off a snake. Killing a movement's leaders rarely solves the problem or changes hearts. Violence begets violence. Eliminate one set of killers and the next generation becomes even *more* radical.

Here's another thing, a concept Americans had better start getting used to: it's not always about *us*. This problem is bigger than Obama, the December 2010 elections, or the 2007 Surge. The tragedy doesn't belong to Lindsey Graham or other likeminded political hawks nestled safely in Washington. The real tragedy is an Iraqi one— millions of human beings living the horror, redux. They lost a dictator, but gained what exactly? Twelve plus years of ongoing terror, rapidly spiraling out of control.

So much controversy surrounds what may ultimately be an inconsequential debate: Did the Surge "work?" Could the military adapt quickly enough to pivot midwar and adjust to counterinsurgency tactics? Was General Petraeus a more effective leader than his predecessors? I'd answer these in the following sequence: (1) Sort of, but only in the extreme short-term sense. (2) Yes, eventually. (3) Maybe. Nonetheless, we might be asking all the wrong questions. Tactics, operations, even transient military commanders are no substitute for sound national strategy. Far more relevant are four crucial inquiries: Was committing the totality of America's ground forces to Iraq ever in our national interest? Did more than eight years of occupation establish a safer, more stable, or tolerant atmosphere for the Iraqi people? Is the current state of Iraq a reliable ally—in other words, did the United States *gain* anything from the invasion? Finally, how well suited was our highly touted all-volunteer military to prolonged conflict, and what are the *moral* implications for a democracy that relies on 1 percent of its citizens to fight a decade-long war? Those answers are far less positive. And here is the tragic part—one hears precious little discussion of *these* questions. Not on the twenty-four-hour news cycle, in Congress, from our presidents, or among private citizens. We ignore such questions at our peril.

Read the memoirs of the administration's architects of invasion or, for that matter, of Bush himself. The Surge, they imply, *vindicates* their reckless decisions in formulating invasion and utter incompetence directing the occupation. And so, I fear we'll learn all the wrong lessons from the Iraq War. In place of a cautionary reminder to blaze balanced, judicious paths in international affairs, Iraq might instead encourage risky, ideological policies. Secure in the knowledge that America's military legions can do *anything*, and unimpeded by an apathetic citizenry, the next generation of Cheneys, Wolfowitzs, and Rumsfelds won't hesitate to do their worst. Why would they? Grounded in false historical assumptions of a Surge analogy, they'll rest easy in a new American confidence. In place of sound strategy we'll substitute our army as a safety net.

# 13

## Staggering to the Finish Line
### Aftermath in a Shattered Platoon

The romantic, spendthrift moral act is ultimately the practical one.
The practical, expedient, cozy-dog move is the one that comes to grief.
Yes, remember that. If it comes to a choice between being a good soldier
and a good human being, try to be a good human being.
— ANTON MYRER, *Once an Eagle*

The day after the memorial ceremony, Sergeant Keenan—one of Fuller's closest friends, and a scout in 3rd platoon—approached me outside the barracks. I'd been sitting alone on a stack of sandbags smoking a cigarette. Keenan handed me a crumpled piece of loose-leaf paper with some scribbled notes. "Hey, Sir, I know you loved Fuller, and I thought you might like to have this. It's one of the rap songs he wrote. I'm not sure if you knew about that. Ya know, Fuller always kinda played down his thug-side to you." I thanked Keenan and he turned to leave. Looking down at the paper, I read the lyrics to myself: "Yo, I'm 19-D [army nomenclature for cavalry scout], till the day that I die!" Turned out he was a pretty good writer. Not very educated, kind of a limited vocabulary, but a certain flow and a way with words that actually worked. Mostly, though, my mind was fixated on what Keenan had said—how Fuller kind of hid his thug-side from me. Well, he hadn't done a very good job; I mean, he told plenty of stories and wore his heart on his sleeve. But still. The fact that he'd even think to try bespoke the nature of our relationship, and as I sat in the sweltering heat lighting another smoke, I couldn't shake my discomfort.

You see, I liked to believe Fuller and me were tight—tighter than tight. In a way, we were. More so than most other LTs and their troops and way more than traditional regulations would deem appropriate. Much as Fuller's identity straddled the line between soldier and "thug," my own self-image depended on a balance between officer and New York street kid. Look, we all have ideas about ourselves, stories we live out in our heads, and that just happened to be mine. Hearing that Fuller might have kept even a slight distance bothered me on some level. Looking back, though, I get it. In many ways I *was* different from the other officers. On the other hand, those guys, the other lieutenants, *were* my friends. I drank, partied, and spent most of my time among peers. Fuller and all the soldiers would inevitably have known that. The LTs, by the way, were a great group of dudes, by and large. That said, we officers inhabited a completely different universe than our soldiers.

It wasn't even the rank or pay. Rather it was about life's prospects. Most of the LTs I served with saw the army as a very temporary thing. They'd sit around and talk loudly—sometimes in front of their soldiers—about things like investments, stocks, and what kind of jobs they planned to get once they left the service. Corporate headhunters did indeed seek out young former military officers—especially West Pointers—for good-paying middle management positions. We all knew that a solid career awaited us on the outside. All we had to do was take it. Not so for most of the young troopers. A scarce few completed any college, some had only a GED, and for many the army wasn't just some fleeting expedient but rather a chance to *make something* of themselves. How must those officers have sounded to the young troopers within earshot? Like a bunch of smug, entitled pricks—that's how. The gap between us would always be there. Perhaps it always was. Our paths were just too distinct.

I didn't have long to reflect on these sorts of things back then. My platoon faced a dire situation. In just three months we'd lost six soldiers killed or wounded. Casualties in Iraq are, of course, lower than those in Vietnam or World War II, but the situations were also different. Far fewer troops were stationed in Iraq. At its peak we had about 160,000 soldiers in the Iraq War, versus more than 530,000 at the height of Vietnam. In Iraq, moreover, the same units and the same guys kept going back for tour after tour. Consider the case of West Point graduates. As of late 2013, ninety-four academy grads had died in Iraq or Afghanistan. That constitutes 1.8 percent of total war deaths—the highest rate of any war in U.S. history with the lone exception of the

Mexican-American War. The stats are rather startling: the West Point death rate was three times Vietnam, eleven times World War II, and forty-two times the Civil War.[1] Why? Well, for starters West Pointers are a higher percentage of the officer corps these days, but more significantly, a smaller group of professional soldiers *in general* are bearing the burden of these wars. Without the swell of draftees to fill out the ranks, the same soldiers—professional enlistees—deployed again and again. An all-volunteer military is a double-edged sword.

You also need to remember how few soldiers, even the deployed ones, are actually on the *line* and in danger. It takes many, many support troops to field one combat soldier. This isn't new, but rather highlights the disproportionate effects of casualties on a relatively small number of combat elements. Platoons in both Afghanistan and Iraq are rather easily rendered combat ineffective. To review where we were at that point: starting with an authorized strength of me plus eighteen soldiers, we had lost DJ, Faulkner, Ducks, Fuller, Balsley, and Rittel. That took us down to twelve. Take away two more on leave and you've got ten. Division policy required a minimum of four vehicles and twelve soldiers to leave the FOB. Do the math—we couldn't even patrol!

To make up the losses, squadron hooked me up with a couple clerks and a staff specialist—none with any combat experience—and sent us out the gate forty-eight hours after the incident. The army rolls along—it's what we do. Sure, the platoon now had the minimum 4/12 configuration, but that ignored the emotional toll. My guys were broke. I overheard their conversations. They felt hopeless and vulnerable. Most didn't understand what we were trying to accomplish, or see a credible defense against the EFPs. They weren't all wrong, either. It was my job, however, to get them out the gate and on patrol. A better soldier, a stronger leader, might have blazed a better path, a tougher one. But I did what I felt was right, and what I was capable of. I knew the boys would follow our sturdy senior scout, SSG South— and he was wavering at best. We had some history, rather close for an LT/sergeant combo, so I gathered myself and walked up to his barracks room. I knocked, he answered, and I told him the new plan.

It was 28 January 2007, and the war was essentially over for me. So we did as South and I planned—the bare minimum on our patrols. I hid us out in safe areas, survived, and tried to protect my guys. For the next few weeks my crew took the lead truck. Traditionally, the LT rolls in the second vehicle and the senior scout takes point, but everything was changed. Everyone knew the first truck was in by far the most danger—especially in the EFP country of east Baghdad. Taking point was my best—and perhaps only—chance of getting those boys out the gate while maintaining their trust and respect. Promises to do everything in my power to avoid dangerous areas for a while, combined with Damian's support, won them over. We headed back out on patrol that day, and every one for the next year.

Those were rough times. All of February I was sure I'd be killed or severely maimed. I lived on cigarettes and high doses of caffeine. In the middle of patrols I'd catch my mind wandering, imagining my life as an amputee or picturing loved ones at my funeral. Who would come? What would they say? I liked to think my old friends would have all kinds of profound, heartfelt things to say about me. Old flames might wax nostalgic about the kind of man I'd have been. Family and friends alike could remember me as perhaps I'd always wanted to be: young, handsome (I hoped), and fun. You get by any way you can, I guess. Back on the FOB, these were also angry times. I read voraciously—history, politics, and current affairs—more than seventy books in a year. I'd obsessively, almost furiously, digest works that appealed to my prevailing attitude. I became—and I suppose, remain—politically quite left-wing, and doubted the very efficacy of force in U.S. foreign policy. Even a certain strand of poetry appealed to me, mostly the British antiwar poets of World War I. I read everything I could find by that holy trinity—Wilfred Owen, Siegfried Sassoon, and Robert Graves. Anger, resentment, and immaturity fueled some of my outbursts. Loud debates over war policy in the dining facility, refusing to keep my hair short or wash my hat, and posting quotes all over my walls were just a few ways to act out. On my locker I posted the poem "Base Details," by Siegfried Sassoon.

> If I were fierce, and bald, and short of breath,
> I'd live with scarlet Majors at the Base,
> And speed glum heroes up the line to death.
> You'd see me with my puffy petulant face,
> Guzzling and gulping in the best hotel,

Reading the Roll of Honour. "Poor young chap,"
I'd say—"I used to know his father well.
Yes, we've lost heavily in this last scrap."
And when the war is done and youth stone dead,
I'd toddle safely home and die—in bed.[2]

The truth is, I actually liked and generally respected *our* squadron's majors, but for me the poem attacked those who sent us to Iraq—the ideologues in the Bush administration, the senior officers who needed a combat command for promotion, and the American people, who didn't give two shits either way.

For a few weeks—at least when it was possible—I'd largely ignore the daily mission and "circle the wagons." We'd drive to a safe area, like the squatter zone—hand out humanitarian aid, kill a few hours, and build up the boys' confidence. I don't know if it was right or wrong, but it felt appropriate at the time. The boys needed it, and I didn't believe we could make a difference anyway. At least, not in a military sense. And I guess I was scared too, just like my guys. But unlike them, I could do something about it—and I did. I have no regrets.

The night of our first patrol after the attack, I thought back to Scripture, and in truth, to a favorite scene from *The Crying Game*: "When I was a child, I spoke as a child, I understood as a child, I thought as a child: but when I became a man, I put away childish things."[3]

I'd been to war, seen death, and suffered loss, but I was not a man. Not in any real sense. The great lie—war makes men out of boys. Horseshit. The truth is, I no longer cared much for conventions, nor was I much of a soldier. And I never could put away childish things. Still can't.

## YOUTH, INTERRUPTED

Living, naturally, is never easy. You continue making the gestures commanded by existence for many reasons, the first of which is habit. Dying voluntarily implies that you have recognized, even instinctively, the ridiculous character of that habit . . . the uselessness of suffering.
— ALBERT CAMUS[4]

Trooper James Smith was nothing if not impulsive. It's what we loved *and* hated about him. People with their shit together—you know, the ones who don't swear, never miss a day of church, and always act polite—have never appealed to me. To steal from Kerouac, "The only people for me are the mad ones, the ones who are mad to live, mad to talk, mad to be saved, desirous of everything at the same time, the ones who never yawn or say a commonplace thing."[5] That was Smith, all right: wild, excitable, and genuinely *alive*. I loved him. Smith and I were both scheduled to take our two weeks' leave in early June. In the months before, he'd met a girl on the Internet, and a few of the fellas warned me that Smith was thinking of marrying her over leave. I still thought you ought to meet a person face to face before committing to matrimony. Then again, life hasn't taught me too much for sure, but I know this—love is a mystery. And judge not, lest you be judged.

Some of the other guys knew Smith's penchant for rash decisions and told Damian and me of his plans. We decided to approach him. That's one of the things that makes the army so different from other jobs. Try to imagine a boss at Verizon or Walmart taking such an active role in an employee's personal life, or giving unsolicited romantic advice. It would never happen, but for us—business as usual. We cornered him on the stairs of the barracks and tried to talk him out of it. We used all the usual rational arguments against a hasty marriage: divorce rates, other fish in the sea, youth, finances, inexperience, the benefit of patience, and so forth. I'm not sure we got through to him. He had that "Smith-look"—a little smirk and eyes looking right past you—on his face the whole time. Best we could get was a promise that he'd think about it. In the end, twenty years old or not, he was a grown man—and would do whatever he wanted. He was in love, and that shit is more powerful than the word of any sergeant or lieutenant; probably stronger than God himself.

James met Rachel online through a mutual friend that January. He spied on her Myspace page and finally worked up the courage to send her a message. He decided to go big: "I just have say, you're the most beautiful girl I've ever seen." It was on. From that day forward, they spent every free minute talking over Yahoo messenger, the phone, and video chats. Rachel flipped her whole life to talk with him, forgoing sleep and staying up all night. The eight-hour time difference was a bitch. They fell fast, and quickly became each other's everything.

Rachel was drawn—as we all were—to his big personality and bigger heart. James, well, he had someone to talk endlessly to and share his thoughts with. They were young, in love, and impatient. It happens. He worked with the fax machine at headquarters and sent her a power of attorney in March; this way she could move to Colorado Springs and set up an apartment for them. They hadn't met in person, but Rachel and James started planning a life together.

Meanwhile, James was living another life in Baghdad—a city and a mission seemingly coming apart at the seams. He stayed in touch with a few people from home, but he shared almost nothing of the war with anyone but Rachel and his sister, Candace. He'd call and video chat with his parents, but he mostly kept it light, talked about the food, and asked for comfort items in their next care package. Nonetheless, David and Susan Smith kept their oven clock on Baghdad-time, always ready for a call or instant message. He stayed in contact with Sara—his old high school friend—but typically they talked about boys and her life at college.

With Rachel, though, he'd discuss the war a bit. During one video chat, James pulled a bottle cap from his pocket and showed it to her. He said that little cap was the one thing that kept him safe. On 24 January, during a routine mission, we'd stopped by a small Baghdad shop and while I talked to the owner, Fuller and Smith each bought a Coke. Fuller handed his cap to Smith and said, "Keep this bro. If anything ever happens to me, I'll watch over you." Alex Fuller was killed the next day. James's hard exterior collapsed as he related this story to Rachel. He'd also been losing faith in the mission and getting frustrated with the war. Many of us were. Mostly, he just couldn't wait until leave so he could finally *touch* his future wife. Rachel never wanted to get off the phone, but we patrolled our asses off that spring, so James would need to get a couple hours' sleep. "I'll tell you what," he'd say. "Let's meet up in our dreams—I'll be waiting under an apple tree." Deal.

James flew into Dallas on 28 May and drove to Houston, where he finally met and got to kiss Rachel. The next few days were busy. James met her parents and attended her brother's graduation party, then they drove up to visit with the Smiths in Hurst, Texas. The couple sat in his childhood bedroom and watched his old high school wrestling videos. It was as if they had to fit in years worth of courtship into just two weeks of leave. After a night in Hurst, they drove out to Lubbock, Texas, to pick up some of James's paperwork from the courthouse and finally put that old reckless driving arrest to bed. As they walked down the street, James pointed to the Justice of the Peace building and said, "Hey, you wanna get married?" And so they did.

James also spoke with his sister Candace over Skype and Yahoo messenger. She was still his rock and the best listener in his life. James's new nephew, Blake, was born that December, and he met his uncle over video chat. Sadey would also jump in front of the screen to see her favorite soldier. When the kids were in bed, James would share details of the platoon's missions and losses with his sister. He told her about Alex Fuller's death and how gruesome the scene was that night. Candace could sense small changes in James. He seemed jaded and cold compared with his predeployment self, but mostly he tried to hide it by acting like the outgoing, fun-loving guy everyone expected. Other people might have been fooled, but not Candace.

▰▰▰ I got the call early in the morning of 7 June 2007. Roused from my sleep in the Fort Wadsworth Navy Hotel on Staten Island, I saw the strange digits of the incoming call, picked up, and immediately heard the voice of BJ Laney—a fellow platoon leader and a close friend. "Look, Danny, I don't know how to tell you this—but Smith's dead. He killed himself." Silence. What the fuck was I supposed to say to that? It felt like I'd been worked over by a whiffle ball bat. I had to sit down. The details were sketchy: something about a fight, closet, belt, and a hanging. I thanked BJ for the call and crawled back into bed. Numbness set in. In an effort to feel *something*, I lay there and tried to make myself cry but couldn't. There would come a time for that, I suppose.

No one will ever know why it happened, not really anyway. After the Lubbock ceremony, James and Rachel had headed north to their apartment in Colorado Springs. The next few days, they mostly spent every waking minute talking and in each other's arms. Every morning he got up early, walked the dog, and picked a few flowers from a neighbor's garden. Then he'd wake her with a bouquet in hand. It began the same way on 6 June, with one difference: after his morning walk, James insisted she take his bottle cap. When she refused, insisting that it was *his* good luck charm, he said, "You don't have to worry about me anymore."

That night, some friends were heading to a local bar and Rachel convinced James to go. It started well with lots of laughs and a bit of dancing. Everyone drank too much, but that wasn't abnormal. James was hitting the double Jack and Cokes hard—same as always. As they sometimes do, things quickly fell apart. Some guy, a friend, was about to leave the bar and Rachel gave him a farewell hug and kiss on the cheek. Then she headed off to the bathroom. When she came back, James was gone. The remainder of the group told her what had happened. James had seen the good-bye hug and freaked out. He closed his tab, left his wedding ring on top of the bar, and stormed out with a few friends. Rachel called him and he was hysterical, upset that she'd kissed the other guy's cheek; he was drunk and crying.

Rachel drove home, and James walked around outside with friends for a while longer. She must have fallen asleep, because when she awoke James was standing over her, swaying from side to side. Rachel tried to get him to come to bed and told him she loved him, but he walked into the bathroom and she fell back to sleep. She awoke to the sound of the dog crying. Rachel got up, walked through the bathroom, turned the corner to the closet, and saw him there. James was hanging by his own belt. She did what she could—cut him down, called 911, and attempted CPR. But he was gone.

The next few days were a blur. David and Susan got the call at 6:30 a.m. and flew to Colorado immediately. Their grief was unimaginable. It is hard to fathom. The truth is often more tragic than fiction, and the flight to Colorado proved it. Flying out of Dallas was convenient, but awful. Dallas/Fort Worth Airport just happens to be one of two hubs for deployed military personnel returning for leave. As he walked through the terminal, while on the phone discussing identifiable tattoos on his dead son's body, David had to watch a few *hundred* young soldiers walk by. From behind, some blond troopers could so easily have been his James.

Rachel had met the Smiths twice before but felt a little like an outsider. I suppose that was inevitable. She was young, brand new to the family, and hadn't shared as much of James's life as his friends and relatives. The rumors started right away. One of James's army buddies called her the next day and said he'd heard James found her in bed with some other guy. Back home in Texas, Rachel could see people staring and whispering as she walked by. Some of James's close friends even said it to her face: "Look, we've just got to say it—we blame *you!*" Initially, only James's old friend Sara and his mother Susan were kind to her. When Sara heard the news, she'd collapsed. Somehow, though, she found the strength to talk with Rachel on the phone—for *hours*—in the days between James's death and funeral.

His sister, Candace, missed about nineteen calls on her cell phone the morning of James's death. She was at the gym and didn't check the phone until she finished. Every call was from her father. When she called back, David Smith told her that James was dead and then immediately broke down. Candace had never heard her father cry like that. She collapsed, started hyperventilating, and must have re-peated "Oh my God," a few hundred times. Candace decided not to fly with her parents up to Colorado. Her son, Blake, was still an infant, and she couldn't leave him for an indefinite trip. The decision was a tough one. When James's body was returned to Texas, Candace had a private viewing. Seeing his hair—he'd dyed it brown over leave—she refused to be believe it was her brother. The funeral was rough. They had a small affair, with only David, Susan, Candace, and Rachel's im-mediate family in attendance. When the ceremonies ended, it was all final. James was really gone; a new wife, loving sister, and an en-tire family were devastated. The ripples of the death spread wide and lasted years. For some—they still remain.

The afternoon of 7 June, my family was heading down to the Jersey Shore, and I went along. As much maligned as the place is (some-times deservedly so) the "Shore" was the setting for all my childhood vacations—a working-class Riviera, if you will. Besides, if you ignore the growing array of fools popularized on the recent MTV reality show *Jersey Shore*, you can have one hell of a good time. Smith's death lin-gered over me all day. I tried hard to keep my game face on and get excited for the upcoming family party, but it was a hard sell the whole drive down. It took—as it often does for people—plentiful alcohol to get me over the hump. I checked into the hotel, changed into my John Mellencamp concert T-shirt—party attire—and headed down to meet my cousins at the Point Pleasant Tiki Bar.

After a couple of strong beverages, I attempted a toast. It was a struggle to explain Smith to friends and family possessed of little understanding about the army or the war. He was my driver, sure, but he was also my friend, my soldier, and teammate. I tried to tell everyone how Smith represented all soldiers as far as I was concerned. How his youth, energy, courage, insecurities, and loyalty were symbolic of a whole *generation* of volunteer soldiers serving in Iraq during this age of increasing divergence between our society and its military. The blank faces told the story. They meant well, and understood I was sad, but it didn't sink in. This might have been the first realization of how inadequate my words would be whenever I tried to explain the war, my perceptions of it, and the connections I saw everywhere between Iraq, our country, and American culture. It's still a problem. We stayed at the Tiki Bar, I got drunk, the band played Springsteen, and everything was all right. At least for one night.

▇▇▇▇▇ The army's got itself a suicide problem. The stats are startling. Here's what happens though: the military is an outcomes-based bureaucracy. It thrives on action, numbers, judgments, and performance. If one of your soldiers gets a DUI—that's a black eye for the unit. Just the same, if one of your boys kills himself—that's on you too. Why didn't you see the warning signs—the risk factors—the senior officers not so subtly imply. The blame game is nauseating. Experience in the army has taught me some limited patience, although anyone who worked in my troop HQ in Afghanistan can attest to the fact that I'll still smash a chair or two against the wall now and again. Back in 2007, though, I was far too emotionally invested to handle that shit. I loved Smith—he was my guy—and for anyone above my level to imply we were somehow to *blame* for his death was infuriating.

Looking back, though, it's striking how many textbook risk factors were there—*if* you were looking for them, that is. Whether these dots only connect because *of* hindsight, I do not know, but some of it seems apparent now. Smith was full of energy. An adrenaline junky and brave to a fault. He needed approval for sure, and possessed all the insecurity of a normal twenty-year-old. Impulsivity was at his core, and I'm reminded of his temper tantrum at the football game before the war. He drank a good deal. Jack, beer, you name it. Sometimes I've thought back on all this and started to question myself, even assign some blame. But I know this too: almost *none* of what I just described is unique to James Smith. He was a young, single, male soldier. He drank a bit, partied hard, and ran full speed all the time. I bet there are a lot of frat-boys at the University of Wherever acting the exact same way right now. The whole blame concept is pure nonsense, the kind of farce brought on when a large bureaucracy is utterly baffled by a complicated problem. And suicide is perhaps the most complex human question of all.

Back then, and even today, there's one thing I am sure of: Smith was a casualty of the Iraq War. The Tragedy Assistance Program for Survivors (TAPS) teaches the term "killed *by* action," as opposed to killed *in* action, for self-inflicted deaths, and I'm a believer in the sentiment. Not everyone agreed. The unit held a memorial ceremony, of course, but his picture was not posted in the squadron headquarters along with the soldiers killed in action, and because he died while on leave, his name is not listed on the online database: icasualties.org. At the time, this caused such irritation that the slightest hint of the topic would throw me into a rage. Smith was a casualty of the war; it killed him as much as it did anyone else. I know this too: he watched his friends die, and he knew we still had a long way to go in an increasingly dreadful tour.

James longed for a connection and for love. He was the kind of guy I had known to put *everything* into whatever he was interested in. The war was deeply troubling for him, but he didn't let most of us know that. Then one night he drank a ton, got jealous over his new wife, and lost control. Too young to process it and unable to see all that was ahead of him, maybe he just couldn't check his impulsiveness. Or maybe it was an accident—a cry for attention and help—and he lost control of the situation before anyone could help. We'd all known Smith to live in the moment. The future was abstract. Life was too real in the here and now—death and love were all around him—and when things fell apart, they fell apart hard. Maybe he couldn't see any way out, and none of us—not me, or Damian, or his buddies in

2nd platoon—were there to show him how wrong he was. Maybe—or perhaps that's just my way of rationalizing, explaining as much for myself as for you. Be that as it may, I do know he died in the Iraq War. Sure, Jack Daniels and heartache played a role, but we'd known him to drink lots of Jack and chase plenty of girls before. He did what he did while on leave from Iraq. That much was no coincidence.

Something else must be said—Smith died a proud Texan, representative of a state that has suffered extensively in this war. Some 420 Texans have died in Iraq, and 2,810 have been wounded.[6] That's nearly *10 percent* of all U.S. deaths. Smith wasn't included in that count, so I'll do the honors: 420 + 1 = 421. James Smith was brave, energetic, fun, impulsive, and *alive*. The very same things that made him a little wild and reckless contributed directly to his courage under fire and fierce loyalty. The men and women who serve, the ones that fight on America's behalf, often reflect this very same tension. We ought to be glad the nation produces such characters, even if the results for the soldiers *themselves* are frequently tragic.

James was not the only self-inflicted casualty of the Iraq War. Since 2001, more than twenty-seven hundred service members have killed themselves. That's more than the total number of deaths from combat in Afghanistan. Some other statistics should come as little surprise. A recent Pentagon report found that half of the troops who killed themselves in 2011 had experienced the failure of an intimate relationship. I'm no expert, but I think it often has to do with unmet expectations. War is the worst—the death, fear, privation, isolation, and loss. We tell ourselves, month after month, that once we get home, everything is going be *perfect*. Amazing fun, mind-blowing sex, and fulfilling relationships. You see, everything's got to be as epic at *home* as it was in Iraq—and then it's not. That kind of disappointment is hard to swallow, and many of us aren't as equipped for the fight as we like to tell ourselves.

In response to the epidemic, the Pentagon has commissioned numerous reports and invested tens of millions of dollars in research and prevention programs. A four-star general took the lead and began having every single division commander (controlling ten to fifteen thousand troops each) brief him personally on the details surrounding *every single* suicide in their units. Somehow, it was hoped, the attention and focus would slow the suicide rate. It didn't. Suicide among active-duty troops rose steadily, hitting a record 350 in 2012—twice as many as a decade before and surpassing the number of American troops killed in Afghanistan that year.[7] Things are worse than they seem. Consider the broader population of past servicemen. Some twenty-two veterans commit suicide daily, a huge increase over the last several years. The recent spike is explained not by elderly Vietnam veterans but by the alarming number of young Iraq and Afghanistan vets taking their own lives.[8]

Troop commanders—as I can recently attest—and a slew of mental health professionals now teach an array of suicide awareness classes to our soldiers. Training is regular and it is mandatory. The effort, itself, is commendable. But, of course, it's typical bureaucracy—trying to explain the unexplainable, attempting to control the uncontrollable. Classes tell us one thing, but reality teaches another. Here's one: send some kids to war, then release them into a society utterly disconnected from the conflict, and trouble will result. Expectations are unmet, disappointment sets in, and hopelessness ensues. Things have reached—as they tend to—their logical extreme. These days, we commanders fill out detailed, quantifiable risk assessments on each and every soldier in the unit. Firearms ownership, past disciplinary incidents, unpaid parking tickets, divorces, youth, riding a motorcycle, and being a PFC can all decrease your score. Classic army: seeking to manipulate and predict everything. Sometime in the next twenty-four hours, when (statistically) the next soldier kills himself, no one is going to see it coming. People are highly complex and in the main—unknowable. That's the reality, and the tragedy.

# 14

## Disappointing Paths
## Iraq, Seven Years On

I still think about Salman Pak. More even than Baghdad. From time to time, I'll Google the city just to see what's happening. I've never fully shaken my sense of responsibility and awe for the place. As in Iraq more generally, the Pak has made some progress yet failed to overcome major structural weaknesses. In March 2007 an entire *brigade*—more than thirty-five hundred soldiers—took over the sector our tiny squadron once held down. The 1-15 Infantry—about seven hundred guys—took over for our troop's three eighteen-man platoons. The new unit's commander summed up the change well: "When you look at it, they [our squadron] really weren't able to do much of anything. They had troops doing what we have battalions doing, and platoons doing what we now have companies doing."[1] We sure as hell *thought* we were doing a lot, and our fight was regularly intense, but his point is well taken. In 2007 someone finally decided Salman Pak was important, so much so that a few thousand soldiers came to town. The move, of course, was temporary. Furthermore, for every Iraqi district loaded with soldiers, another was, by necessity, all but ignored. Fires put out in one spot inevitably crop up elsewhere.

In the meantime, the new battalion literally flooded the area with troops and extended control, slowly but surely, down into the ball sack. They had some legitimate success, using their huge numbers to put checkpoints and combat outposts both in and south of the city. They also convinced a battalion of Georgian troops (that is, troops from the former Soviet Republic) to take over quieter parts of the sector. This allowed 1-15 Infantry to use their main elements in numerous helicopter air assaults to drop soldiers deep behind insurgent lines south of Salman Pak.

The real turning point, however, was the use of Sons of Iraq volunteers from the Sunni Awakening movement to secure outlying areas and clear out the remnants of Al Qaeda. These Sunni militiamen were paid, sometimes armed, and empowered by U.S. forces desperate to bring security to the region. Motivations were complex, but most Sunnis who signed on either hated Al Qaeda groups, sought empowerment in a post-American Iraq, needed some cash, or a combination of all. It worked. In the short term, that is. Of course, hindsight being 20/20, we now know that many of these Sons of Iraq became sons of the Islamic State by 2014. Nevertheless back in 2007 and 2008, after months of hard, costly fighting, most of the ball sack temporarily fell under U.S. control and AQI insurgents fled elsewhere.

It wasn't easy. During 2007, 1-15 Infantry suffered heavy losses in the battle for Mada'in Qada. Ten 1-15 soldiers died in the Salman Pak area. Dozens more were wounded.[2] In the process, they achieved more than we'd ever dreamed of during our tough months back in late '06. Nevertheless, whether in Mada'in or elsewhere in the country, the Sons of Iraq program—upon which so much of the Surge's "success" rested—confronted some inherent limitations. Paying Sunnis to arm and patrol their own areas most certainly lowered violence and did initially root out some of the more extreme insurgent elements, but it did not solve the root causes of conflict. Sunnis continued to distrust the Shia-dominated government, and Shias vowed never to let the Sunnis regain their past hold on power. Many of the young men manning the Sons of Iraq checkpoints could, and as we are seeing play out now, *would* quite easily return to war as members of ISIS.

The overall situation in Salman Pak, and to be honest, Iraq more generally, though billed a massive success remained highly tenuous. The Iraqi people were far more cautious than American proclamations of victory might seem to warrant. They moved back to the city only slowly, and many stayed away for fear of Salman Pak's dreadful reputation. Iraqis knew the limits of our Surge alliances. It was their country, and they knew its foundational flaws. They knew that Salman Pak's future security, like that of the nation at large, was entirely fragile. At present, bombs still go off in Salman Pak and nearby Jisr Diyala. February and March 2014 saw several explosions rock both cities, leaving several dead and more wounded.[3] It was all well and good for Americans to declare victory and make haste for the exits, but Iraqis have to *live there*. In contrast to American optimism, Iraqi caution is much in the way of prudence.

The 3rd Infantry Division left Iraq in the spring of 2008. The division entitled the concluding chapter of their official campaign history "What Winning Looks Like." I sure hope their triumphalism is someday justified. Seven years later, though, it reads as farce. One must debate whether or not the ends justified the means. The counterfactual is dangerous, yet tempting: what if we had never invaded? After all, there was no sectarian war in Salman Pak before the American occupation. Let's assume that the Surge worked. So what? At best, we fixed the problem we caused, and finally shoved the genie back in the bottle? At what cost? How many dead soldiers? How many dead Iraqis? In Mada'in Qada alone, the count is scores and thousands, respectively.

Personally, I wish the people of Salman Pak well. I genuinely do. Indications though, are not good. Violence continues—twelve years and counting now—in Mada'in. On 13 February 2014 a car bomb exploded on a crowded Salman Pak street, killing two.[4] On 21 April, a suicide car bomber drove into an army checkpoint, killed three soldiers and two nearby civilians, and wounded a dozen more.[5] On 4 May, Iraqi police found the bodies of seven people, an entire family, kidnapped and murdered in the Sunni section of town.[6] On May 8, a gunman on a motorbike opened fire on a crowd in central Salman Pak, killing one and wounding four.[7]

By late summer, Salman Pak and the whole Mada'in Qada was a veritable battleground in the fight between ISIS and the central government in Baghdad. On 14 September, a masked gunman equipped with a silenced pistol executed five members of a moderate Sunni council previously allied with U.S. forces.[8] On 16 October 2014, three Iraqi soldiers were killed in a roadside bomb attack.[9] These are just the highlights—in one small city. I wish the people of Mada'in had found peace; that the efforts of 1-15 IN, 3-61 CAV, 1-61 CAV, 3-7 CAV, and the USMC had permanently ended the madness in Salman Pak. Unfortunately, I'm afraid Salman Pak's long history makes that rather unlikely. So does Iraq's. During the brief respite from violence in 2010, "only" 4,114 civilians were killed. In just the first ten months of 2014, that number reached 13,749.[10] I'm still uncomfortable with the word "victory." Like the Iraqis, I choose cautious prudence.

▰▰▰▰ The ultimate and tragic irony of an insincere "Surge as savior" narrative was its direct responsibility for failed application of a similar strategy in Afghanistan. True to form, senior civilian and military policy-makers ignored distinct differences in geography, demographics, culture, and political situation to force one strategic model onto a widely dissimilar Afghan context. Soldiers, like anyone else, do what they *know* and apply past experiences to new problems.

Consider just one example: my brigade commander, in heavily rural and depopulated Kandahar province, decided that the best way to secure a local village was to create—you guessed it—a "gated community." No shit, he and my battalion commander wanted to surround this tiny farming town of *maybe* fifty mud houses with a couple hundred concrete T-walls! A few problems: (1) the people were absolutely opposed (no matter—we know what's best for them); (2) half the Taliban insurgents were *from* the village and members of the same tribe, families, and religious sect, *not* some foreign element; (3) the area was crisscrossed by a few dozen irrigation canals that fed the surrounding farms. Any T-wall enclosure would block those canals, flood the village, and dry out all the fields—the absolute *lifeblood* of the farmers. It took months to talk the boss out of it, and in the end the determining factor wasn't my logic or Afghan preference, but a simple matter of dollars and cents—the T-walls were too costly. No matter, the commander had a solution. We just surrounded the place with triple strand, chest-high barbed wire. The village looked like a POW camp. So the man got his gated community after all. Where did the boss do his previous command? You guessed it—west Baghdad, 2007.

▰▰▰▰ "Surge" has entered the military lexicon to a preposterous degree. Once, the term was hardly known. Now, to "Surge" is to exert extra energy, time, or attention to any military task. Not even the most mundane aspects of soldiering are spared the semantic abuse. If a battalion staff needs to work late updating some PowerPoint slides, well, their major will warn them: "Hey fellas, we're gonna be surging on the briefing slides this evening." It's nauseating. But I get it. The army was handed a pair of unwinnable wars in Afghanistan and Iraq. Iraq, in particular, fell apart and cost us thousands of lives and years of our collective youths. Defeat, even a bloody stalemate, is hard for a professional army to swallow, especially given the energy and resources expended. The institution needed a victory, and the Surge appeared to provide one. Civilian bureaucrats and senior military officers sold it as such. That combat soldiers largely bought it derived partly from a deep psychological need to justify all the death and sacrifice. And so the Surge came to Afghanistan. I witnessed Surge 2.0 down in Kandahar province. The results were predictable.

Iraq cost somewhere between 2 and 5 trillion dollars, depending on the flavor of official report you prefer.[11] Just before the tenth anniversary of the 9/11 attacks, a 2011 Watson Institute study (even *before* ISIS, mind you!) attempted to assess the gains and losses of the Iraq War. This report concluded that the United States had "gained little from the war while Iraq was traumatized by it. The war reinvigorated radical Islamist militants in the region, set back women's rights, and weakened an already precarious healthcare system."[12] At that time, supporters of the war attacked the Watson report and pointed to the gains of the 2007 Surge as proof of the war's worth. Steven Bucci, military assistant to former defense secretary Donald Rumsfeld, said that "action needed to be taken," and he claimed that "it was really in Iraq that 'al Qaeda central' died; they got waxed."[13] Looking backward from 2014, with the Iraqi Army fighting to recapture much of western Iraq from reinvigorated Sunni militants, the flag of ISIS raised over Fallujah—a city that nearly one hundred marines died fighting for— and the conflict now spread to Syria, Bucci's "they got waxed" borders on farce.

With the invasion more than a decade in the rearview, a generation of Iraq War veterans are divided about the meaning and purpose of the war. According to a recent *Washington Post*/Kaiser Family Foundation Poll of post-9/11 veterans, only 44 percent felt "somewhat" or "strongly" that the war was worth fighting. Some 50 percent were now against the invasion, with 34 percent of those indicating that they "strongly" believed that the Iraq War was not worth it.[14] More significantly, 69 percent indicated that they believed most Americans didn't understand the veterans' experience in Iraq or Afghanistan. These were all volunteers, disproportionately from the South or Midwest, and more likely than the population at large to self-identify as Republican or conservative. In other words, the men and women polled were far from some lunatic, pacifist fringe. These were our veterans, lauded by countless millions of Americans' bumper stickers and yellow ribbons across the landscape. Even so, they—we—aren't so sure the fight was worth it. Perhaps that says something.

### LOW THRESHOLDS

At the tenth anniversary of the 2003 Iraq invasion, the *New America Foundation* held a debate on the question, Can we call Iraq a success? Journalist Peter Bergen moderated the disputing parties. In favor of the resolution was Douglas Ollivant, a former military officer and member of General Petraeus's plans section during the Surge. Ollivant later served as a senior civilian counterinsurgency advisor in Afghanistan. Opposing him was still active Lieutenant Colonel Joel Rayburn, an army intelligence officer with experience in both Iraq and Afghanistan. He had also been my history professor at West Point back in 2004 and 2005. Rayburn, incidentally, had displayed his wide knowledge base and even won some money on *Who Wants to Be a Millionaire* back in 2005. Both men are highly experienced experts in political-military affairs and possessed personal experience in Iraq. Nevertheless, Rayburn was wholly more convincing. Once each panelist had completed prepared remarks, Bergen asked his first question: "I'm going to ask you a very basic question, then. Is it possible today in Baghdad to go out and have a meal in a restaurant [safely]?"[15] Rayburn answered first: it depends, he said, on who you are, your religious sect, and whether you're a foreigner.

Then Ollivant chimed in with a smile: "Baghdad is much safer today. . . . As I tell my friends, there are really only three ways to get hurt in Baghdad. . . . If you follow three rules, you're probably gonna be safe."

Not a great start, I thought, but please continue.

[Ollivant went on] "One—don't stand outside a Shia mosque on Friday. . . . Two—don't stand around Iraqi policemen. . . . And three, don't hang out with any moderate Sunnis, because they're also likely to get blown up. If you follow those three rules, your chances of getting hurt in contemporary Baghdad are fairly slim."

[Rayburn interrupted] "And I would say the fact that you have to follow Doug's three rules indicate that the country is fundamentally not stable."

Ollivant, it seems, has a staggeringly low threshold for success. Perhaps it's because he witnessed Iraq at its worst. A better explanation, though, is the typical American inability to empathize with foreigners. They think that Iraqis ought to be content, and on some level *thankful*, for the degree of security they now possess. But that depends on when you think history begins. If your starting point is January 2007, then yes, Iraq looks fairly safe. But what if you start in February 2003, July 1958—the date of the revolution that ushered in an Iraqi Republic—or AD 600, for that matter? Perhaps, then, the current state of affairs doesn't measure up so well. It's all very interesting. Many Americans will effortlessly jump back 250 years to describe *exactly* what our Founding Fathers meant in the words of our "inerrant" Constitution. Iraqis, however, should forget ancient quarrels and just be happy things are better now than they were in 2007.

Today, Iraq is far from stable. Reinvigorated ISIS militants continue to seize territory in Iraq's northern and western provinces. Suicide bombs are still a regular part of life in Baghdad. Iraq's western border is more fluid than ever. In the wake of the Syrian civil war, the region witnessed, during 2011 through 2013, the irony of a refugee swap. Syria, once the destination for nearly a million Iraqi migrants, flooded *Iraq* with evacuees. Many were Iraqi refugees returning to their still unstable homeland. The problem is that almost none of them actually went back to their old homes. Instead, they remained internally displaced, moving to slums and squatter camps that are safe for their own sectional group.

Some pointed to continued violence and argued that it was American *withdrawal* that's to blame. Had U.S. troops remained in Iraq, they claim, violence would have remained low and democracy could bloom. Enter ISIS. Forged in the bloody chaos of not one but *two* civil wars (in Iraq and Syria) in 2014, ISIS militants stormed out of Syria and across the porous border. Within months, nearly all of western and northern Iraq fell. Fingers pointed in all directions, and the very same hawks who had devised our 2003 invasion sounded the war drums. Not only had the president abandoned Iraq, they said, but he'd ignored the problem in Syria far too long. The disaster that followed (so went the narrative) was America's fault.

Much of this, of course, is motivated by partisan rancor. Obama is a pacifistic, socialist, traitor—you know the drill. Yet even intelligent, experienced military intellectuals fall prey to political pejorative. Army Colonel Peter Mansoor (ret.) is a classic case in point. Appearing on C-SPAN's *Book TV* in early February 2014 to promote his newest work, *Surge: My Journey with General David Petraeus and the Remaking of the Iraq War*, and after a thirty-minute introductory briefing—replete with PowerPoint graphs, charts, stats, and pictures—Mansoor ended with one final slide. Recurring violence in Iraq, Mansoor concluded, is attributable mainly to a failure of resolve by our current president, Barack Obama. With plenty of historical frameworks to choose from, Obama's predecessor, George W. Bush, had used South Korea. Sure, the country was devastated by the three-year Korean War, and of course it took time, money, and energy to stabilize the place. But look at it now! "But President Bush wasn't able to see this through to the end," Mansoor said. President Obama, on the other hand, looked at Iraq and saw Vietnam—"an unwinnable quagmire that U.S. troops needed to get out of as soon as they could." Indeed, Mansoor continued, "unfortunately, by removing U.S. forces, in my view, it removed the glue that was holding the security situation together."[16]

Hold on. Which of those two historical analogies was, in fact, more accurate? Sure, the Korean War was brutal and devastated the South Korean peninsula. But North Korea *invaded* South Korea in 1950 and U.S. troops, along with a multinational *United Nations* contingent (conspicuously absent in 2003), intervened to preserve South Korean independence. The South Korean government *wanted* us to intervene. After the war, Mansoor correctly noted, "South Korea wasn't always South Korea," at least as we know it today.[17] True, the country faced internal turmoil, economic stagnation, and political infighting, but U.S. troops didn't face a broad insurgency in Korea, nor were they targeted in widespread attacks.

Other differences also stand out. Korea, particularly when compared with Iraq, possessed a strong degree of social cohesion. There were no major historical, religious, or ethnic splits lurking beneath the surface. And then there is this—simple geography. South Korea is a *peninsula*. Iraq, conversely, is essentially landlocked and afflicted with more than 2,000 miles of porous borders. Which sounds easier to stabilize, control, and guide toward a functioning democracy: a small, ethnically and religiously homogenous state with one highly militarized international border, *or* a large, highly unstable, colonial fabrication of a country cursed with both ethnic and sectarian divides and a 2,000-mile border? The answer doesn't require strategic training.

The 2003 invasion of Iraq was a war of choice, plain and simple. Our occupation was poorly planned, bungled from the start, and almost immediately contested by a range of nationalist and Islamist insurgents—both Sunni and Shia. More than four thousand dead and thirty thousand wounded U.S. troops attest to that.

How long *should* we have stayed in Iraq? I've never heard a truly emphatic consensus on the answer. Mansoor, for starters, seemed to imply sixty years, per our South Korean experience. Proponents of Operation Iraqi Freedom loved to invoke the example of America's post–World War II occupation of Japan as the putative "model" of transformation and success. Omitted from this illustration, of course, is that Japan did not even regain its sovereignty until 1952: seven *years* after Hiroshima and the surrender.[18] And Japan, unsurprisingly, bears far more in common—socially, ethnically, religiously, and geographically—with Korea than Iraq.

While not a perfect analogy, the situations in postwar Iraq and Vietnam bore more in common than Iraq and *South Korea*. Think counterinsurgency, porous borders, and political corruption. But in reality, neither Vietnam *nor* South Korea provided an accurate comparison. When planning for America's adventure in Iraq, policymakers should probably have looked not to postwar Germany, Japan, or South Korea, but to Israel's occupation of Lebanon or the Palestinian territories. Here they might have found a closer, and altogether more troubling, analogy. Words matter. So do comparisons. Truly, though, how long would have been long enough to usher in lasting peace and security in Iraq? And was that our role, or in our long-term national interest? Furthermore, what about Iraqi opinions on the question—do those matter? Perhaps my central gripe with all Mansoor's talk about troop levels and American policy is that it tends to treat Iraq as a black box, a pawn in America's national security game, a place to be "fixed," "molded," and essentially tinkered with until it meets *our* needs. The people of Iraq, the ones I grew to know and sometimes love, are rarely a factor. They should be.

██████ Structurally, the Iraqi state we left behind is far from ideal, and is, in fact, utterly unstable. In January 2014, UN chairman Ban Ki-Moon visited, and, in a joint press conference with Prime Minister Maliki, urged political reconciliation to "address the root causes of the problems," calling for "inclusive dialogue." Maliki immediately rebuked the chairman, snapping, "Talk about dialogue in Al-Anbar is rejected because we do not hold dialogue with al-Qaeda."[19] The prime minister, true to form, seemed to insist that all residents of Anbar were terrorists and ignored this salient fact: "Protesters in Anbar, along with five other provinces, have been peacefully demonstrating since December 2012."[20]

There's more. Current Iraqi law allows the death penalty for forty-eight separate offenses. In 2013, 169 people were executed, the most since the 2003 invasion. That ranks third worldwide, behind only China and Iran. (Awkwardly, the United States was fifth on that list.)[21] Corruption and incompetence hinder prosperity. While millions of Iraqis lacked basic services, the Maliki government took in more than $100 billion annually in oil revenues.[22] That income was not evenly divided among the population or across sectarian divides. Worse still, violence and instability spread throughout the region and is now being visited back upon Iraq, in a sort of cruel boomerang effect.

The current Syrian civil war is brutal, yet familiar. Watching footage from Homs and Aleppo propelled my mind back to the Baghdad of late 2006. Even before the ISIS invasion, the passions and violence of Syria had spilled into Iraq. Sympathies were divided along strict sectarian lines. Iraq's Sunnis waved Free Syrian Army flags and supported toppling the Alawite (Shia) Assad regime.[23] The Shia, Maliki's government included, supported the Assad regime. Iraq, along with Lebanese Hezbollah and the Iranians, are all active allies on the Syrian question.[24] Syria has become a proxy battleground for Iraq's sectarian groups. The conflict further invigorated AQI, elements of which morphed into Al Qaeda in Iraq and the Levant, or as it is more commonly known, Al Qaeda in Iraq and Syria (ISIS), to reflect a new regional role. In 2012 and 2013, Sunni insurgents, who once flowed into Iraq through the Damascus airport—one assumes with Assad's tacit support—drifted west to attack the Alawite regime and carve out a new Islamic caliphate spanning the border.[25] Shia militiamen also entered the fracas, using social media to highlight their role in defending Damascus against (Sunni) insurgent attacks.[26] Then, in 2014, the situation reversed itself once again, as ISIS militants swarmed into western and northern Iraq.

Watching the Syrian crisis unfold, one wonders how much of the chaos is attributable to the Iraq War, or for that matter, the once lauded "Arab Spring." The sectarian bloodshed of 2006 and 2007 slowed down drastically in 2008 and 2009, but the central foundations of conflict were never resolved.[27] Iraqi Sunnis still feel excluded from the power structure. The Shia simply cannot forgive past repression, and so they fear and stymie Sunni influence. The Maliki government, parts of which actively participated in sectarian cleansing in 2006 to 2008, remained Iraq's sovereign rulers until August of 2014. If anything, Maliki *further* centralized power and control over the nation's security forces in the years after American withdrawal.[28] Iraq's opposing parties fight one another in Baghdad, Anbar, and across the Syrian borderlands. The region is plagued with reciprocal violence. Syria helped destabilize Iraq, and the resultant chaos has washed back upon the homeland.

Where did it all start? Some might say (and there is some merit here) that it began with the death of Mohammed and subsequent split in the faith. Such an argument, however, ignores abundant historical evidence. Rather, the current millennial Sunni-Shia conflict is manifesting itself in dangerous *new* ways.[29] A conflict triggered, in large part, by a reckless and ill-considered American invasion of Iraq. Deposing a despotic dictatorship had the unintended, but altogether foreseeable, consequence of handing the Iraqi government to Shiite political parties. The resultant Pandora's Box emitted not only internal strife but also regional instability. A new Shia bloc composed of Iraq, Iran, Syria, and much of Lebanon formed an arc coursing through the heart of a majority Sunni Middle East. Never mind that Iran and Iraq possess the fourth and fifth highest crude oil reserves in the world, threatening Saudi Arabia's position and utterly altering the regional power balance.[30] A Cold War–like stand-off now envelops the Middle East, divided not by respective economic systems, but rather religious sects. We mustn't forget what our Iraq invasion wrought.

As for the ISIS threat, the current struggle within Iraq and Syria lacks simple solutions. The tough problems usually do. Make no mistake, these ISIS militants are terrible people. Living under their occupation is tragic. Ultimately, though, this must be viewed as a regional problem. Saudi Arabia, Jordan, and the various Gulf sheikdoms must realize that despite a common Sunni faith, ISIS poses a major threat to their governments. They are more likely to take action if the U.S. government suppresses the urge to take the lead role.

Here's where it gets even trickier: in *this* fight, Iran's ayatollahs and Syria's Assad regime have common strategic interests with the United States. The ISIS problem is a Shia problem, perhaps first and foremost. If the United States is to get involved at all, one hopes it's solely in a counterterror role against active ISIS plots. Anything further, and especially ground troops, while perhaps politically popular, and scratching America's recurring itch to do *something*, is likely only to inflame the region and ally nationalists with Islamists. People—we ought to have learned by now (but haven't)—don't take kindly to being occupied. As for myself, I'm left skeptical as to the efficiency or wisdom of using U.S. military force to reorder societies or solve Mideast problems—without creating new ones, that is. As the Hippocratic oath would warn: first, do no harm.

Syria and Iraq; Iraq and Syria. The tragedy is the same, but our role, one hopes, will be different. Sixteen veterans of Iraq and Afghanistan served in the last U.S. Congress. Fifteen were Republicans. In

September 2013, after Syria's dictator Bashar al-Assad crossed President Obama's "red line" and used chemical weapons, only *two* congressional Iraq War veterans supported U.S. military strikes. At a time when the two parties can't agree on much of anything, *nine Republican* veterans joined their Democratic colleagues in strident opposition to intervention. Four others were undecided but leaning toward an antiwar stance. For these vets, Iraq colored the Syrian conflict. Representative Tammy Duckworth (D-IL) lost both her legs in the war. Should U.S. forces enter Syria, she said, "it's military families like mine that are the first to bleed." "Until I feel it's imperative to our national security, I will not support pre-emptive intervention."[31] An undecided Republican, Steve Stivers of Ohio, said before making a decision, "I want to understand the end state [in Syria], the strategy to achieve it, and the exit strategy—all of which must be tied around America's national interest."

Violence, repression, and dictatorships still flourish all around the world—especially in the turbulent Middle East. Always have, always will. Thucydides was correct: human nature being what it is, war and death remain eternal. But some wars we *choose*, and Iraq was most certainly one of those. Perhaps Iraq taught a few of us—at least those who experienced the war—that intervention and a foreign military presence have unforeseen consequences. Here is one: by the end of 2001, nearly 80 percent of Al Qaeda fighters were killed in Afghanistan. It took our Iraq invasion to replenish them.[32] In 2006, Osama Bin Laden himself observed that "Iraq has become a point of attraction and restorer of our energies."[33]

I'd hope that our long tragedy in Iraq would at least give us pause when the war drums once again start beating. But at a time when fewer Americans than ever serve in the armed forces, a shrinking number of veterans sit in Congress, and most people scarcely look up from their iPhones long enough to notice, I fear that our national caution will be brief. The next time our leaders ignore John Quincy Adams's two-century-old warning and storm off "in search of foreign dragons to slay," let us hope that enough vigilant citizens raise a wary voice. That would, of course, first require attention and self-awareness on the part of a distracted populace. Perhaps others are more hopeful than I.

# 15

# War in the Rearview
## On Life after Iraq

Point me out the happy man and I will point you out either extreme
egotism, selfishness, evil—or else an absolute ignorance.
— GRAHAM GREENE, *The Heart of the Matter*

DIVERSE PATHS: 2ND PLATOON
ON THE LONG JOURNEY HOME

In April 2007, we moved into the Rusafa neighborhood of
east-central Baghdad. Five more squadron soldiers died, and several times that number were wounded. Violence slowed for a number of reasons, mostly unrelated to the Surge of troops. None of that,
of course, was apparent at the time. In fact, that summer, U.S. casualties peaked and things looked worse than ever. Hindsight, of course,
allows all kinds of explanations. Personally, I prefer to remain fixated
on the time—those moments in Baghdad, 2006 and 2007—because
everything seemed clearer then than in any of the grand explanations
I've heard since. Around that time, I left 2nd platoon and bumped up
to Troop Executive Officer (XO)—second in command to the captain.

The job was all right. I still spent a ton of time around the Ghost
Riders and could protect them in a few different ways. I tried to shield
the boys however I could, but mostly my job was different now. I
counted equipment, organized maintenance, wrote patrol schedules,
and more often than not—which was a product of our command climate—planned and led troop operations. Truth is, I was shot. Worn
out and overstressed. BJ Laney, from London, Ohio—my West Point
classmate, friend, and fullback on the army football team—took over
the platoon. I was glad. BJ was just what the boys needed: a fresh, excited, and personable LT. Ironically, BJ commanded a completely different platoon. About half the guys had been killed or wounded and

a few others had been moved around. By the time we went home, 2nd platoon had a whole new crop of soldiers. That's just how it goes. People change, the unit is forever.

The war was over for me, though I still had to survive another eight months. I got by—we all did. I did my job, led some patrols, planned a few operations, and kept studying my Arabic. Mostly though, I upped my smoking habit to two packs a day and read anything subversive I could find. By this, of course, I mean works by anyone intelligent and independent—Kurt Vonnegut, Graham Greene, Tim O'Brien, Robert Graves, Joseph Heller, and dozens more. For the first time in my life, I'd have trouble sleeping, but endless episodes of *The Office*, replete with that catchy theme song, helped me nod off. The Jim and Pam, will-they or won't-they romance and the very setting of Scranton, Pennsylvania, represented, for a distinct moment, all that was good and comfortable about home, about America. From there my path was to surviving the war, redeployment, a baby boy, promotion, and a move to Fort Knox, Kentucky. It all happened so fast. We all had our own path, some fine and others tragic. We made our own way—there was no plan guiding us along. More's the pity. I wish life were more like the movies.

After fourteen months and twenty-two days at war, we landed in Colorado Springs on New Year's Eve—December 31, 2007. After a few weeks of leave, we went back to work, and on the surface things were largely the same. Damien and I still drank at the Hatch Cover. In fact, we started drinking together quite a bit. The best part about coming home was the lax work schedule. We'd put in half-days for the first few months, and that left plenty of time for trouble. My second day back I made my first big purchase—a nice bar for the basement of my new house. For a while, Damian and I would leave work about noon and drink either at Hatch Cover or the "Sjursen Tavern" in my basement. Some days I'd pass out on the couch by 5:00 p.m. and have trouble sleeping at night. Mostly, they were harmless times, and being with Damian made me feel normal and safe. Besides, after no alcohol for fifteen months, I decided we had a lot of catching up to do.

My platoon sergeant, Malcolm Gass, signed a few of us up for a

Tuesday evening bowling league in Colorado Springs. Gass, Damian, Rittel, SSG Kevin Bailey from 3rd platoon, and I were all pretty decent bowlers and stayed competitive all winter. We ragged on each other, threw back pitchers of beer, and crafted a variety of new "Gass is so old . . ." jokes. I liked the predictability of Tuesday bowling, and just being around the guys. The hardest thing for me about coming home, paradoxically, was *missing* my army friends. Odd, of course, because after fifteen months in extremely close quarters, you'd think we'd be sick of each other. Not the case. After a few hours alone in my house, I'd get stir crazy and start calling Steve, BJ, Scott, Keith or Damian— desperate to be close to the guys and to have someone to drink with. It got to where I didn't feel comfortable or relaxed around anyone else. Tuesday night bowling was the closest I got to feeling *right*. I've missed it in times since.

In May 2008, I received orders to attend the Captain's Career Course (CCC) at Fort Knox, Kentucky. Before leaving, we threw one final 2nd platoon bash at my house. All the original Ghost Riders attended. The night was a blast, but kind of surreal. The platoon bore an array of scars—physical and psychological. We carried DJ down to my basement in his wheelchair. Faulkner showed off his scar, and everyone toasted the fallen. A round for Fuller, a shot for Balsley, and *two* for Smith. The night ended—as such events do—with a few die-hards left standing at 2:00 a.m. South, DJ, Faulkner, Frunk, and I sat around my kitchen table, a bottle of Jack Daniels at the center, and started dropping truth bombs. The bottle passed, you'd take a swig, then profess love and loyalty to the platoon, the dead, and each other. It went like that for a while. Faulkner went to the bathroom and didn't return—he'd passed out and collapsed face first in the doorway. We gathered him up and said our good-byes, complete with abundant "man-kisses"—cheek to cheek embraces followed by the Arabic phrase, *habibi*—"my love." Years have passed, but I've never stopped loving such events. It's the rawness, honesty, and extravagance of these parties that only the army seems to produce. The boys left for the night and I left for good. I haven't seen most of them since. I think of them always.

## ED FAULKNER'S JOURNEY

Ed Faulkner was one of the only original Ghost Riders to stay in the unit. Most everyone else either left the service or moved to a new post. After he was wounded, Ed needed surgery to repair his shattered forearm, and he spent several months recovering at Fort Carson. While home on leave we met up, and he came to a backyard BBQ at my house. We drank and had more than a few laughs. He showed off one hell of a scar, visible for all to see, and got to explain it to a few young civilian ladies in attendance. This being America in 2007—they couldn't care less. A few months later, Ed volunteered to come back. He finished out the last few months of our deployment in Baghdad—one hell of a gutsy move. He didn't make a big thing about it, just said he missed us. It was Ed's quiet way.

After barely a year back in Colorado, 3-61 CAV deployed to the mountains of eastern Afghanistan. Our troop—mostly full of new people—manned an isolated outpost named COP Keating. The place was situated in the bottom of a valley, dominated by high peaks on all sides. You don't need to be a military professional to know this much: you *never* put a base at the *bottom* of a mountain! Keating served little legitimate military purpose and was only occupied because it was *there*. We don't like to give ground *back*, even after holding on loses any intrinsic tactical meaning. Call it an institutional flaw. The official army report spells out the disaster far more eloquently than I, but suffice it to say, the outpost—just about to be closed down anyway—was surprised by a massive Taliban attack. At dawn on 3 October 2009, more than three hundred insurgents attacked and nearly overran COP Keating. Only the heroic defense of the fifty-three defenders saved the outpost from complete destruction. Eight soldiers died, twenty-two were wounded, and two received the Congressional Medal of Honor for their heroism—the first time since Vietnam that two living veterans from a single battle received the award.

During the battle, Ed got pinned down in a HMMWV and was injured by shrapnel from a succession of *eight* rocket-propelled grenades that smashed into the vehicle. Realizing their position was untenable, the troopers inside attempted an escape. Ed was the only survivor.[1] Evacuated after the battle—now twice wounded, once in each contemporary American war—he underwent several surgeries during a prolonged recovery. He earned another Purple Heart and an addiction to painkillers. Ed also suffered from a severe case of PTSD. While still recovering at Fort Carson, he told his own parents that something was terribly wrong and he'd need some serious psychological help. Ed had an impressive combat record, of course, and no one wanted to do him wrong, but he was incapable of soldiering at that point. He received an honorable discharge and left the army in the spring of 2010.

Unfortunately, leaving the service and his unit was probably the worst thing for him. At least in the old troop he had NCOs and comrades keeping an eye on him and providing credible empathy. Back in Elon, North Carolina, Ed withdrew to his bedroom. He'd obsessively view YouTube videos of the COP Keating battle. Nightmares and flashbacks haunted him both day and night. One evening his mother found him huddled in the bushes in front of their home, warning of incoming Taliban fire. The next day, he remembered none of it. That July, local police responded to one of Ed's severe hallucinations and what turned out to be a full-blown nervous breakdown. They hospitalized him at the Alamance Regional Medical Center. Once he had been released, doctors recommended Ed seek thirty days of treatment at the local VA hospital. The VA facility was inundated with patients and kept him just two days. On 16 September 2010, Ed died of an accidental overdose after mixing methadone and Xanax. His parents believe he'd been self-medicating to suppress his crippling PTSD. Ed Faulkner suffered too much. He'd served his country in two complicated, difficult wars, and bled in both, but the more difficult battle was in his own mind. One hopes he's found peace. His headstone reads: "You are safe. You are at home. You can rest."[2]

Post-traumatic stress disorder (PTSD) cases are abundant and growing—exponentially—as a generation of veterans return from prolonged wars in Iraq and Afghanistan. A Congressional Research Service report from December 2012 identified 103,795 *diagnosed* cases of PTSD among Iraq/Afghanistan vets.[3] Just six months later the numbers spiked as the Veterans' Health Administration released a new figure of 310,746 VA-diagnosed PTSD cases. That said, most experts estimate less than 50 percent of PTSD sufferers actually seek help or receive a diagnosis. War is expensive, and we mortgage the bill onto our children and grandchildren. Consider the hidden costs about to be unleashed on the American taxpayer. Some 914,193 Iraq and Afghanistan veterans have already filed VA disability claims. This number will undoubtedly rise.[4] No one knows exactly how much this will cost in the long run. Some of these VA claims will be denied, some veterans will receive only partial benefits, but thousands upon thousands will—deservedly—receive benefits for life. When we go to war, our society ought to consider the totality of long-term expenditures. We owe it to our veterans. Besides, an honest national conversation weighing the advantages versus costs of war should be the minimum prerequisite for unleashing the military. Such was the design of our democracy. Limited government, small "c" conservatives—above all other groups—ought to subscribe to such a sentiment, but *war* seems to be the only thing they *will* fund—indefinitely.

In August 2013, Staff Sergeant Ty Carter—the second Medal of Honor recipient of the COP Keating battle—called up the Faulkners at home in North Carolina. He wanted Ed's parents to attend his award ceremony at the White House. They were hesitant at first but SSG Carter insisted they be there, and the Faulkners relented. During the ceremony, they were stunned when President Obama recognized Ed in his speech. Obama spoke of Carter's heroic bout with PTSD and said Carter "urges us to remember another soldier from COP Keating who suffered too, who eventually lost his own life back home, and who we remember today for his service in Afghanistan—Private Ed Faulkner, Jr."[5] Later, at the Pentagon, the army officially designated the Faulkners a Gold Star Family—a distinction given to the families of soldiers killed in action. It was fitting. He truly was the ninth casualty of the battle.[6] The war killed Ed as much as any overdose. Years after we left Baghdad, Ghost Riders were still dying. Ed, at least, was recognized, but he was one of many delayed casualties of a nasty war: one that for some, will never really end.

### DUCKS FLIES HOME

Things continued not to go well for Ducks the night he was wounded. As they sped toward the Green Zone, a flight medic on the MEDEVAC helicopter kneeled directly onto Ducks's shattered arm. The noise of the rotors ensured she couldn't hear his screams. After the EFP attack, Ducks's recovery was long and arduous. These things often are. After a few days in the Baghdad CSH, they flew him up to Landstuhl Medical Center. In Germany, congresswoman and future House speaker Nancy Pelosi visited his bedside. After a few days, Ducks boarded a medical flight en route to Brooke Army Medical Center (BAMC) in San Antonio, Texas. In flight his vitals crashed, and the plane made an emergency landing in Bethesda, Maryland. There he was quickly stabilized, then put on the first flight to San Antonio.

Thanks to a heavy and regular dosage of potent painkillers, Ducks doesn't remember much of this journey. Once he had landed in BAMC, however, everything came into focus. His wife and mother were in Texas waiting for him. His first instinct was utter reticence. Glad as he was for the support, he remained shy about loved ones *seeing* him in such a condition. Thus began eighteen long months of recuperation. He underwent several surgeries as well as regular physical and occupational therapy. The doctors recommended he keep the devastated left arm as long as possible, and they conducted a marathon ten-hour-long reconstructive operation. The surgeons filmed the procedure and used it for future teaching purposes. The good news was he kept the arm, if not all of its functions. And he finally got that promotion—pinning sergeant in July 2008. Though offered the chance to switch jobs and stay in the army, Ducks couldn't fathom a career behind a desk and opted instead for medical retirement. Receiving 100 percent disability from the VA, he'd be well taken care of—financially—for the rest of his life. But there were also dark times.

One of the first things to fall apart was his marriage. His wife was neither interested nor emotionally equipped to handle his injury. When a *four-star general*—Army Chief of Staff Peter Schoomaker— came to BAMC and held a ceremony awarding Ducks the Purple Heart, she was an outright embarrassment. She refused to wash her hair or dress in decently appropriate clothing for the formal event. After a while, Ducks's condition improved enough that he could move into a small apartment on base. His wife—unable or unwilling to cope with his worsening night terrors—made the wounded man sleep on a recliner. In his *own home*. One day, finally fed up, Ducks took her out on the porch for a talk, and they simultaneously suggested a split.

That was the low point. Out of disaster, however, came hope. Ducks was sure he'd never marry again. "How could anyone ever want me like *this?*" he thought. Then the Balsley family invited him to attend a memorial birthday party for Michael. With nothing else to do, Ducks got in his car and drove straight through to California. At the party he met Jennifer, one of Michael's old hometown friends. It wasn't long before they married. Life is funny. As he drove out to the Balsley's home, Ducks had no idea his life was about to pull a 180. Then it did. Nothing's perfect—but everything's been better ever since.

The new couple bought a home just outside Chicago, in Bensenville, Illinois. Ducks still suffers from significant PTSD, traumatic brain injury (TBI), and physical pain, but he's learned to manage. He sees a chiropractor weekly, and that eases the aches and helps him sleep. In 2012 a nonprofit organization, Working Dogs Making It Home, provided him a service dog—Spanky. The two are now inseparable. Spanky helps remind Ducks to take his meds, snuggles close during night terrors, aids in anger management, and provides persistent companionship. Perhaps most important, Spanky draws attention. Before, he says, "everywhere I went I'd catch everyone staring at me—not saying anything—just *staring*." He'd actually have preferred them to *ask* about the wound, because the incessant gawking bred insecurity. Now, though, "everyone just watches Spanky and wants to pet him. He's the center of attention, and I like it that way!"

The Duzinskases have a solid, happy marriage, and they're financially taken care of by the VA benefits. And they are thankful. Life, naturally, still presents its challenges. Ducks, who once relished the glorified images of old World War II movies, is now less certain about his own war. "At least in the first deployment, I could rationalize that we were there to secure the Iraqi elections," he'll say, "but the second one, in 2006-7, when it became more like an occupation—I'm not sure it was worth it." We all try to make sense of the war, more so even as the years pass, but it's particularly pressing for the wounded veterans. Ducks wears the evidence of his severe wound every single day. He can't take it off.

Physically, there are still tough times. Jennifer gave birth to their first child, a son—Dominick—two years ago. Dominick is the pride of the family, and Ducks's whole life; yet raising the boy presented early challenges. He was scared to hold Dominick—in fact he was one of the last to do so—terrified he'd drop the boy. The nerve damage in his left arm left him with little feeling and very limited fine motor skills. One day Jennifer tried to show Ducks how to cradle the boy's fragile neck, and demonstrated for him. "Look down at your hands," he told her. "See how both your palms face *up*—I can't *do* that."

Despite these early struggles, Ducks figured it out. He's a stay-at-home dad now—and completely dedicated to his family. In a few months, his parents will move in; they're building an extension on the Bensenville home. Someday, Ducks might like to volunteer for a veterans' support organization, but for now Dominick keeps him busy enough. Ducks misses the army, the old platoon, and thinks about Fuller and Balsley all the time. That may never stop. Nonetheless, Ducks and Jennifer frame their memories differently now. Every 25 January, they celebrate Ducks's *alive* day. He turned seven this year.

### DAMIAN SOUTH

Life has had its highs and lows for even the strongest among us. Damian South returned home the most successful senior scout in the squadron—he'd had the most IED finds in the unit and received stellar evaluations. Still, something was wrong. Before Iraq, Damian had been hard-charging, type-A, and highly motivated. He'd impressed his superiors, including our squadron commander. Inside, though, Damian just didn't feel it anymore. His drinking grew intense, loneliness magnified, and his coping mechanisms were simply shattered. Despite the birth of a son, Xavier, that May, his marriage was suffering under the weight of stress, drinking, and detachment. Before the New Year, he was divorced.

In the middle of it all, Damian left the army. I'd tried to talk him out of it, as had SFC Gass and lots of other guys. The squadron commander even spoke with him—offering Damian a job mentoring cadets at West Point if he'd agree to stay on. He was on the fast track to promotion, and by all measures, Damian could have been a first sergeant or a sergeant major someday, but it just wasn't in him anymore. All the combat, stress, and death weighed heavily on the young sergeant. He'd managed to perform all year—compartmentalizing the bad and focusing on the mission—but now, back in the States, his heart was no longer in it. "I just wasn't able to deal with it, the loss of Fuller, Balsley, and Smith," he says. Besides, he was handling a divorce and just needed to get out.

The next couple of years were the hardest. He'd landed a pretty solid job with a telecom company, but then the economy collapsed. He didn't *love* the job anyway. It wasn't like the army, and he found civilian life draining. "In the army, I was a sergeant so I was used to giving instructions, planning complex operations, and watching everyone just get to it," he remembers, "but in the civilian world, some people don't do shit and there's really no consequences." The recession caused his hours to evaporate anyway, and suddenly Damian had too much time on his hands. Before the deployment, he'd slept like a baby and had no problem being up and ready each morning. Now, for the first time in his life, he was plagued with dreams and the thoughts racing in his head kept him up all night. Once an extrovert, Damian now lost touch with everyone from the old platoon. "I loved those guys—still do—but I just wrote everyone off," he says. "I guess I just couldn't deal with it." Smith's suicide weighed heaviest. South had spoken to Smith right before he'd left. A few guys from other platoons had gone AWOL—refused to come back from leave—and Damian had asked Smith point-blank—"Yo, dude, you're coming back to us, right?" Smith looked him in the eye and said yes. The answer has haunted Damian ever since. When he heard about Faulkner's death, it sent him into another tailspin. There were some hopeless days.

His break came when an old friend offered him a job with the police department back home in Panama City, Florida. As hard as it had been to leave Xavier back in Colorado, Damian knew he needed a fresh start. He moved home and re-enrolled in Gulf Coast State College. He needed a degree before entering the police force, so he went to school all day and managed the old club he'd once bounced for at night. It was a tough time, and he rarely slept more than a few hours, but the prospect of a new career infused in him more energy and motivation than he'd felt in years. He also met and eventually married Melissa. She was, and is, Damian's complete opposite. He calls it like it is and can be abrasive; she stays calm and measured at every turn. Melissa is everything Damian, and his world, needed. "She, no shit, saved my life," he'll say, and he means it. He's now stepdad to her daughter Cloey, and they have a new daughter, Piper. Catch her from the right angle, and she looks a bit like Damian. Poor girl.

Don't try to tell him the Surge, or the Iraq War in general, was some sort of victory. "We didn't win *shit*, we've got nothing to show for it," he says. The only certainty is, "We *lost* some of the best people this world ever produced—my guys." As for the future? He's just looking for stability and happiness. At times he misses the army—"every day, in fact," he says, but law enforcement has been a good fit. Truth is, Damian could have been a sergeant major, no problem, had he wanted it, but his current life is healthier. Policing is the closest thing to military leadership he can find and still maintain normalcy and a family life. For a while it was tough. On isolated traffic stops he'd get out of his cruiser with a bad feeling and have to fight off shaky hands. He'd seen so much hurt, been through such horror, that the shakes really bothered him—it just didn't make sense. One day he called up his old gunner, Brian Longton—now a deputy sheriff in Fort Worth, Texas—to ask about the problem. "That's gonna happen," Brian said. "It was that way for me too, but it passes." And so it has. On the job and in his life, Damian's making it work—one day at a time.

DJ

It was one of the lowest points of Sergeant Ty—"DJ"—DeJane's life. Just like any other day, he'd dropped the cherry of a cigarette butt on the floor and proceeded to light another. After a couple minutes DJ noticed a strange smell—almost like something cooking in the oven. Looking down, he saw that the cigarette butt was actually burning a hole through his right foot. The paralysis was so severe that he hadn't felt a thing. Back then, he'd never have imagined the transformation his life would soon undergo. Financially, the army took care of Sergeant DeJane—medically retiring him with 100 percent disability. In 2008, he bought a beautiful house on the east side of Colorado Springs. Physically, his recovery has been nothing short of miraculous. Dozens of doctors tried to temper DJ's expectations, but he never quit on walking. About a year ago, he joined a gym and now lifts weights five days a week. The routine, discipline, and added core strength substantially altered his physical condition. After more than seven *years* in a wheelchair, DJ *willed* himself to walk. With the aid of a walker, he can now walk around the block, in and around a store, and up to the bar to order his own drink.

The emotional recovery, however, was far more instrumental. Not too long ago, DJ spent much of his time doing midday drinking at local bars. Those days are gone. In 2010, DJ's former wife offered him full custody of his son, Taber—now eight years old—if he'd clean up his own life. She knew that DJ adored the boy and that only Taber could motivate him to turn things around. He's now a full-time, high-energy stay-at-home dad. The boy is his whole world, and they're good for each other. DJ got his life in order in preparation for full-time fatherhood. He quit binge drinking and as of 1 January 2014 went cold turkey—at Taber's request—on all tobacco products. He drops Taber at school, hits the gym, and takes care of errands before class lets out. The guy who in his own youth so hated academics can now be found hunched over Taber, helping with nightly homework. After that, the pair are usually off to cub scouts or jujitsu practice. Taber, in fact, was the 2013 Colorado state champ in his Brazilian jujitsu age bracket. There is no prouder father.

It hasn't been an easy journey, but a positive attitude and a singular commitment to improving his life have made all the difference. DJ knew he could potentially wallow in despair, alcohol, and self-pity. He consciously chose another path. Leaving the bar and joining that gym changed his routines. The gym, DJ says, gave him "a healthier attitude about *everything*." He eats better, got fit, and *feels* good. Most important, he's made a new crop of friends—a much better influence than his previous bar-fly acquaintances. The army is a small family. DJ's sister—Matte—is still in the service and stationed at Fort Leonard Wood, Missouri. She was injured almost one year *to the day* before DJ was shot. They've *got* to be about the only serving brother/sister combo wounded in the same war—maybe in American *history*. Seriously.

Life is still hard, for DJ as for all of us, but he opts for a positive attitude. The hardest thing is "trying not to dwell on the past, or think too much about Fuller, Faulkner, Balsley, or Smith." For a long time, Fuller's death was particularly tough to swallow. After all, the night of the IED, Fuller was sitting in DJ's seat and doing his old job. His views on the war have done a 180, as well. Looking back, he doesn't see much purpose in the eight-year conflict, nor does he think the costs, in blood or money, were remotely worth it. Wealthy interests, he feels, prolonged the war to make a boatload of cash—money that didn't trickle down to us soldiers.

It's a cliché—time heals all—but there's some truth to the phrase. DJ needed a few years, but he's left most of that guilt behind, and generally manages to keep the past where it belongs—*in* the past. Ask him today, and DJ will say, "Look, I *can't* make a difference by dwelling on Fuller, Smith, or any of those guys, but I *can* make a difference with Taber." And he does. The boy adores him, and DJ dedicates everything he has to his son. As for the future? DJ doesn't have goals, for say, ten years from now—just a mission. "I *will* be walking and hopefully sending Taber off to a good college." I believe he will.

### REMEMBERING JAMES

No one, except James, can ever really explain why he did it. All of us who loved him—his fellow soldiers, parents, sister, friends, and wife—can't help but wonder, of course. What emerges is ultimately speculation, often driven by our *own* needs to rationalize the death of a big-hearted, well-loved, beautiful young man. The loss of a child is unnatural—perhaps the most unnatural thing. So too is the death of a healthy, youthful soldier—not even old enough to legally buy a beer—at his own hands. No one knows that as well as David and Susan Smith. For all we've been through, in spite of all the casualties, it's been James's death—above all others—that has stayed with many of us. That is no accident.

There wasn't a note. Rachel searched for weeks, combing every square inch of the apartment, even the inside of James's cowboy boots. Nothing. He left us no record of his final thoughts. Everyone has worked to process James's death in his or her own way. Sara struggled for a long time. She spent countless days at his gravesite and couldn't stop wishing James had just *called* her that night. "I'd have gotten on a plane that minute and calmed him down—same as I'd done a hundred times before," she says. After seven years, she has managed to cope, telling herself she couldn't have stopped James's "0 to 60" decision-making. She still visits the cemetery fairly often and keeps in touch with both Rachel and the Smiths. She's married now and her first child, a daughter, was born on 8 June. Now, the days surrounding James's death give her reason to be happy and something to celebrate.

Rachel fell apart in the months after the death. She stopped taking care of herself, took to binge drinking whiskey—James's favorite—and living rather recklessly. One night around Thanksgiving, she nearly drank herself to death and still got behind the wheel of her car. Somehow she made it home safely, and that night she dreamed her first dream of James. He spoke directly to her, and it was so real. "Rachel, there's nothing you could have done," he said. "It wasn't your fault." That simple vision changed her life, and she credits James with giving her the strength to carry on and eventually become the person she is. She has two children now, and takes them to visit his grave once a year. Although it was hard for her, Rachel gave James's prized bottle cap to Sergeant DJ. That heirloom remains within the 2nd platoon family. Sometimes she'll be driving along and slam on her brakes— sure that someone on the roadside looks *just* like him. James is with her still, always, but she's learned to cope. Nonetheless, some nights, when she drifts off to sleep, she's still hoping to meet him under that apple tree.

Letting go hasn't been easy for James's sister Candace. For a long time, she was convinced that her brother had a reason for not visiting her during his leave. James *knew* his sister always had a sixth sense about him. He might have known Candace would suspect something was bothering him—severe PTSD, depression, doubts, or *something*. She's moved on as best she can, finishing a master's degree and now happily remarried. But sometimes she's still angry with God. She was never *supposed* to be an only child. It hits her hardest when she thinks about her children. Sadey is nine now, and Candace dreaded telling her the truth about James's death. Blake, seven, will ask his mother to take him fishing. Candace, not exactly an outdoorsman, thinks to herself, "Your stupid uncle is supposed to *be here* to take you!" But when she looks at Blake, especially when he cracks a certain smile—there he is. Her son is a spitting image of his uncle, and that alone brings Candace much joy and solace. She's also close to Sergeant Ty "DJ" DeJane, who has become a dear friend of the entire family. Sadey has heard the story about Uncle James and his tattoo. When Sadey met DJ, she said: "You see, I'm *not* a cow." The dead can live forever in the stories we tell.

### REMEMBERING ALEX

Alex Fuller's life should have been a movie. So wrote a journalist covering his funeral, and so I always thought too—long before Alex was killed. The sentiment itself is bullshit—I realize that—but reflecting on his death, and everything since, I can't stop thinking it was never supposed to turn out this way. Stacey was just nineteen when an officer in full dress uniform knocked on her door and informed her that Al—just twenty-one himself—had been killed. She was five months pregnant, and carried the combined weight of impending motherhood and crippling grief to her husband's funeral. Hundreds of mourners attended the ceremony at St. Francis Xavier's church in Hyannis, Massachusetts. The audience included Governor Deval Patrick, a two-star general, sheriffs, state legislators, town officials, Russian immigrants, and old friends.[7] Notably absent was Katie Fuller—still serving time in a Florida State correctional facility—but she sent her love in the form of a poem for the occasion, read by their Uncle Leo:

> I'm free / don't grieve for me.
> For now, I'm free / I'm following the path God laid for me . . .
> I could not stay another day / to laugh, to work, to play.
> I found heaven at the close of day.[8]

Zack Hallet, Al's best friend—the guy he'd lived with before moving in with the Zinovs—followed Uncle Leo at the podium. "This is going to be a hard day for all of us," he began. "I can't tell you the number of bad days I had when Al would say, 'Need a hug?'" Hallet continued. "Well, Al, I could use one now."[9] Struggling through tears, he went on: "Al was the funniest guy I ever knew. He told the funniest stories—stories that I will tell his daughter someday." Hallet and other friends remembered Al for his five necklaces, gold teeth, boxing, and love of hip-hop. Then the Reverend Frechette led the formal service and spoke about Sergeant Alex Fuller: "By the way we live our lives, we say something."[10] He may not have known Al personally, but there were no more fitting words. He might have added that we also say something by the way we die. Al did both.

Aliciah "Allie" Fuller—named for her dad—was born in April 2007. She'll never know her father. The Fuller family saw its share of discord in the years after Al's death. His mother, Linda Fuller, died in Delray Beach, Florida, in 2009. Stacey Fuller, only nineteen when Al was killed, has had her ups and downs. She bought a nice house on Cape Cod and enrolled in community college to pursue a nursing degree. Then, in January 2010, DEA and local police officers served a warrant on her Centreville home and allegedly found 255 Percocet tablets hidden in Aliciah's teddy bear. Stacey eventually pleaded guilty to possession with intent to distribute narcotics and received a two-and-a-half-year prison sentence. In October 2012, a judge stayed her sentence, but Stacey landed back on house arrest after missing a court date and allegedly testing positive for oxycodone.[11] I like to think none of it would have happened were Al still alive, but maybe that's naive. Nevertheless, life is hard and people make mistakes—especially young mothers confronted with a traumatic loss. Every soldier's death sent ripples in all directions, aftershocks that went on for years. In this sense, Fuller was no different.

In other ways, he was the exception. Fuller could have gone a thousand different ways—drugs, crime, jail, or just plain bumming around. He had more distractions and risk factors than most people combined. No, he wasn't an angel. Who is? But at eighteen years old, he'd put all his chips on the table, volunteered for the U.S. Army, and went all in. Nobody tried harder, with more sincerity and downright *gratitude*, than Alex Fuller. In a world full of irony, doubt, and hypocrisy, this guy inspired us all. Everyone from the lowest private to the squadron commander knew his name and what he was about. We were all better for knowing the man.

His death, from the instant it occurred, left me wanting to tell his story and spread the gospel according to Fuller. It goes something like this: no one is perfect, life deals you shit, but if you want it badly enough, give every ounce of yourself and live in the service of *others*, maybe, just maybe—you can inspire a whole lot of people and intrinsically *matter*. As I look at those words, they seem entirely inadequate. Because they are. Fuller defied simple explanation; maybe we all do. And few Americans know a thing about those who live, fight, and die in their name. A writer covering the funeral wrote: "If the life of Army Sgt. Alexander Henry Fuller were a book, it would be an all-American story of pride and pain."[12] True enough. Al *was* a proud man—all twenty-one years of him—but life, from the start and up to his death, dealt him much pain. He smiled through it all and served with integrity and devotion. This much is true: he was funny, he was beautiful, and he was our friend. If his story was one of pride and pain, so too was 2nd platoon's—and that of the entire army in Iraq. For me, Alex Fuller will always and forever embody that essential truth. Some nights I can still hear his voice: *"Yo, Sir. Sir, yo, Artis in jail, cuz."* And when I do, its 2006 all over again—I am young and still believe anything is possible. But each time I wake, Fuller is dead, the war remains a disaster, and that is that.

━━━ For all the army's modernist impulses and egalitarian progress, a wide gulf remains between the paths of officers and enlisted men. Postwar life for the lieutenants was wholly different. We always knew it would be, and that forever irked me. The difference is this: when officers get out, jobs come looking for *them*; when Joes get out they search desperately for jobs. Corporate headhunters sign many young officers—especially West Point grads—for good-paying, upwardly mobile, middle-management jobs in New York, LA, Houston, or Chicago. I know guys, former peers, working for Texas oil firms, managing a Walmart, trading stocks on Wall Street, and finishing up an MBA at Harvard. They're all doing well. And why not? They'd served honorably, *volunteered* for wartime service, and mostly gave it their all. For the officers, military service, and even Iraq, is seen by employers as a *positive*, a stepping stone to future management positions. Not so for the Joes. Delaying college to drive a HMMWV or kick in doors isn't exactly a plus on most job applications. Such is life, I suppose.

Personally, though, I couldn't fathom going off to corporate America—especially after all this. Only half-joking I used to say that when I left the army, I wanted to teach kindergarten on a South Dakota Indian reservation. Basically, I'd be looking for a job as distant and opposite from the army and Iraq as possible. Most of my friends *did* get out; some are doing quite well. In the end I stayed in, for a variety of reasons—some good, others shabby and lazy. Our soldiers, though, had much more limited options. Life hasn't turn out great for many of them. The Iraqis, well, they've had it even worse—much worse. And no one cares.

### MARK

Akeel, "Mark," is still looking for love. Only now he does so on this side of the Atlantic. After years of appeals, and receiving probably the longest letter of recommendation in history from yours truly, Akeel was approved for a visa. In 2010—after *seven years* of wartime service with American soldiers—the U.S. State Department settled him in Raleigh, North Carolina. Before he left, Akeel spent the remaining savings—which he'd earned working as an interpreter—on a house for his brother's family in Baghdad. Ever the family man, he left the country without a penny.

Moving to the United States was the culmination of a lifelong dream, but reality hasn't been quite so promising. Struggles to hold a good job and fit in socially, and grapples with loneliness posed early and lasting challenges for Akeel. He holds two separate degrees from the University of Baghdad, in English and Germanic studies. Unfortunately, those credits will not transfer to accredited American colleges. Akeel—clever as ever—jokes that his English proficiency is great among ignorant Iraqis, but not quite as impressive around academics at the nearby Duke campus. Besides, "Even *Americans* with degrees in German can't find a job!" Perhaps he should have studied finance. Akeel came to the States just as the national economy collapsed and jobs contracted. Finding steady, good-paying work has been his foremost obstacle.

When he first arrived, the refugee agency got him a job washing dishes at a local restaurant. He wasn't exactly thrilled. After seven years of combat duty with the U.S. Army and earning two university degrees, Akeel felt understandably insulted by the work. Nevertheless, he needed money and wanted to make a good impression, so he took the job. On his second day, after breathing in the heat and detergent fumes for several hours, he suddenly collapsed. Akeel, unbeknownst to him, had developed asthma. Baghdad is overcrowded, lacking top-notch emissions standards and regular sanitation, and the climate is *far* different from that of North Carolina. Perhaps some combination of these factors contributed to the affliction. Akeel returned to work the next day and was promptly fired. His manager said he couldn't keep a guy on who might require a daily ambulance trip.

Soon afterward, Akeel landed a solid job as a contracted "role player" for the army at Fort Bragg, North Carolina. The pay was solid and he generally liked the work. Day and night, he'd dress in traditional Arab garb and play the *role* of an Iraqi—sometimes a policeman, some days an insurgent, still others a tribal sheik. The upside was money, predictability, and familiarity. It was also fun, and he met a lot of other Iraqi refugees. One problem—within a couple of years, the work dried up. The contracts were canceled and all role-playing jobs simply disappeared. Ironically, as U.S. military involvement finally ended, the army had little use or budget for Iraqi contractors. The only role left to play was as himself, Akeel—unemployed refugee.

He bounced around at a few different jobs after that, employed for a while at the refugee placement agency he'd gone through. Unfortunately, after 2011, the number of Iraqis entering the country slowed, and fewer placement counselors were required. He lost that job, too. He spent four months working in a North Carolina electronics factory, but the plant closed down. In a sense, Akeel dealt with the same structural problems facing many low-wage American earners in the postrecession economy. Yet, for an Iraqi refugee without family support, savings, or a long resume, difficulties were magnified. The vulnerable among us struggle most, and Akeel, as a foreigner, was more susceptible than others to the whims of an unstable economy.

Some of Akeel's most difficult barriers are social. Now thirty-five years old, he longs, above all, for love, marriage, and companionship. His years at war, living the stressful double life of an interpreter and American "collaborator," did not lend themselves to romance or courtship. Now that life has finally settled down, he faces a new set of challenges. The pool of eligible Iraqi, or even Muslim, women is small in Raleigh, and finding a connection even more difficult. He did fall in love, though, with an Iraqi woman he met at the airport while working for the refugee agency. They dated for a year, but after some disputes with her family, the relationship ended. Akeel now largely stays away from the Iraqi-American community and the drama they bring over from the old country. He doesn't rule out American, or Christian, women, but they too are hard to meet. Akeel still abstains from alcohol and can't stand bars or clubs. That *alone* makes it hard to connect with single women. Besides, he says, "American women don't like my style, man. They all think I'm Mexican!" His sense of humor, strong as ever, masks genuine disappointment. He needed to try something new.

Last summer, Akeel returned to Baghdad for an extended visit. His family had missed him terribly, and he wasn't working much anyway. He hoped to find a wife. Maybe, he thought, a traditional Iraqi woman would be a better match than he'd found in North Carolina. At first he was nervous to return, with the war memories and recurring fears for his own life. But once in Sadr City he felt surprisingly at home. At least at first. His mother cried when she first saw him, amazed by how much older and thinner he looked. He met one woman that he liked some, but it didn't pan out. She was perhaps *too* traditional, and Akeel had changed during his time in the States. Besides, her father was a constant annoyance, always pestering him about visas for the whole family. Akeel enjoyed visiting with his parents and especially seeing his many nieces and nephews, but he decided to return to the United States. His family tried to hold him, begging him to stay and get married. Akeel, though, had changed too much and felt trapped between two worlds—not quite American, but no longer fully Iraqi.

He returned to Raleigh in the fall, probably just in time to avoid some of the worst violence to hit Iraq in years. Summer 2013 saw plenty of violence, and as Akeel observed: "It's a little better, sure, but the situation is the same—nothing really changed." Car bombs still exploded in Shia neighborhoods, and policemen were regularly shot. After he left, things went from bad to worse. As 2013 turned to 2014, Al Qaeda–linked Sunni groups reclaimed much of Anbar province, and attacks on Shia civilians in Baghdad multiplied. Shia militias responded in kind, and the increasingly autocratic Maliki regime did little to attract moderate Sunnis. For Akeel's family, that meant once again living in fear of suicide bombers and dreading trips to public places. At the time of this writing, a motorcycle bomb has blown in

Sadr City, taking at least fifty-two lives.[13] Days later, an explosion tore through a neighborhood café, killing four and wounding fifteen.[14] These were the highlights of only *two days* worth of attacks in Akeel's old neighborhood. In the first two months of 2014, 1,750 Iraqis died in sectarian and communal violence, the worst rate since 2008.[15] The cycle continues.

Akeel returned to North Carolina—a world he "doesn't love, but . . . still better than life in Iraq." He tries to keep busy, and has made a few friends—acquaintances, really—in the area. He plays in a weekly soccer game with a mixture of Americans, Moroccans, Egyptians, and Iraqis. He's even taken up some occasional ice skating in downtown Raleigh! Mostly, though, he stays alone in his apartment and watches hours of cable news—in both English and Arabic. Ever the intellectual, he reads, thinks, and follows current affairs. Mostly, he's just very lonely.

He has rent to pay, however, and he recently started driving for a local taxi service. He doesn't really care for the work, but it makes ends meet. Sometimes driving drunk college kids around Duke is frustrating. Occasionally, a patron will ask where Akeel's from and seem not to know a *thing* about Iraq. Amazed, Akeel will then ask how that could possibly be the case, when the United States was at war for eight years and sent hundreds of thousands of soldiers to Iraq. How quickly Americans forget. The excitement and sense of purpose that came along with working as an interpreter is long gone. Perhaps that's just as well. He likes the peace and privacy of the U.S. Living in Sadr City all those years, Akeel lived *next door* to brutal militiamen—some of whom he'd grown up with—and knew full well what they'd do if they found out. The stress and anxiety were overwhelming. Sometimes, he says, "when I think back to what I did, the secret life I lived, and all the danger I was in—I can't imagine how I did it." It never really leaves you.

He's still looking for government work—preferably contracting or teaching Arabic, but jobs are hard to come by. For now, Akeel drives that taxi—often all night. Sometimes, he told me, when he felt down, he'd pull out the long recommendation I wrote for him years back—a letter highly charged and brimming with emotion, a time capsule of *me*, circa 2007—and remember how much he'd hoped for this day, the day he'd get to America. Next year, maybe, he'll apply for citizenship. He deserves it, and has earned it, more than any natural-born American I know. We've reconnected now, and discuss the old days and current Middle East turmoil for hours over the phone. Nothing's changed, really—he's still the most informed guy I know, and a kindred spirit—only he's not in back of my HMMWV anymore. And I finally call him Akeel.

# CODA
# The Power of Memory

We grew up way too fast
now there's nothing to believe
and reruns all become our history.
— "Name," The Goo Goo Dolls

There can be no easy moral answer to this war, no one-sided
condemnation of American actions.
— SENATOR ROBERT F. "BOBBY" KENNEDY, antiwar speech
at Kansas State University, 18 March 1968[1]

### IN DEFENSE OF THE ARMY

With hindsight, and after commands in both Iraq and Afghanistan, I've grown more sympathetic toward the army itself. My anger
has been (mostly) redirected. In both wars, the U.S. Army and Marine
Corps were dealt a losing hand. Despite some of the highest defense
budgets on record, we've never had enough troops or resources to
do what was asked. The missions themselves were Kafkaesque,[2] and
bordered on the absurd. Make no mistake, U.S. troops were given
unattainable goals in Iraq before, during, *and* after the Surge. Without pause, our soldiers charged head on into often-farcical quests. In
February 2007, MNC-I (Multi-National Corps—Iraq) published our
overarching mission statement for the war. It stated that by *December*,
U.S. forces would: "Secure the population, defeat terrorists and ir-
reconcilable extremists, neutralize insurgent and militia groups, and
transition responsibilities to the ISF (Iraqi Security Forces) in order
to reduce violence, gain the support of the people, stabilize Iraq, and
enable GoI (Government of Iraq) security self-reliance."[3]

The U.S. military embarked upon this enterprise and later declared conclusive victory, largely by itself. Sure, there were token
civilian government employees on board for the ride, but this is true:

I never saw a *single* member of the State Department, U.S. Agency for International Development (USAID), or the Department of Justice in nearly fifteen months of combat. That's not to say these folks weren't in certain areas, and for sure hundreds were hunkered down in Baghdad's Green Zone, but I never dealt with any. And that's too few. Diplomacy? That's the army's job. Economic aid and development? We handled it. Law enforcement? That's us too. That the army did as well as it eventually did is all the more remarkable when you consider the mentality of the common soldier. Here's a dirty little secret: the vast majority of American troops didn't and don't give a *shit* about Iraq or Iraqis. They were combat soldiers, trained for war. No matter how fancy the senior commanders' mission statements or varied the daily tasks, this salient fact remained: each morning soldiers strapped on their gear, adjusted bullet-proof vests, loaded a rifle, and mounted HMMWVs. They can be forgiven for emphasizing the *military* component of the business over the thirty other odd jobs they weren't trained for. We do what we know—its human nature.

That said, with some notable and unforgiveable exceptions (one thinks of Abu Ghraib, and the Haditha massacre, for starters), the U.S. military conducted itself with decency and integrity throughout the Iraq War. Insurgencies are, at their core, exceptionally Hobbesian affairs—nasty and brutish to the core—but not short. Under constant threat of attack, facing an invisible enemy, and overburdened with the unworkable combined tasks of governance, economics, policing, diplomacy, and combat, the army somehow held together. By and large, soldiers maintained discipline, honor, and—I think tragically—a "can-do" optimism that our civilian policy-makers probably didn't deserve.

This doesn't dismiss atrocities like Abu Ghraib and Haditha, or the numerous smaller acts of indecency perpetuated by some American soldiers. Rather, it encourages one to consider the counterfactual—the paths not taken. Military occupation and counterguerrilla warfare are a dirty business. Just ask the French in Algeria, and the Brits in Malaya, Israel, Ireland, India, Afghanistan, Cyprus, Yemen, Kenya, South Africa, Greece, Iraq, and well, come to think of it—just about everywhere. Or consider our own history in the Philippines and Vietnam. No, counterinsurgency isn't pretty. It's war. War among, and for, the loyalty of the people. Most officers, sergeants, and individual soldiers decided to treat Iraqis with a reasonable degree of dignity every day of our eight-year occupation. In the age of YouTube, Twitter, and independent journalism, the fact that we can count major American atrocities on our hands is evidence of this relative benevolence. I write this as an outspoken critic of the U.S. invasion and subsequent occupation of Iraq. Nonetheless, fairness demands such context.

For all its flaws, and there are many, the U.S. Army outpaces the country at large on a number of progressive benchmarks. These include class, race, and, recently, sexual orientation. Let's begin with economics. It's a well-known fact that American income inequality is on the rise. Across the nation, elite salaries are aggressively outpacing middle-class earnings. Not so in the military. Consider this: in 2014, a four-star general, potentially responsible for the governance, diplomacy, economics, and security of an entire occupied *country*, as well as hundreds of thousands of American troops, will earn a base salary of approximately $204,000. The newest private first class (PFC) to join an infantry platoon, responsible for only a personal weapon and listening to his sergeant's every direction, makes $21,600 annually.[4] To review, the nation's top military officer earns less than ten times what's earned by the newest eighteen-year-old recruit. Compare that to Walmart. In 2012, CEO Michael Duke earned $23.2 million, or *1,260 times* more than an entry-level employee—who earned approximately $18,700. The newest associate at Walmart has to work the register every day for 750 years to earn Duke's 2012 annual compensation.[5]

Or contemplate healthcare differentials. General Petraeus had exactly the same health benefits as my youngest private.[6] We have no gold or platinum "Cadillac" health care plans in the army. Imagine the CEO of Goldman Sachs visiting the same doctor, in the same hospital, as the office janitor.[7] Never happen. At one time, say back in the 1960s, the head of a major bank and his lowliest clerk still ran in very different circles. The bank president would probably belong to an exclusive country club, send his kids to private school, and vacation in the Caribbean. The clerk, at best, owned a small split level ranch, bowled on Tuesday nights, and vacationed on the Jersey Shore. *But*, the banker and the clerk likely shared at least one thing: military service, with the mutual hardship and equalizing force of basic training. Should they get stuck in an awkward social situation at the company party, they'd at least be able to discuss their military experience.

Today, even that collective experience is absent, and the two worlds—that of the worker and that of the CEO—are utterly separate. The boss may conceivably waltz through an entire lifetime with no occasion or motivation to circulate in the everyday world of his employees. My point is that the army remains, by most measures, the most egalitarian institution in the United States. Perhaps this rests on the core mission of the institution—warfare. The highest-ranking general remains, at root, a soldier. He still takes a semiannual physical fitness test, qualifies with his assigned rifle, and may conceivably die in combat. In a final sense, the general knows that the private is more likely to lose his life in battle, but shared sacrifice bolsters the meritocracy.

Racial segregation and inequality have always represented the dark side of the American national project. While most de jure racial barriers are gone, de facto residential and educational segregation, as well as major economic and criminal justice inequities, remain firmly in place. The military, however, is one place that tends to be on the cutting edge of personal and institutional integration. Admittedly, the armed forces have a spotty track record here, with segregated units being the norm until after World War II. That said, the military *has* often been far ahead of many states with regard to acceptance of race, gender, and most recently, sexual orientation. For all its flaws, the army is a place where—theoretically, at least—merit alone generally determines promotion and opportunity. No matter the racial or socioeconomic strata that divide a group of new recruits, each individual possesses the same potential for advancement, based only on training, discipline, and competence.

Look only at the huge number of black and Hispanic sergeants major across the army. Personally, of the four first sergeants I've had over the last several years, two were Hispanic, and one was black. The military had African American generals before the *New York Times* had a single black editor. In fact, far more blacks and Hispanics sit at the top of the U.S. military than anywhere on Wall Street. Nearly twenty years ago, military sociologist Charles Moskos wrote that "the military is the only place in America where African-Americans routinely boss whites around."[8] The U.S. Military Academy at West Point consciously strives to admit a reasonable percentage of African American cadets in order to ensure that the officer corps reflects the enlisted men they command. Yet there is little outcry against such blatant affirmative action. Why? Because it *works*—highly talented and professional cadets enter West Point from a range of ethnic and racial backgrounds.[9] They quickly meld together and leave the academy a single shade of army green. It's not perfect, but as of this writing the army comes closer to replicating progressive national ideals on race, gender, and sexual orientation than do many states and most private institutions. This is particularly true when the army is contrasted with states from the Deep South, the very states—ironically—that provide a disproportionate number of their new recruits.

This is part of why we lose something in our lack of shared, common national service. Once upon a time, eighteen-year-olds from Alabama, Massachusetts, and California all left their towns, families, and provincial frameworks behind to spend at least two years serving a federal, *national* project. Such forced amalgamation forged travel, friendships, and empathy; it had the potential to break stereotypes and forge a sense of selflessness. For a generation of veterans, even those who served in peacetime, the experience of national service, however brief, was one of the most memorable and formative of their lives. Then, and now, the military served as a catalyst for expanded civil rights, social progress, and civic action. The army I've served ought to be recognized for its strengths, and, compared with the deified corporate world—it has many. That much should be said.

One more thing deserves mention. Although in my own view the wars in Iraq and Afghanistan have been wildly mismanaged, expanded outside the scope of our natural resources, and—in the case of Iraq—waged under false pretenses, I am *not* an outright pacifist. As a serving officer, I suppose that would be awkward. The fact remains that the world is a deep shade of gray and power still matters. Schemes for world peace are admirable and ought to be pursued, but never at the expense of preparedness. We do not live in a black and white Manichean universe of American "good guys" and terrorist, communist, or Eastern "evildoers." The world is far more complicated. Consider only one example: the population of "evil" Iran is generally far more pro-American than the citizens of "allied" Saudi Arabia. It's messy like that. Hewing the middle path I'm describing entails many complex things, and here is one: don't get spun up when the military budget shrinks by some small percentage. Maybe, in fact, security doesn't demand a bloated Cold War force, but rather a sizable, professional and deployable force that can expand to include citizen soldiers in times of true crisis. As I write this, I can just hear the shocked rebuttals of the professional military analyst class!

Nevertheless, a strong and capable permanent force is necessary to form a credible defense and provide the nation options in global affairs. That professional *army*—the marines, navy, and air force are remarkable but incapable of taking on the army's role—can and should form the core around which to train and lead an expanded force of citizen soldiers in the event of either large-scale conventional war or extended counterinsurgency (both of which ought to be waged only when vital national security issues are at stake—which is to say, rarely).

Tragically, but just as certainly, it seems that Thucydides was right, and human nature being what it is, we are likely stuck with the phenomenon of war. One hopes, however fruitlessly, that we might at least learn from Iraq, and reassess which conflicts are *actually* in our national interest. This much Clausewitz knew, and this much a generation of veterans knows: war is chaos and uncertainty. Once a nation commits to war, neither the method of fighting, initial goals, nor predicted enemy responses are likely to turn out as planned. Not even close. If the population isn't invested, they are less likely to scrutinize the need for war, and God help the professional soldiers once this happens. We've seen the results firsthand: endless war, repeated deployments, and an exhausted, overstretched core of volunteer troops. Let us never forget that cost.

Unfortunately, Americans will likely have to relearn these lessons. I can see it all so clearly. The army will shrink in size—not in itself a tragedy, were we to pare down its responsibilities—and soon be called upon to perform miracles again. Our nation's soldiers will answer the call, bear unthinkable burdens, and by sheer force of will and professionalism, keep an irresponsible, bombastic foreign policy afloat. Willfully oblivious, a civilian population unaffected by prolonged wars—in fact knowing little else and absent any fear of *personal* service—can and will look the other way.

The United States, it seems, has two choices: gracefully accept the approaching multipolar world, or fight this eventuality kicking and screaming the whole way. I fear the latter path will involve an over-reliance on the government's ultimate trump card. Our powerful volunteer military will then be utilized around the globe in ill-advised interventions seeking the impossible dream of absolute security. There is a history here, by the way. Blessed with decisive victories in early wars of survival (French and Indian/Revolutionary War), then protected by two oceans for a full century of "free security," at least from foreign enemies (1815 to 1917), the United States developed a binary approach to foreign policy.[10] It has stayed with us. Either the country is safe or it is not—period. Little else in the world is quite so black and white, and unfortunately such an all-or-nothing approach inevitably leads to disappointment, and in global affairs—folly.

Clear vision and prudent policy require honest assessment of the past. Americans, apparently, lack a certain cultural proclivity for this kind of self-awareness. Military men and women don't like to lose, and they can't tolerate the thought of so many friends dying "in vain." With little time or inclination to consider the merits of a given deployment, most professional soldiers lower their heads, put in twenty-hour days, redouble efforts, and attempt the impossible. Against incredible odds, and in the absence of a sound national strategy, America's servicemen managed some astounding feats. But they cannot and will not effectively *remake* entire societies. We ask too much of them. Tragically, the soldiers' very competence may seal their fate. Were we to fail more obviously, the ideologues and militarists would be unable to hide behind us. More's the pity. In the next Iraq, those who will suffer are the very same soldiers that fought, died, and repeatedly deployed the last time around. It appears irony knows no bounds.

## DEATH, LIFE, AND MEMORY

The thing about a story is that you dream it as you tell it, hoping that
others might then dream along with you, and in this way memory and
imagination and language combine to make spirits in the head. There is
the illusion of aliveness.

— TIM O'BRIEN, *The Things They Carried*

My son was born in late September 2008 at Ireland Army
Hospital in Fort Knox, Kentucky. I was there for the Captain's Career
Course—a year-long academic school for newly promoted captains,
and coincidentally, so was my old platoon sergeant, SFC Malcolm
Gass. Malcolm landed a gig training new recruits in 5-15 CAV. That
night, my son decided to flip over and force an emergency C-section.
Then he went ahead and stopped breathing and got himself rushed
into critical care. A doctor cornered me with the news and advised
that I find someone to drive me—because I'd be too emotional, I suppose—up to the Children's Hospital in Louisville. My new baby, apparently, would be flown by emergency helicopter. Only a few minutes old and the kid needed his first MEDEVAC.

I pulled out my cell and instinctively dialed Gass's number. Without a moment's hesitation he mounted up and was out front within
ten minutes. By that time, thankfully, my son had started breathing. I
guess he didn't like the idea of intubation, because he started breathing as soon as they tried to stick the tube down his throat. I met Gass
out front and thanked him profusely for coming out in the middle of
the night. With shaky hands—another gift from Baghdad—I pulled
out a smoke and we talked for the length of its burn. We were all
so close, for so long—the boys of Ghost Rider platoon. Even at the
birth of my son, 2nd platoon asserted itself in my life. Then, just as
soon as it had begun, it was all over. The army sent me to Fort Riley,
Kansas, and, because I'm the last American alive without Facebook,
I lost touch with everyone. I've missed them and the closeness more
than I'd have ever thought, and next time I'm in a crisis, I don't know
*who* I'll call.

I'm afraid I haven't adjusted very well in the intervening years. I'm
still in the army—probably a bad sign. Alex Fuller is still very much

alive with me. He, Smith, Balsley, Mark, and a thousand Iraqi faces contribute to my affliction. Look, other soldiers had it worse than me. For all the combat and losses we suffered, there is always a unit that saw more shit. But life still hasn't been easy. My own followed a path eerily similar to that of many of my soldiers. After a couple of years I got divorced, then remarried. My wife, Kate, holds me together now, which can be quite a task. Redemption, it seems, came in a petite frame. I'm a great guy to have a beer with—solid in small doses— but living with my mood swings, rants, and intolerant idealism would wear on someone who loved me even a little less. Kate's the straight man to my dramatic compulsiveness. Damian says opposites really do attract, and at least when it comes to certain underlying person- ality traits—that's probably true. A second marriage added two step- sons to my life, so now we've got three boys—AJ, my six year old; Ryan, 12; and Brady, 9—running all over the house. They don't know or care one bit about Iraq. I guess it is better that way. Kate's my part- ner, and I'm doing ok these days. Nevertheless, I've got a range of lingering issues, many of which thousands of other veterans share; others, I'm sure that are unique to me. No one knows how each com- plex, individual brain will respond to war—there are just too many contingent circumstances.

Me, I can't stop worrying about being happy all the time. Iraq left me with a profound need to make up for lost time and live each day to the fullest. Life doesn't always cooperate. I refuse to care about "trivial" things like money, household chores, or my "career." I freak out about people watching *Jersey Shore*, or the *Real Housewives of Where-ever-the-fuck*. I yell at television screens and cable news—a lot! Some days my brain overflows with self-penetrating questions: am I wasting the good, solid days of my youth? Should I be having more fun? Must I do something more with my life—run a refugee camp or work for Human Rights Watch? I do anything and everything to avoid unnecessary stress. Being happy becomes an obsession. I'll handle big problems with ease and crack under the strain of the smallest things: a phone call I don't feel like making, arguing with a sales agent, or having a minor disagreement with my wife. I'm rather ill equipped, I fear, for everyday life. The problem is I want—in fact, expect—every day to *feel* the way Gin Blossoms's music *sounds*: free, easy, fun, and stress free. When it's inevitably *not* that way, I don't handle it so well. Spells of depression set in, and it can take days to fight my way out.

For purposes of stress avoidance, staying in the army was a disaster. Another round of intensive training followed by command of a Cav Troop in Afghanistan didn't help. Rural southwest Kandahar province was the spiritual home of the Taliban, and in 2011 they were fighting *hard* for that ground. "Terry" Taliban had my troop boxed in on a tiny outpost, attacked us daily, and we suffered a few dozen casualties—including three dead. In terms of actual legitimate firefights, Iraq had nothing on Afghanistan. Shit, my troop engaged in over five hundred separate gun battles that year. As the *troop commander*, I personally fired my rifle more in a few weeks than I did in the whole Iraq deployment. Maybe it's because Iraq was my first war, or because my platoon's casualties were so concentrated, but Baghdad remains—even now—the more formative of the two experiences. Mostly, though, I think it's the idealism and dedication I brought to Baghdad, and my emergent love for the Iraqi people. By 2011, I was in Afghanistan to keep my boys alive, survive, and beat the Taliban away from our base. I never allowed myself to develop much of an attachment to those people and entered Kandahar with profound cynicism about the war itself. That had not been the case in 2006.

▬▬▬ As we come to the end, I wish there were larger lessons to draw from all this. There's so little I'm sure of, and even less about Iraq that I'm certain actually *matters* in a general sense. I'm left with a few certainties: I remain a mess and can't fully understand why. Sometimes I wake up in the middle of the night with some profound conclusions and promise myself to write them down in the morning. Usually, I forget. It's all so clear in my head at the time, but never so when I try to verbalize or write it down. Fact: this book is shit compared with the eloquence of my bedtime thoughts—I assure you.

I'm suffering from some sort of long-term arrested development. I think I'll always be twenty-three, a lieutenant, and recently returned from Baghdad. I come at everything in life from that place, that perspective. As a captain and troop commander in Afghanistan, I never really stopped being the LT. Soldiers and platoon leaders were amused; some of my superiors—less so. That said, my lens has mostly served me well. The army has handed me good report cards, some great friends, and a master's degree from a civilian university at government expense. But Baghdad was the moment I stopped growing, stopped truly learning. For all the trouble this causes me, I sort of hope it stays that way. I don't ever want to lose the intense feelings I brought home from the war—the empathy, the anger, the love.

Salman Pak, the Ghost Riders, Operation Dolphin, Mark, Fuller, Smith, and all the Iraqi people stay with me and color everything I do, say, and think about the world around me. Maybe because it was the most honest time of my life—when I felt most real, most alive, most scared. In those days, we were so young, yet in some sense so independent and powerful. It was also the rawness of emotion; the connection and dependence on other human beings. The sense that once it was over, life would be epic. That I would live *right*, without conventions, and could bottle those feelings in order to feel alive each and every day. Then I got home. It never really pans out. Perhaps that's why the divorce rates among veterans are so high; and the suicides. Epic adrenaline, experiences, and expectations are like so many taut rubber bands—eventually they snap.

The war took its toll on me and on a couple million other guys. Whether we realize it or not, it's affecting our entire society and concept of democracy. My twelve-year-old stepson was born into a war. For the first time in American History, he and his fellow sixth graders know nothing else. Without even the *memory* of peace, how can they be expected to grasp war's meaning and sacrifices? How will they respond, as voters—citizens even—six years from now, when they partake in their first election? The damage is deep, but its bleeding is internal. We don't realize the gravity or significance.

Again, I'm not sure what it all means—maybe because it *doesn't have* the intrinsic meaning I so badly want it to. There's really no way to know for sure. Day-to-day life presents its own reality—its own lessons. Mostly it's the guys who stay with me. I think of them every single day. I don't have a commemorative tattoo—although I've often wanted one. My memorial is more permanent. It's in the sights and sounds I can't forget. Some nights, I can still see Balsley's face lying on that Baghdad street. I'll imagine Faulkner sitting up on that pile of dirt, inhaling a cigarette and taking it easy. Smith's smile and Fuller's laugh are as real now as on my first day in the unit. Perhaps even more so. The dead come alive in such conjured visions, but also in the stories we tell, and the memories we share.

So one day I looked down at my son as we read together, watched cartoons, and built Legos. I knew he was only five, but for some reason I decided to sit him down and try to explain why he has three names—AJ Sjursen—Alexander James Michael Sjursen. I told him about a brave, impetuous boy named James, and the finest soldier I ever knew, a sometime juvenile delinquent called Alex. He listened intently for a few minutes, looked up and asked—"Daddy, can we play Power Rangers?" I smiled faintly—and so we did.

*This book is written in honor and loving memory of*
ALEXANDER H. FULLER, JAMES D. SMITH, MICHAEL BALSLEY, and EDWARD FAULKNER

And with eternal gratitude and awe for the "original" Ghost Riders

SFC Malcolm Gass (Ghost 4)
SSG Damian South (Ghost 2)
SSG Micah Rittel (Ghost 5)
SGT Ty "DJ" DeJane (Ghost 6)
SGT John Pushard (Ghost 3)
SGT Caleb Holloway
SGT Richard "Ducks" Duzinskas
PFC (now SGT) Edsel Keith Ford
SPC (later SGT) Matt Singleton
SPC Jon Bynum
SPC Tyrone Artis
SPC Brian Longton
SPC Jeremy Frunk
SPC Chris Shuman
SPC Tim Cloutier
SPC Josh "Doc" Schrader

# Acronyms and Abbreviations

The following acronyms and abbreviations appear throughout the text.

| | |
|---|---|
| ADA | Air Defense Artillery |
| AO | area of operations |
| AQI | Al Qaeda in Iraq |
| AVF | All-Volunteer Force |
| AWOL | absent without leave |
| BAMC | Brooke Army Medical Center (San Antonio, Texas) |
| CAV | cavalry (reconnaissance units) |
| CCC | Captain's Career Course |
| CENTCOM | U.S. Central Command (responsible for all military operations in Middle East) |
| COP | combat outpost |
| CSH | Combat Support Hospital |
| CWIED | command wire improvised explosive device |
| DEA | U.S. Drug Enforcement Administration |
| EFP | explosive formed penetrator |
| EML | environmental and morale leave |
| EOD | explosive ordnance disposal |
| FOB | Forward Operating Base |
| FSO | fire support officer |
| HHT | headquarters and headquarters troop |
| HMMWV | high mobility multi-purpose wheeled vehicle |
| HQ | headquarters |
| HUMINT | human intelligence |
| IED | improvised explosive device |
| IIA | Iraqi Islamic Army |
| IN | infantry |
| IRA | Irish Republican Army |
| ISF | Iraqi Security Forces |
| ISIS | Islamic State of Iraq and Syria |
| KIA | killed in action |
| LT | lieutenant |
| LTC | lieutenant colonel |
| LZ | landing zone |
| MNC-I | Multi-National Corps, Iraq |

| | |
|---|---|
| MND-B | Multi-National Division, Baghdad |
| MOI | Ministry of the Interior |
| MP | military police |
| MTOE | modification table of organization and equipment |
| NCO | non-commissioned officer |
| NP | National Police |
| NTC | National Training Center (Fort Irwin, CA) |
| OBC | Officer Basic Course |
| OIF | Operation Iraqi Freedom |
| OP | observation post |
| OPFOR | Opposing Forces |
| PFC | private first class |
| PIR | passive infrared |
| PKM | Kalashnikov machine gun, or *Pulemyot Kalashnikova* |
| PLT | platoon |
| POW | prisoner of war |
| PT | physical training |
| PTSD | post-traumatic stress disorder |
| RCIED | remote controlled improvised explosive device |
| ROTC | reserve officers training corps |
| RPG | rocket propelled grenade |
| SCO | squadron commander |
| SFC | sergeant first class |
| SGT | sergeant |
| SLC | Scout Leaders Course |
| SOP | standard operating procedures |
| SPC | specialist |
| SSG | staff sergeant |
| TAPS | Tragedy Assistance Program for Survivors |
| TBI | traumatic brain injury |
| TIC | troops in contact |
| USAID | United States Agency for International Development |
| USMC | United States Marine Corps |
| VBIED | vehicle-borne improvised explosive device |
| VOIED | victim-operated improvised explosive device |
| WIA | wounded in action |
| WMD | weapons of mass destruction |
| XO | executive officer |

# Notes

This book's second epigraph comes from Dylan Thomas to Caitlin, Letter, 1936, to Caitlin, later his wife. *The Collected Letters of Dylan Thomas* (1985).

### PROLOGUE

1 The term "cookbook" in this context is lifted from LTC Joel Rayburn, my brilliant former West Point history and serving army intelligence officer.

### PREFACE

1 Bing West, *The Strongest Tribe: War, Politics, and the Endgame in Iraq* (New York: Random House, 2008): 191–93.

2 We learned of this (probably unauthorized) local arrangement from the platoon leaders in B Troop, 1-61 CAV, who explained the reasons for the truce and the need to take sides or come under attack from all. Unfortunately, the power of Al Qaeda–linked Sunni insurgents continued to grow during this period. In fairness to 1-61 CAV, they did what they perceived as best to survive and quell violence. It was difficult to forecast second- and third-order effects. We were guilty of just as many miscues.

3 In fairness, this guy worked one level above 3-7 CAV, and one wonders whether the 3-7 commander or operations officer would have risked such a grand statement.

4 Task Force Baghdad Public Affairs Office, "News: Iraqi Tip Leads U.S. Soldiers to Weapons in Salman Pak," 27 April 2005, accessed at www.dvidshub.net/news/1698/iraqi-tip-leads-us-soldiers-weapons-salmanpak#.UvpUSSDnaP8#ixzz2t2 8rWU9Y.

5 Dale Andrade, *Surging South of Baghdad: The 3rd Infantry Division and Task Force Marne in Iraq, 2007–2008* (Washington, DC: Center of Military History, 2010), 27.

6 In this instance, "Al Qaeda" refers to the local Iraqi affiliate, known officially as Al Qaeda in the "Land between the Two Rivers," known more commonly as Al Qaeda in Iraq (AQI). AQI was loosely affiliated with Al Qaeda proper, headquartered in Pakistan, and while reinforced by many foreign fighters, the core majority were local Iraqis.

7 Andrade, *Surging South of Baghdad*, 27.

8 Ibid., 39.

9 Ibid.

10 Ibid., 38–39.

## CHAPTER 1: ENTER THE "GHOST RIDERS"

1 Military Occupational Specialty 19D—cavalry Scout: essentially, a reconnaissance soldier that populates U.S. Army cavalry squadrons. All my soldiers, apart from the medic and artillery forward observer, were 19D Cav Scouts.

2 Rose Avenue—a residential street in the New Dorp neighborhood on the East Shore of Staten Island, New York—blue collar, middle class, Irish and Italian to the core.

3 A reference to the 1960 Hollywood feature film *The Great Escape*. In that famous movie James Garner plays the role of "scrounger" in the German POW camp, stealing or bribing to get whatever contraband the British and American pilots needed to escape the Luftwaffe prison.

## CHAPTER 2: CITIZENSHIP AND SACRIFICE

1 That deployment was Afghanistan, February 2011 to January 2012.

2 2010 U.S. Census data, accessed at http://factfinder2.census.gov/faces/nav/jsf/pages/community_facts.xhtml.

3 Based on the 2006 U.S. military pay scale, at the rank of private first class. This includes only basic pay and not allowances for hazardous duty and family separation during deployments; accessed at www.navycs.com/06militarypaychart.html.

4 Andrew J. Bacevich, *Breach of Trust: How Americans Failed Their Soldiers and Their Country* (New York: Metropolitan Books, 2014), 21.

5 Kathy Roth-Douquet and Frank Schaeffer, *AWOL: The Unexcused Absence of America's Upper Classes from Military Service—and How It Hurts Our Country* (New York: Harper Collins, 2006): 43.

6 One thinks of Fort Devens, Massachusetts (once home to the 10th Special Forces Group) and Fort Ord, California (former base of the 7th Infantry Division) for starters.

7 Roth-Douquet and Schaeffer, *AWOL*, 44–45.

8 Bacevich, *Breach of Trust*, 20.

9 Bob Greene, "Two Guys You'd Love to Have on Your Side," *Chicago Tribune*, 30 April 2002.

10 See "Players Who Lost Their Lives While in Military Service," *Baseball's Greatest Sacrifice*, accessed at www.baseballsgreatestsacrifice.com/table_of_all_players.html.

11 Bacevich, *Breach of Trust*, 20.

12 "Use of Force against Iraq/Passage, (in Sen.) S J Res 2," in Congress and the Nation, 1989–1992, vol. 8, CQ Press, Washington, DC, 1993, accessed at http://library.cqpress.com/congress/catn89-11-5254-269397, accessed 13 September 2013.

13 "Roll Call Vote Results," CQ Press, Washington, DC, dynamically generated 4 October 2013 from CQ Press Electronic Library, CQ Congress Collection, ac-

cessed at http://library.cqpress.com/congress/rollcall.php?PHPSESSID=juc1j
outo2cbe4ds1grjhdtn54&congress=226&vote=1068&yearlimit=0&milservice=
Served.

14 George Bush, *All the Best, George Bush: My Life in Letters and Other Writings*
(New York: Scribner, 1999), 49–52.

15 Edward J. Renehan, Jr., *The Lion's Pride: Theodore Roosevelt and His Family in
Peace and War* (New York: Oxford University Press, 1998).

16 See ibid., and Richard Connolly, "Presidents' Sons at War," *Houston Press* blog,
May 28, 2012, accessed at http://blogs.houstonpress.com/hairballs/2012/05
/presidents_sons_in_war.php?page=2.

17 See Franklin Delano Roosevelt, Jr., in the *Biographical Directory of the United
States Congress*.

18 See Connolly, "Presidents' Sons at War."

19 Ibid.

20 Jim Geraghty, "A Rude Question about Romney's Sons Yields an Off-Key Answer,"
*National Review*, 8 August 2007, accessed at www.nationalreview.com/campaign
-spot/12104/rude-question-about-romneys-sons-yields-key-answer.

21 Ibid., 56–57.

22 Roth-Douquet and Schaeffer, *AWOL*, 171.

23 Ibid., 170.

## CHAPTER 3: LIFE AS A COUNTDOWN

1 I have a theory. It is based on absolutely zero hard evidence, but it goes like this:
New Yorkers and Bostonians hate each other precisely because they're so similar. This applies to the blue-collar culture, sports fanaticism, and equally intense,
though obviously distinct regional accents.

2 2nd Lieutenant Daniel A. Sjursen, Officer Evaluation Support Form (DA Form
67-9-1), June 2006.

3 For detailed data and history on NTC, see Fort Irwin's homepage, at www.irwin
.army.mil/Pages/default.aspx.

4 The Joads stop in Needles, California, in *The Grapes of Wrath*.

5 Soldiers generally preferred tours in Italy, Germany, and Hawaii, but in the con-
tiguous forty-eight states Fort Carson, Colorado, was considered preferable to
duty at more rural outposts such as Fort Polk, Louisiana, or Fort Leonard Wood,
Missouri.

## CHAPTER 4: DOING MORE WITH LESS

1 Excluding D Troop—the assigned Maintenance and Logistics Company from the
Forward Support Battalion as well as ancillary attachments.

2 This is *not* meant to denigrate the service or importance of the many staff positions under the HHT. In fact, intelligence and logistics drove and facilitated

combat operations every step of the way. On the contrary, our scout platoons were useless without their vital support. As for danger, both from mortar attacks on the FOB and IEDs directed against logistics convoys, D Troop and HHT soldiers faced far more risk than their historical counterparts in earlier U.S. wars, such as World War II.

3  In all fairness, a SCO *needs* a security element to facilitate his movement around the battlefield. It allows him to visit his subordinate commanders and control disparate elements in combat. There just weren't any extra soldiers to be had. Everyone was short.

4  Jaysh al Mahdi, the Mahdi Army, formed by Moktada al-Sadr, son of famed Shia imam Mohammed al-Sadr. Moktada's father and older brothers were murdered by Saddam's henchmen in 1999. Soon after the U.S. invasion, Moktada formed the Mahdi Army, allegedly to protect the Shia community. In 2004, the self-styled nationalist leader called for U.S. withdrawal and declared war on the U.S. military.

5  Pamela Hess, "Fight and Rebuild: Squaring Iraq's Circle," United Press International, 10 October 2005, accessed at www.spacewar.com/news/iraq-05zzzzc .html.

6  Ibid.

7  The Mahdi Army, Shia militiamen under the nominal command of Moktada al-Sadr, a Sadr City–based nationalist/populist/opportunist, living off his father's and grandfather's good names to organize resistance both to U.S. troops and Sunni insurgents/civilians.

8  Data from Iraq Body Count Project, accessed at www.iraqbodycount.org/data base/.

9  Irish Republican Army (IRA)—nationalists in favor of uniting Northern Ireland with the rest of the republic. To the British—terrorists.

### CHAPTER 5: "THESE DUDES ARE TRYING TO *KILL* US"

1  Mike was from Fords, New Jersey, and went on to command an infantry company in Kandahar province. He liked to wear fancy suits and order bottles of Dom Perignon in his off time. He grew on you.

2  Scott hails from Akron, Ohio, loved Ohio State football, and was my West Point classmate. He divided his time fairly evenly between playing the stock market and bedding random girls from the bars. He excelled at both. He's now out of the army. A good dude.

3  Dale Andrade, *Surging South of Baghdad: The 3rd Infantry Division and Task Force Marne in Iraq, 2007–2008* (Washington, DC: Center of Military History, 2010), 39.

4  Fedayeen: Iraqi irregular forces organized for defense, ostensibly by the Saddam regime.

5  Terri Weaver, "U.S. Troops in Salman Pak Find That the Most Important Part of

Joint Force Is Sharing Information," *Stars and Stripes*, 7 June 2009, accessed at www.stripes.com/news/u-s-troops-in-salman-pak-find-that-the-most-important -part-of-joint-force-is-sharing-information-1.92313.

6  One dollar per pack for Miamis—the most disgusting cigarettes of all time— similar to inhaling fiberglass and asbestos. I smoked them anyway.

7  Regulations and an impressive penchant for euphemism required that we call it "tactical questioning." Oh, how we love to take the life out of meaningful words!

## CHAPTER 6: INDISPENSABLE FRIENDS

1  Most personal information stems from conversations in Iraq and recent phone interviews with the author, dated 9 February 2014.

2  See "Sadr City [Saddam City/Al Thawra]," *GlobalSecurity.org*, accessed at www .globalsecurity.org/military/world/iraq/sadr-city.htm.

3  "Profile: Moktada al-Sadr," *Al-Jazeera Online*, 7 March 2010, accessed at www .aljazeera.com/news/middleeast/2008/04/200861517227277282.html.

4  Ernesto Londano, "U.S. Ban on Masks Upsets Iraqi Interpreters," *Washington Post*, 17 November 2008, accessed at www.washingtonpost.com/wp-dyn/content /article/2008/11/16/AR2008111602040.html.

5  Ibid.

6  Vivian Tan, "Feili Kurds in Iran Seek Way Out of Identity Impasse," UN Refugee Agency News Story, 28 May 2008, accessed at www.unhcr.org/483d60872.html.

7  Doug Bandow, "Endangered Wartime Interpreters: The U.S. Should Protect Those Who Protect Us," *Forbes Magazine*, 25 February 2013, accessed at www .forbes.com/sites/dougbandow/2013/02/25/endangered-wartime-interpreters -the-u-s-should-protect-those-who-protect-us/.

8  U.S. Department of State, Department of Consular Affairs, Special Immigrant Visa Statistics, accessed at http://travel.state.gov/content/visas/english/law -and-policy/statistics/immigrant-visas.html.

9  Ibid.

10  Only while at war with the U.S. Army could one find designated *areas* where smoking cigarettes was authorized *outdoors*. This "smoking area" was right next door to the former headquarters of Saddam's Directorate of Internal Security, a huge multistory building that bore the catastrophic wreckage marks from a few massive U.S. Air Force guided bomb units (GBUs). Our military will level a building but prohibit outdoor smoking. That's how we roll.

11  Green Zone: the nickname for the central Baghdad location of both the U.S. embassy and the Multinational Corps—Iraq Headquarters.

12  That being said, my memory might be affected by future experience in Kandahar province, Afghanistan. That place made Baghdad seem like Brooklyn. It was straight biblical in the villages of my subdistrict of Pashmul, southwest of Kandahar City.

13 In all fairness, they usually referred to "terrorists" and not Iraqis in the broad sense, but few of the insurgents in Iraq were transnational terrorists. In truth they were a hodgepodge. Nationalists, Islamists, criminals, drug traffickers, guns for hire, desperate poor kids, sociopaths, and the mentally ill.

### CHAPTER 7: BREAKING POINT

1 Courtney Marulli, 2nd Brigade Combat Team, 2nd Infantry Division Public Affairs, "Army Commendation Medal for Valor for Joshua R. Schrader, *DVIDS*, 30 July 2007, accessed at http://northshorejournal.org/pfc-josh-r-schrader.

2 Colonel Erin P. Edgar, "Baghdad ER—Revisited," in *Strategic Studies Institute* (Carlisle, PA: U.S. Army War College, 2009), 2.

3 Ibid., 13.

4 John Fleck, "ABQ's VA Hospital Is Praised but Still Faces Complaints about Long Waits," *Albuquerque Journal*, 19 March 2007, accessed at www.abqjournal.com /news/metro/547907metro03-19-07.htm.

5 John Fleck, "VA Hospital No Walter Reed," *Albuquerque Journal*, 11 March 2007, accessed at www.abqjournal.com/news/metro/545457metro03-11-07.htm.

6 Leonia C. Knight, Major, "Casualty Evacuation in the Contemporary Operating Environment," School of Advanced Military Studies Monograph (Fort Leavenworth, KS: U.S. Army Command and General Staff College, 2002), 12.

7 Incident Report, Lubbock Police Department, Report # 06-0045735, 2 September 2006.

8 Military.com, overview of the Servicemen's Civil Relief Act, accessed at www .military.com/benefits/military-legal-matters/scra/servicemembers-civil-relief -act-overview.html.

9 Dale Andrade, *Surging South of Baghdad: The 3rd Infantry Division and Task Force Marne in Iraq, 2007–2008* (Washington, DC: Center of Military History, 2010), 49–50.

10 Brenda E. Rodgers and Ronald K. Chesser, "What We Found at Tuwaitha," *Bulletin of the Atomic Scientists*, 19 May 2009, accessed at http://thebulletin.org/what -we-found-al-tuwaitha.

11 Ibid.

### CHAPTER 8: SUNNI VERSUS SHIA

1 Michael O'Hanlon, "Iraq Index Tracking Variables of Reconstruction & Security in Post-Saddam Iraq," *Brookings Institute*, 1 October 2007, accessed at www .brookings.edu/fp/saban/iraq/indexarchive.htm.

2 The Economist Explains, "What Is the Difference between Sunni and Shia Muslims?" *Economist*, 28 May 2013, accessed at www.economist.com/blogs /economist-explains/2013/05/economist-explains-19.

3 Ibid.

4 Derek Hopwood, "British Relations with Iraq," *BBC Recent History*, 2 February 2003, accessed at www.bbc.co.uk/history/recent/iraq/britain_iraq_01.shtml.

5 Ibid.

6 John W. Dower, *Cultures of War: Pearl Harbor, Hiroshima, 9-11, Iraq* (New York: W. W. Norton, 2010), 92–93.

7 Ibid.

8 Ibid.

9 Ellen Knickmeyer and K. I. Ibrahim, "Bombing Shatters Mosque in Iraq," *Washington Post*, 23 February 2006, accessed at www.washingtonpost.com/wp-dyn/content/article/2006/02/22/AR2006022200454.html.

10 Ellen Knickmeyer, "Blood on Our Hands," *Foreign Policy*, 25 October 2011, accessed at www.foreignpolicy.com/articles/2010/10/25/Blood_on_Our_Hands.

11 CNN.com World Desk, "Rumsfeld: Situation in Iraq 'Exaggerated' by Media," *CNN Online*, 7 March 2006, accessed at www.cnn.com/2006/WORLD/meast/03/07/rumsfeld.iraq/.

12 Knickmeyer, "Blood on Our Hands."

13 "Documented Civilian Deaths from Casualties," Iraq Body Count Project, accessed at www.iraqbodycount.org/database/. Of note, the project estimates a total of 121,000 to 134,000 deaths during the war, but admits: "Further analysis of the WikiLeaks Iraq War Logs may add 10,000 civilian deaths." This almost certainly refers to the updated Pentagon reports released in the wake of Knickmeyer's and the WikiLeaks revelations.

14 Knickmeyer, "Blood on Our Hands."

15 "Profile Moktada al-Sadr," *Al-Jazeera Online*, 7 March 2010, accessed at www.aljazeera.com/news/middleeast/2008/04/200861517227277282.html.

16 Miranda Sissons and Abdulrazzaq Al-Saiedi, "A Bitter Legacy: Lessons of De-Baathification in Iraq," *International Center for Transitional Justice*, March 2013: 10, accessed at https://www.ictj.org/publication/bitter-legacy-lessons-de-baathification-iraq.

17 Michael O'Hanlon and Kenneth Pollack, "Iraq Trip Report," *Brookings Institution*, August 2007, 6–7, accessed at http://www.brookings.edu/research/reports/2007/08/iraq-trip.

18 Lory M. Fenner, "Stand Up and Be Counted: The Continuing Challenge of Building the Iraqi Security Forces," *U.S. House of Representatives*, Committee on Armed Services Subcommittee on Oversight and Investigations, July 2007, 81.

19 Lisa Burgess, "Iraqi VP Says Police Help Prevent Food, Medicine from Reaching Sunnis," *Stars and Stripes*, 7 February 2007, accessed at www.stripes.com/news/iraqi-vp-says-police-help-prevent-food-medicine-from-reaching-sunnis-1.59991.

20 Natalie Rostek, "Salman Pak Leaders Work Together to Revitalize Neglected

Hospital," *Free Republic*, 8 February 2008, accessed at www.freerepublic.com /focus/f-news/1967366/posts.

21  "Salman al-Farsi," encyclopedia entry, *Encyclopedia Britannica online*, accessed at www.britannica.com/EBchecked/topic/519481/Salman-al-Farisi.

22  Youssef Aboul-Enein, ed. *Iraq in Turmoil: Historical Perspectives of Dr. Ali al-Wardi, From the Ottoman Empire to King Feisal* (Washington, DC: Naval Institute Press, 2012).

23  Bing West, *The Strongest Tribe: War, Politics, and the Endgame in Iraq* (New York: Random House, 2008), 196.

24  Ibid., 238.

25  Burgess, "Iraqi VP Says Police Help Prevent Food, Medicine from Reaching Sunnis."

26  Ibid.

27  Jomana Karadsheh, "Arrest Warrant Issued for Iraqi Vice President," *CNN Online*, 19 December 2011, accessed at www.cnn.com/2011/12/19/world/meast /iraq-vp-arrest/index.html?hpt=hp_t2.

28  Omar al-Jawoshy and Michael Schwirtz, "Death Sentence for a Top Iraqi Leader in a Day of Bloodshed," *New York Times*, 9 September 2012, accessed at www .nytimes.com/2012/09/10/world/middleeast/insurgents-carry-out-wave-of -attacks-across-iraq.html?_r=0.

29  Karin Brulliard, "'Gated Communities' for the War-Ravaged," *Washington Post*, 23 April 2007.

30  Rick Hepp and John P. Martin, "2 More Jerseyans Make Ultimate Sacrifice in Iraq," *Newark Star-Ledger*, 21 June 2007, accessed at http://blog.nj.com/njwar dead/2007/06/army_sgt_eric_snell_june_18_20.html.

31  Brulliard, "'Gated Communities' for the War-Ravaged," 2.

32  Ibid., 1.

33  Account comes from Ambassador Peter Galbraith, son of the economist John Kenneth Galbraith, first publicized in his book *The End of Iraq: How American Incompetence Created a War without End* (London: Simon and Schuster, 2007).

34  The vast majority of east Baghdad was Shia, even before the civil war. West and central Baghdad had been far more mixed. One notable exception was the northeastern Sunni stronghold, mentioned earlier in the text—Adhamiyah.

35  Hajis: pejorative term for Iraqis—similar to "Charlie" or "Gooks" in the Vietnam War.

36  "Ashura," encyclopedia entry, *Encyclopedia Britannica*, accessed at www.bri tannica.com/EBchecked/topic/38434/Ashura.

CHAPTER 9: USHERING IN THE "SURGE"

1  Central Command—responsible for all U.S. military forces in the Middle East and North Africa—General Casey's immediate boss.

2 President George W. Bush, "President's Address to the Nation," Office of the Press Secretary, 10 January 2007.

3 Damien Cave, "Helicopter Crash Claims 13 on Deadly Day for U.S. in Iraq," *New York Times*, 21 January 2007, accessed at www.nytimes.com/2007/01/21/world /middleeast/21iraq.html?fta=y&_r=0.

4 Ibid.

5 See Zeke Minaya, "Losses in Iraq Hit Schweinfurt Unit Hard," *Stars and Stripes*, 6 August 2007, accessed at www.stripes.com/news/losses-in-iraq-hit -schweinfurt-unit-hard-1.67352.

6 See www.salon.com/2007/01/22/ieds/.

7 For information about early British counter-IED tactics in Northern Ireland, see Col. Norman L. Dodd, "The Corporal's War: Internal Security Operations in Northern Ireland," *Military Review* (July 1976): 58–68, and "Send for Felix!" *Military Review* (March 1978): 46–55.

8 The attacks were almost exclusively conducted by Shia militias such as the Jaysh al Mahdi (Mahdi Army), with technical support from their sectarian allies, the Iranian Revolutionary Guards. East Baghdad was the home turf of the vast majority of these Shia insurgent elements, though there were sizable enclaves in parts of West Baghdad.

9 Neta C. Crawford, *Accountability for Killing: Moral Responsibility for Collateral Damage in America's Post-9/11 Wars* (New York: Oxford University Press, 2013), ii.

10 Ibid. Casualties refers to dead *and* wounded in this statistic.

### CHAPTER 10: TROOP SHORTAGE, TROOP SURGE

1 See Iraq Coalition Casualty Count, http://icasualties.org/Iraq/ByMonth.aspx.

2 Ibid.

3 Dale Eisman, "Sen. Webb's New GI Bill Gets Overwhelming OK in Senate," *Virginia Pilot*, 27 June 2008, accessed at http://hamptonroads.com/node/470399.

4 Ibid.

5 Sam Stein, "Larry Craig Taps His Way into Webb GI Bill Debate," *Huffington Post*, 22 May 2008, accessed at www.huffingtonpost.com/2008/05/14/larry-craig-taps -his-way_n_101688.html.

6 Ravi Shankar, "Post 9/11 Veterans Educational Assistance Act of 2008," *Harvard Journal on Legislation* 46 (February 2009), accessed at http://journals.law.harvard .edu/jol/files/2013/10/Shankar-Article.pdf.

7 Frank Rich, "The Swift-boating of Cindy Sheehan," *New York Times*, 21 August 2005.

8 Patrick Winn, "Troops Unite to Save Soldier Knifed in Head," *Army Times*, 22 October 2007, accessed at http://archive.armytimes.com/article/20071022 /NEWS/710220304/Troops-unite-save-soldier-knifed-head.

9 Ibid.

10 Ibid.

11 Ibid.

12 Ibid.

13 Ibid.

### CHAPTER 11: A NIGHT TO REMEMBER

1 Robert Salladay, "Army Pfc. Michael C. Balsley, 23, Hayward; Killed by a Roadside Bomb," *Los Angeles Times*, 11 February 2007, accessed at http://articles.latimes.com/2007/feb/11/local/me-balsley11.

2 Something to keep in mind is this fact: our occupation enforced a "no-movement" outside curfew for *years* in Iraq. Imagine having everything shut down in your town at 9:00 or 10:00 p.m. and being required—on pain of arrest or even death—to stay indoors. That was the average Iraqi's reality for most of a decade.

3 Salladay, "Army Pfc. Michael C. Balsley, 23, Hayward; Killed by a Roadside Bomb."

4 Matt O'Brien, "Hayward Soldier Dies in Iraq Blast," *Oakland Tribune*, 2 February 2007, accessed at www.insidebayarea.com/search/ci_5100822.

### CHAPTER 12: SHOUTING AT LINDSEY GRAHAM

1 Bestselling author Thomas Ricks, *The Gamble: General Petraeus and the American Military Adventure in Iraq* (New York: Penguin Books, 2010); senators McCain, Lieberman, and Graham; the Bush administration; the entire Republican Party; and any military officer even loosely associated with General David Petraeus—for starters.

2 See Colonel Gian Gentile's (West Point professor and former battalion commander in Baghdad) *Wrong Turn*; Andrew Bacevich's (West Point class of 1969, retired colonel, Vietnam veteran) *The Limits of Power, Washington Rules*, and *Breach of Trust*; and Professor Douglas Porch's *Counterinsurgency: Exposing the Myths of the New Way of War.*

3 Bing West, *The Strongest Tribe: War, Politics, and the Endgame in Iraq* (New York: Random House, 2008), 330.

4 The 1st Brigade, 1st Armor Division, stationed in Friedberg, Germany, and commanded by Colonel (now Major General) Sean MacFarland.

5 "Iraq: Four Years On—Mapping the Violence in Baghdad," *BBC News*, accessed at http://news.bbc.co.uk/2/shared/spl/hi/in_depth/baghdad_navigator/.

6 Operation Iraqi Freedom, "Iraq," accessed at www.iCasualties.org.

7 David Wood, "U.S. Wounded In Iraq, Afghanistan Includes More Than 1,500 Amputees," *Huffington Post*, 9 November 2012, accessed at www.huffingtonpost.com/2012/11/07/iraq-afghanistan-amputees_n_2089911.html.

8 Michael M. Phillips, "After Wars in Iraq and Afghanistan, Brain-Injured Vet-

erans Search for Solace: Returning U.S. Veterans Face Physical and Mental Hurdles," *Wall Street Journal*, 19 February 2014, accessed at http://online .wsj.com/news/articles/SB10001424052702304899704579391454059654682?mg =reno64-wsj&url=http%3A%2F%2Fonline.wsj.com%2Farticle%2FSB1000 1424052702304899704579391454059654682.html.

9 Hannah Fischer, "U.S. Military Casualty Statistics: Operation New Dawn, Operation Iraqi Freedom, and Operation Enduring Freedom," *Congressional Research Service* Study, dated 7 February 2013, 6, accessed at www.crs.gov. www.fas.org /sgp/crs/natsec/RS22452.pdf.

10 "Iraq Body Count database," available at Iraqbodycount.org.

11 Brad Knickerbocker, "Iraq War 10 Years Later: Was It Worth It?," *Christian Science Monitor*, 17 March 2013. See www.csmonitor.com/USA/Military/2013/0317 /Iraq-war-10-years-later-Was-it-worth-it.

12 Arwa Damon, "Iraq Refugees Chased from Home, Struggle to Cope," *CNN World News Online*, 21 June 2007, accessed at www.cnn.com/2007/WORLD /meast/06/20/damon.iraqrefugees/index.html.

13 Ibid.

14 Iraq Body Count Project, accessed at www.iraqbodycount.org/database/.

### CHAPTER 13: STAGGERING TO THE FINISH LINE

1 Colin Carroll, "West Point Combat Casualties Are High in Post-9/11 Era," *Army Times*, 21 August 2013, accessed at www.armytimes.com/article/20130821/NEWS /308210022/West-Point-combat-casualties-high-post-9-11-era.

2 Siegfried Sassoon, "Base Details," accessed at www.haverford.edu/engl/english 354/GreatWar/Sassoon/SassDeL.html.

3 1 Corinthians 13:11, King James Bible.

4 Albert Camus, *The Myth of Sisyphus and Other Essays* (New York: Random House, 1955), 6.

5 Jack Kerouac, *On the Road*, Penguin Classics Edition (New York: Penguin Books, 2002), 5.

6 Casualty statistics from Iraq Coalition Casualty Count, accessed at http:// icasualties.org/Iraq/USCasualtiesByState.aspx.

7 James Dao and Andrew W. Lehren, "Baffling Rise in Suicides Plagues the U.S. Military," *New York Times*, 15 May 2013.

8 Leo Shane III, "Report: Suicide Rate Spikes among Young Veterans," *Stars and Stripes*, 9 January 2014.

### CHAPTER 14: DISAPPOINTING PATHS

1 Dale Andrade, *Surging South of Baghdad: The 3rd Infantry Division and Task Force Marne in Iraq, 2007–2008* (Washington, DC: Center of Military History, 2010), 48.

2 Ibid., 336.

3 See assorted articles: "12 Killed in Iraq's Violence," *China Radio International's English Service*, 12 February 2014, accessed at http://english.cri.cn/6966/2014/02/12/2561s812602.htm. Sameer N. Yacoub, "Bombings Kill at Least 32 in Iraqi Capital," *Navy Times*, 5 February 2014, accessed at www.navytimes.com/article/20140205/NEWS08/302050022/Bombings-kill-least-32-Iraqi-capital. *Reuters*, "Bombs Kill at Least 17 across Iraq: Police and Medics," 12 February 2014, accessed at http://ca.reuters.com/article/topNews/idCABREA1B1ZA20140212.

4 "Day of Violence Leaves 17 Dead across Iraq: Sources," *Press TV*, 13 February 2014, accessed at www.presstv.ir/detail/2014/02/13/350450/bomb-attacks-kill-17-across-iraq/.

5 Murtada Faraj, "Suicide Bombings, Attacks in Iraq, Kill 33 People," *USA Today*, 21 April 2014.

6 Xinhua News, "29 Killed in Wave of Attacks across Iraq," *Xinhua English News*, 4 May 2014, accessed at http://news.xinhuanet.com/english/world/2014-05/04/c_126460575.htm.

7 Sameer N. Yacoub, "Attacks in Iraq, Including Cafe Bombing, Kill 15," *ABC News*, from the Associated Press, 8 May 2014, accessed at http://abcnews.go.com/International/wireStory/officials-attacks-iraq-kill-people-23640796.

8 Sinan Salaheddin, "Rights Group Calls for Probe into Iraqi Airstrike," *Associated Press*, 14 September 2014, accessed at www.wtop.com/220/3701575/Rights-group-calls-for-probe-into-Iraqi-airstrike.

9 Lizzie Dearden, "Iraq Crisis: At Least 50 Killed in Wave of Terrorist Attacks across Baghdad," *The Independent*, 16 October 2014, accessed at http://www.independent.co.uk/news/world/middle-east/iraq-crisis-at-least-50-killed-in-wave-of-terrorist-attacks-across-baghdad-9800049.html.

10 The Iraq Body Count Project, accessed at https://www.iraqbodycount.org/about/.

11 Daniel Trotta, "Iraq War Cost U.S. More Than $2 Trillion, Could Grow to $6 Trillion, Says Watson Institute Study," *Reuters*, 14 March 2013, accessed at http://www.huffingtonpost.com/2013/03/14/iraq-war-cost-more-than-2-trillion_n_2875493.html.

12 Ibid.

13 Ibid.

14 Kaiser Family Foundation Poll, "After the Wars: Post-Kaiser Survey of Afghanistan and Iraq War Veterans," Q: All in all, considering the costs to the United States versus the benefits to the United States, do you think The war in Iraq was worth fighting, or not? (if worth/not worth fighting) Do you feel that way strongly or somewhat? *Washington Post*, 29 March 2014, accessed at http://www.washingtonpost.com/page/2010-2019/WashingtonPost/2014/03/30/National-Politics/Polling/release_305.xml.

15 Peter Bergen, "Can we call Iraq a Success?" Debate, *The New America Foundation*, 04 March 2013, accessed at http://newamerica.net/events/2013/can_we _call_iraq_a_success.

16 Peter Mansoor, "Book Discussion on *Surge*," *C-Span Book-TV*, 06 February 2014, accessed at http://www.c-span.org/video/?317658-1/book-discussion-surge.

17 Ibid.

18 John W. Dower, *Cultures of War: Pearl Harbor, Hiroshima, 9-11, Iraq* (New York: W.W. Norton, 2010): 315.

19 Haifa Zangana, "Here Is a List of the Real Forces behind the Violence in Iraq," *Al-Jazeera online*, 14 January 2014, accessed at www.aljazeera.com/indepth /opinion/2014/01/here-list-real-forces-behind-violence-iraq-201411613100570 815.html.

20 Ibid.

21 "The Death Penalty: An International Perspective," *Death Penalty Resource Center*, accessed at www.deathpenaltyinfo.org/death-penalty-international -perspective.

22 Ibid.

23 Alawites are a mystical Muslim group that follow a brand of Shia Islam. Alawite means "followers of Ali," the father of Shia Islam. They are a highly secretive mystical sect and control the government of Syria, despite being only approximately 10 to 12 percent of the population.

24 Joel Rayburn, "Iraq Is Back on the Brink of Civil War," *New Republic*, 8 May 2013, accessed at www.newrepublic.com/article/113148/iraqs-civil-war-breaking-out -again.

25 Joel Rayburn, " 'Blowback' Comes to Syria," *Hoover Institution*, Stanford University, 23 February 2012, accessed at www.advancingafreesociety.org/author/joel -rayburn/.

26 Rayburn, "Iraq Is Back on the Brink of Civil War."

27 Ibid.

28 Ibid.

29 At least in its current, relative state of parity, of armed camps divided in a Cold War–like scenario.

30 CIA World Fact book, "Country Comparison: Crude Oil, Proven Reserves," accessed at https://www.cia.gov/library/publications/the-world-factbook/rank order/2244rank.html.

31 Carlo Munoz, "Congressional Veterans Line Up against Military Intervention in Syria," *New York Times*, 7 September 2013.

32 Dower, *Cultures of War*, 136.

33 Ibid.

CHAPTER 15: WAR IN THE REARVIEW

1 Michael D. Abernethy, "Local Veteran's Bout with PTSD Gets National Attention," *Burlington Times-News*, 10 October 2013, accessed at www.thetimesnews .com/news/top-news/ed-will-live-on-now-1.216637.

2 Ibid.

3 Hannah Fischer, "U.S. Military Casualty Statistics: Operation New Dawn, Operation Iraqi Freedom, and Operation Enduring Freedom," *Congressional Research Service* Study, dated 7 February 2013, 6, accessed at www.crs.gov.

4 Jess Walker, "VA Releases New Iraq and Afghanistan War Statistics," Bergman and Moore, LLC, accessed at www.vetlawyers.com/va-releases-new-iraq-and -afghanistan-war-statistics/.

5 President Barack Obama, "Medal of Honor Ceremony for Staff Sergeant Ty Carter," *C-SPAN*, 26 August 2013, accessed at www.c-span.org/video/?314727-2 /medal-honor-ceremony-staff-sergeant-ty-carter.

6 Abernethy, "Local Veteran's Bout with PTSD Gets National Attention."

7 Sean Gonsalves, "Fallen Soldier Mourned in Hyannis," Cape Cod online, 7 February 2007, accessed at www.capecodonline.com/apps/pbcs.dll/article?AID= /20070207/NEWS/101019864&cid=sitesearch.

8 Ibid.

9 Megan Tench, "Soon to Be a Father, Now Gone Too Young: Mourners Remember 21-year-old Iraq Casualty," *Boston Globe*, 7 February 2007, accessed at www .boston.com/news/local/articles/2007/02/07/soon_to_be_a_father_now _gone_too_young/.

10 Ibid.

11 Steve Doane, "Freed Centerville Drug Dealer Now on House Arrest," *Cape Cod Online*, 1 November 2012, accessed at www.capecodonline.com/apps/pbcs.dll /article?AID=/20121101/NEWS/21101032.

12 Gonsalves, "Fallen Soldier Mourned in Hyannis."

13 Kareem Raheem, "Baghdad Motorbike Blast, Other Attacks Kill 52 in Iraq," *Reuters*, 27 February 2014, accessed at www.reuters.com/article/2014/02/27/us -iraq-violence-idUSBREA1Q1Y420140227.

14 Sinan Salaheddin and Qassim Abdul-Zahra, "Bombings, Clashes, in Iraq Kill at Least 42," *Associated Press*, 6 March 2014, accessed at http://abcnews.go.com /International/wireStory/officials-attacks-kill-iraqi-capital-22787366.

15 "Armed Men Seize Iraq's Samarra City Council," *Al-Jazeera*, 4 March 2014, accessed at www.aljazeera.com/news/middleeast/2014/03/gunmen-seize-city -council-iraq-samarra-201434937425837.html.

CODA: THE POWER OF MEMORY

1 Norman MacAfee, ed. *The Gospel According to RFK: Why It Matters Now* (New York: Basic Books, 2008), 33.

2 Of, relating to, or suggestive of Franz Kafka or his writings; especially: having a nightmarishly complex, bizarre, or illogical quality. Definition from Merriam-Webster's Dictionary, accessed online at www.merriam-webster.com/dictionary/kafkaesque.

3 "MNC-I in Brief to General David Petraeus," 8 February 2007, unclassified and published by the *Washington Post*.

4 U.S. Military Base Pay Scale, 2014, accessed at www.militaryfactory.com/military_pay_scale.asp.

5 Christopher Harress, "Wal-Mart Says 'Save Money Live Better,' but Workers Don't Make Living Wage and Rely on State Benefits," *International Business Times*, 12 November 2013, accessed at www.ibtimes.com/wal-mart-says-save-money-live-better-workers-dont-make-living-wage-rely-state-benefits-1487598.

6 Kathy Roth-Douquet and Frank Schaeffer, *AWOL: The Unexcused Absence of America's Upper Classes from Military Service—and How It Hurts Our Country* (New York: Harper Collins, 2006), 162.

7 Of course, many janitors are hired part time precisely *so* the companies don't have to provide them health insurance, but the point remains.

8 Charles C. Moskos and John Sibley Butler, *All That We Can Be: Black Leadership and Racial Integration the Army* Way, quoted in Roth-Douquet and Schaeffer, *AWOL*, 161.

9 In all fairness, much work remains—the officers corps is still only about 8.7 percent black, and general officers only 5.5 percent black, compared with approximately 17 percent of enlisted men, *but* compared with corporate America this is still impressive. For statistics, see Michael Fletcher, "Blacks Lose Ground in the Military," *The Root*, 31 May 2010, accessed at www.theroot.com/articles/politics/2010/05/blacks_lose_ground_in_the_us_military.2.html.

10 The notion of an "era of free security" derives from C. Vann Woodward, "The Age of Reinterpretation," *American Historical Review* 66 (1960): 1–19. The other ideas reference absolute security come from John Shy, *A People Numerous and Armed: Reflections on the Military Struggle for American Independence* (Ann Arbor: University of Michigan Press, 1976).

# Index